Lavery Library

EX LIBRIS
ST. JOHN FISHER COLLEGE

Battered Women
Who Kill

Battered Women Who Kill

Psychological Self-Defense as Legal Justification

Charles Patrick Ewing
State University of New York at Buffalo

Lexington Books
D.C. Heath and Company/Lexington, Massachusetts/Toronto

Library of Congress Cataloging-in-Publication Data

Ewing, Charles Patrick, 1949–
 Battered women who kill.

 Bibliography: p.
 Includes index.
 1. Self-defense (Law)—United States. 2. Women—Legal status, laws, etc.—United
States. 3. Abused wives—Legal status, laws, etc.—United States. 4. Women—United
States—Crimes against. 5. Wife abuse—United States. I. Title.
KF9246.E9 1987   345.73'04   86-21323
                     347.3054
ISBN 0-669-14827-X (alk. paper)

Published simultaneously in Canada
Printed in the United States of America
International Standard Book Number: 0-669-14827-X
Library of Congress Catalog Card Number: 86-21323

The paper used in this publication meets the minimum requirements of American National
Standard for Information Sciences—Permanence of Paper for Printed Library Materials,
ANSI Z39.48-1984. ∞™

Year and number of this printing:

91 10 9 8 7 6 5 4 3

For Elaine.
May she grow up to find a world free of the kind of violence
described in this book.

Contents

Acknowledgments   ix

1. Introduction   1

2. Battered Women   7

    Defining Characteristics: The Physical and Psychological Plight of the
        Battered Woman   7
    Barriers to Seeking Help or Terminating the Battering Relationship   12

3. Battered Women Who Kill   23

    Walker's Fifty Women   24
    Browne's Forty-Two Women   25
    Jones's Thirty-Seven Women   27
    Other Women Who Have Killed Their Husbands   28
    One Hundred Battered Women Who Killed   31
    Battered Women Who Kill and Those Who Do Not   34

4. The Legal Response to Battered Women Who Kill   41

    The Law of Homicide   43
    Legal Defenses to Homicide Charges   45

5. Expert Testimony Regarding the Battered Woman
    Syndrome   51

6. Why Battered Women Kill: A Theory of Psychological
    Self-Defense   61

    Self Psychology: Ontological Insecurity, Disintegration Anxiety, and the
        Victimized Self   63
    Psychopathology: Learned Helplessness, Depression, and Suicide   66
    Victimology: The Psychological Effects and Aftereffects of Violent
        Crime   70

The Psychology of Terrorism: The Effects of "Conjugal Terrorism"   73
Summary   76

7.   **Psychological Self-Defense as Legal Justification**   77

The Proposed Doctrine   78
The Legal Basis for a Doctrine of Psychological Self-Defense   79
Practical Objections to a Legal Doctrine of Psychological Self-
   Defense   85

8.   **Conclusion**   95

Appendix: 100 Battered Women Who Killed   99

Notes   143

Index   171

About the Author   177

Acknowledgments

This book, like most, is the product of many minds. As the author, I take full responsibility for its content. But I cannot take full credit. Too many others have made significant contributions, which I gratefully acknowledge:

John Rowley served as my research assistant throughout the project. He, more than anyone, helped me make this book what it is. Other research assistants who provided help were Jay Goldstein, Daniel Lukasik, Caroline Silk, Eric Snyder, Leslie Stroth, and Monte Warren. Monte deserves special recognition for having served as skeptic-in-residence.

My colleagues, Professors Murray Levine and Philip Halpern, and my wife, Sharon Harris-Ewing, read earlier drafts of the manuscript and offered valuable criticisms and suggestions.

Nina Cascio, law librarian at SUNY Buffalo, provided invaluable assistance in the computerized search that led us to most of the cases described in the Appendix to this volume.

My daughter, Elaine, made her own special contribution. I spent much of the second year of her life writing this book, and I owe her a special debt which cannot ever be repaid. Her daily reminder to "close up shop" (that is, shut off the computer and come to dinner) never failed to help put things in their proper perspective.

Finally, I wish to note that my work on this volume was supported in part by a William J. Magavern Fellowship, a generous grant from the law firm of Magavern and Magavern.

1
Introduction

The Emick case is not a pleasant one to read about. But there is something to be learned from it.[1]

On the morning of February 25, 1983, in a small rural town in Western New York, 22-year-old Leslie Ann Emick shot her common-law husband, Marshall Allison, five times in the head as he was sleeping. Emick then telephoned the police, who arrived shortly and determined that Allison was dead. Emick admitted killing Allison but claimed that the shooting was done in self-defense.[2]

Emick was charged with first degree manslaughter. In New York State, first degree manslaughter is defined as an intentional killing committed by a person acting under "extreme emotional disturbance for which there was a reasonable explanation or excuse."[3] Conviction on this charge carries a maximum sentence of 25 years in prison.[4] At trial Emick told the following story of her relationship with Marshall Allison.[5]

Emick and Allison had lived together since 1978 and Allison was the father of Emick's two young children. Their relationship had been fairly normal until the summer of 1981 when, following the birth of the couple's second child, Allison began to abuse Emick physically and accuse her of having sexual relations with other men. On one occasion in 1981, Allison beat Emick's head against a tree. On another, he stabbed Emick in the foot with a pencil, which required a trip to the hospital to have part of the pencil removed.

Allison's abuse of Emick escalated further in the fall of 1982 after Allison found a bullwhip in a nearby utility shed. Allison then began using the whip to beat Emick while she was hogtied. On one occasion, Allison forced Emick to bring him a piece of wood from a woodpile and then used the log to beat Emick about the head and body. He also abused Emick with a variety of other devices: ropes, belts, a homemade wooden dildo, a lighter, a vacuum cleaner attachment, needle-nosed pliers, and a hunting knife. Allison also constantly accused Emick of sexual infidelity and insisted that Emick call him "master."

By the week of Allison's death, his violence toward Emick had escalated even further. Three days before the shooting, Allison told Emick that he intended to prevent her from having sex with other men. He then placed an electric immersion coil into her vagina. When Emick removed the hot coil, Allison applied the coil to other parts of her body.

On the same day, Allison attempted to hang Emick in the shed. As Emick struggled to keep herself from choking, Allison repeatedly struck her in the head with a mallet, eventually beating her into unconsciousness. When Emick regained consciousness, Allison forced her to place her hands on a table so that he could beat them with the mallet.

On the day before Allison's death, he punched Emick and beat her head against a cupboard. Later that day, just hours before the shooting, Allison told Emick that he was going to kill her and her children and then commit suicide. Allison gave Emick the choice of killing herself or being killed by Allison the next day.

Prior to Allison's death, Emick had informed family members and a friend about the abuse she was suffering but had never complained to legal authorities or made any effort to leave Allison.

Emick's version of the events which culminated in Allison's death were corroborated in part by the testimony of Allison's former brother-in-law, Richard Meyers.[6] Prior to 1983, Emick had informed Meyers of her domestic problems with Allison, including the fact that Allison had physically abused her with various devices. On one occasion when Meyers attempted to visit Emick while Allison was not at home, Emick told him that she could not let him in because Allison had glued the door shut.

On the day prior to Allison's death, Meyers had visited Emick and noticed a burn mark on her face and various bruises on her legs. Meyers offered to remove Emick and the children from the home and take her to a battered women's shelter. Emick declined, saying she feared that Allison would find her.

Later that day, Meyers spoke with both a hotline counselor and the police about Emick's situation. He told the counselor that he felt that Emick was suicidal and he asked the police to go to the home and distract Allison so that he could help Emick leave. The police offered to go to the home the next day and speak to Emick while Allison was away at work.

Still later that same day, Meyers returned to the Allison-Emick home and confronted Allison with his observations of Emick's injuries and his belief that Emick was suicidal. Allison told Meyers that the couple was going to see a counselor at some time in the future. Meyers then called the hotline again and put Emick on the phone. Meyers heard Emick arrange an appointment for counseling.

After the phone call, Meyers told Emick privately that he wanted to leave, but Emick asked him to stay because she was afraid that Allison would kill her if Meyers left. At about 2:00 A.M., Emick and Allison retired to the bedroom and Meyers remained in the living room, where he slept until sometime after 4:00 A.M.

Upon awakening, Meyers knocked on the bedroom door to tell the couple that he was leaving. As Meyers did so, he heard an alarm clock go off and saw Emick motion to him to be quiet. Meyers then left.

According to Emick's testimony, when she saw Meyers' car pull away, she assessed the situation and decided that Allison would abuse her or possibly kill her when he awoke. It was then that Emick decided to kill Allison.[7]

Emick's account of the abuse inflicted upon her by Allison was also corroborated by medical testimony.[8] A physician testified that he had examined Emick shortly after the shooting and had found multiple wounds in various stages of healing covering her body. The physician found abrasions over Emick's eye and on the front and back of her neck. According to the physician, these abrasions could have been rope burns. The physician also found several puncture wounds, welts, and bruises on Emick's upper body; a contusion and abrasion inside her vagina; and burns, abrasions, and contusions on her legs and feet. The physician concluded that these injuries were anywhere from a few days to three weeks old and might have been a result of physical abuse.

Finally, Emick's self-defense claim was bolstered by the testimony of a psychiatrist, who described the battered woman syndrome:

> [T]he abused wife undergoes a personality change as the abuse increases. She becomes frightened and unable to project her thinking into the future. She lives her life from one beating to the next and her thoughts relate solely to her efforts to avoid the next beating. The wife is usually hopeful that, if she pleases the husband, the abuse will stop. For his part, the husband usually expresses remorse after a beating and attempts to reconcile with gifts and/or promises to refrain from abuse in the future. The wife then sees the husband in a different light and is filled with false hope. Another aspect of the syndrome is that the wife eventually feels that she cannot escape her tormentor and that she will be tracked down if she attempts to flee the situation. Her self-esteem vanishes and her confidence is shattered. She feels that no one would believe her if she told them about the abuse and, thus, she keeps it to herself.[9]

Having examined Emick a few months after the shooting, the psychiatrist concluded that Emick displayed the classic signs of this syndrome. The psychiatrist also testified that she had "no doubt" that when Emick killed Allison she was reasonably in fear for her life as well as for the lives of her children. Furthermore, the psychiatrist told the jury that Emick was neither psychotic nor emotionally disturbed at the time of the killing.[10]

To the contrary, the prosecution maintained that "the very ongoing nature of the abuse prove[ed] that Miss Emick was under no imminent danger, particularly from a sleeping man."[11] In support of this contention, the prosecutor called several witnesses.

A police investigator, who had taken Emick's statement immediately after the killing, testified that Emick had mentioned no instances of abuse by Allison in the 24-hour period immediately preceding the killing, other than the "choking incident." The investigator further testified that he did not feel that this incident had been serious and that he did not believe that Emick regarded it as serious.[12]

The prosecutor also called as a witness the hotline counselor to whom Meyers had spoken the day before the killing. She testified that her conversations with Meyers had been "odd" in that Meyers had expressed concern for Emick's safety but had refused to accept any of the alternatives she suggested: medical care, assistance in seeking police protection, or removal of Emick to a shelter for battered women. The counselor also testified that Meyers told her repeatedly that Emick's only option was to kill Allison:

> Q.: Did this particular issue come up more than once?
> A.: Over and over again with every option I gave, that was his pretty standard reply.
> Q.: With every option you gave, he told you that Leslie would have to kill [Allison]?
> A.: Yes.[13]

At the conclusion of Emick's trial, the judge instructed the jury that, in accordance with New York's self-defense law:

> If the defendant, Leslie A. Emick, was confronted by the appearance of danger on February 25, 1983, which aroused in her mind an honest and reasonable conviction that she was about to suffer death or serious physical injury, she would be justified in using deadly physical force in her self-defense.[14]

The jury, clearly rejecting Emick's claim of self-defense, found her guilty of first degree manslaughter. Emick was then sentenced to an indeterminate prison term of two to six years.[15]

On appeal, Emick's conviction was reversed because the trial court, over the objections of Emick's attorney, had allowed the testimony of the hotline counselor described above. This hearsay testimony, the appellate court concluded, impermissibly allowed Meyers' impressions to be imputed to Emick, thereby undermining Emick's claim of self-defense.[16]

Although the case was remanded for a new trial, it was never retried because Emick entered a plea of guilty to a reduced charge of second degree manslaughter. As part of the plea bargain, Emick was sentenced to five years probation on the condition that she perform 3,000 hours of community service, seek vocational training, and continue to receive psychological counseling.[17]

At sentencing, the judge told Emick that if she violated the terms of her probation in any way, she would be "brought back . . . and placed in state prison." The judge also noted that Emick had remarried and become pregnant since the killing, questioned her motives for doing so, and told her that these actions did not "show good sense."[18]

After Emick was sentenced, Allison's father gave his reaction: "As far as I'm concerned, the justice system is going down the drain. There will be no justice for us."[19]

Leslie Ann Emick's case is not unique. A substantial percentage of American women are subjected repeatedly to varying degrees of physical, sexual, and psychological abuse by their mates.[20] Further, a small but increasingly visible number of these women put an end to such abuse by taking the lives of their abusers.[21] When that happens, these women generally are charged with murder or manslaughter and most, like Emick, raise self-defense as a justification for their homicidal actions.[22] While results vary, many of these defendants are convicted, despite their claims of self-defense and abundant evidence that they were severely abused by the men they killed.[23] Moreover, unlike Leslie Ann Emick, who was sentenced to strict probation, many of these women receive stiff prison sentences including, in some cases, life imprisonment without parole.[24]

Who are these women who kill their batterers? Are they different from battered women who do not kill their batterers? Why and when do they kill? How does and should the law deal with them? Are these killings instances of self-defense?

These and similar questions are addressed in this volume. The analysis includes both psychological and legal perspectives. Ultimately the two perspectives are synthesized into an argument for a new legal justification for homicide: psychological self-defense.

The analysis begins in Chapter 2 with a description of the physical, psychological and social characteristics of battering relationships and of the women in such relationships—what some have termed the *battered woman syndrome*.[25] The focus there is largely psychological. Battered women are not only physically battered but generally subjected to severe psychological abuse as well. Indeed, the psychological consequences of the battering relationship are frequently the more significant because they prevent the battered woman from seeking help or terminating the relationship.

Chapter 3 examines the physical, psychological, and social characteristics of battering relationships which culminate in the killing of the batterer. This chapter reviews several empirical studies as well as 100 cases in which battered women have killed their batterers. This review provides a graphic and detailed aggregate picture of: (1) the physical, psychological, and sexual abuse suffered by battered women who ultimately kill their batterers; (2) the reasons these women do not leave their batterers instead of killing them; and (3) the circumstances under which these women kill. The chapter concludes with a brief comparison of battered women in general and those who kill their batterers in particular.

Chapter 4 describes the legal doctrines under which most battered women who kill are convicted of murder or manslaughter despite pleas of self-defense and abundant evidence of the physical, psychological, and sexual abuse suffered at the hands of the men they have killed. In particular, this chapter focuses on the legal requirements of self-defense and explains why so many battered women fail to meet these requirements because it did not reasonably appear that they were threatened with imminent death or serious bodily injury at the moment they killed their batterers.

Chapter 5 provides a critical analysis of the use of testimony on the battered woman syndrome to support the self-defense claims of battered women who kill. This chapter questions the usefulness of this form of expert testimony and explains why it often fails to achieve its intended purpose.

Chapter 6 lays the theoretical and empirical foundation for the argument that many battered women who kill do so primarily as a matter of *psychological* self-defense—that is, to prevent their batterers from destroying them mentally and emotionally. This argument, which draws upon self psychology, psychopathology, victimology, and the psychology of terrorism, goes well beyond the existing doctrine of self-defense and consequently would justify some homicides by battered women not regarded as self-defense under current law.

Finally, Chapter 7 suggests how the theory of psychological self-defense could be assimilated into existing legal doctrine. Specifically, Chapter 7 outlines the contours of a carefully circumscribed legal doctrine of psychological self-defense that would be responsive to the realities of the situation confronting the battered woman; would be consistent with the historical, moral, and utilitarian underpinnings of traditional self-defense doctrine; and would be workable in practice.

2
Battered Women

L ittle is known about battered women who kill their batterers. Our limited knowledge about these women is not surprising. Until relatively recently, we knew very little about battered women in general. Indeed, it was not until the 1970s that the plight of the battered woman was identified as a significant social problem worthy of major scientific and scholarly attention.[1]

Many questions about battered women are still unanswered. Nevertheless, we have learned a great deal about these women and their relationships with the men who batter them. Battered women who kill their batterers are, of course, a subset of battered women in general. Thus, the growing base of knowledge about battered women in general provides both a convenient and essential point of departure in any attempt to understand battered women who kill.

Who are battered women? What sorts of abuse do they suffer? What are the physical and psychological consequences of that abuse? Why and how do these women remain with the men who abuse them?

Once these questions are explored in this chapter, the following chapter examines the same concerns with regard to battered women who kill. It will then be possible to compare the two groups of battered women and to at least speculate as to what characteristics, if any, distinguish battered women who kill from those who do not.

Defining Characteristics: The Physical and Psychological Plight of the Battered Woman

The term *battered woman* is often used loosely by the mass media, the courts, and legal commentators. Even scholars conducting careful research on this phenomenon frequently fail to provide any operational definition of the term. Despite these definitional problems, however, a rather consistent picture of battered women has emerged from a variety of studies and reports.

Physical Abuse

Gayford, a British physician who pioneered in the study of battered women, used the term "battered wife" to mean "a woman who has received deliberate, severe and repeated demonstrable physical injury from her marital partner."[2] He defined marital partner as either the woman's spouse or the man with whom she cohabited.[3]

In Gayford's study of 100 battered wives, he carefully documented the nature of the "demonstrable physical injury." The women he studied had been punched, kicked, attacked with knives, razors or broken bottles, beaten with belts and buckles, burned and scalded. Forty-two had been assaulted with various weapons. All 100 of these women had, at some time, been bruised by their batterers. Eleven had suffered lacerations, 32 had suffered fractures, including broken noses, teeth and/or ribs, and four had experienced dislocations. Nine of these women had been beaten to unconsciousness.[4]

Similarly severe physical batterings and injuries have been observed in other studies of battered women. For example, in their study of 60 battered women, Hilberman and Munson found that these women had been battered with "hands, fists, feet, rocks, bottles, phones, iron bars, knives and guns."[5] They had been scratched, slapped, punched, thrown down and kicked, their faces and breasts being the most frequent targets of the abuse. Many had also been choked into unconsciousness and shot at with guns. Injuries included "multiple bruises, black eyes, fractured ribs, subdural hematomas, and detached retinas."[6]

In a study of battered women who sought medical or psychiatric treatment, Rounsaville and Weissman found that 19 percent had suffered severe head injuries as a result of being battered, 5 percent had suffered lacerations requiring sutures, while 62 percent had received contusions and soft tissue injuries. Eighty-four percent of these women had been injured severely enough to require medical treatment on at least one occasion.[7]

In Walker's study of 435 battered women, she found that two-thirds of the battering incidents included pushing, slapping, shoving, hitting and arm twisting. In half the incidents, women reported having been punched or thrown about by their batterers. Roughly a third of these women reported being choked or strangled, and almost 10 percent said they had been attacked with an automobile. A small (unspecified) percentage had been burned, subjected to attempted drowning, or injured with a knife or gun. Injuries included fractures (broken bones, ribs, backs, and necks), stab and gunshot wounds, loss of teeth and a kidney, serious internal bleeding, bruises, and concussions.[8]

Similar sorts of physical abuse have also been documented by in studies by Kuhl, Pagelow, and Hoeffler. Among the 420 women studied by Kuhl, half reported being physically battered by their mates at least once a week.[9] Among the 350 women studied by Pagelow, 75 had been beaten with weapons, including chains, clubs, chairs, lamps, wrenches, hammers, and golf clubs.[10] In Hoeffler's study of 50 battered women, 24 reported that their batterers had beaten them while they were visibly pregnant.[11]

Psychological and Sexual Abuse

Gayford's definition has the advantage of precision, which is so important to the law, and it is well supported by empirical research. But, by his own admission, it fails to include what some battered women have called the worst form of abuse, psychological cruelty.[12] Gayford's definition also fails to recognize the sexual abuse to which many women are subjected.

A less precise but probably more accurate definition has been offered by Walker. Based upon her extensive research on battered women, Walker defines a battered woman as "one who is repeatedly subjected to any forceful physical or psychological behavior by a man in order to coerce her to do something he wants her to do without concern for her rights."[13] This definition encompasses many cases of psychological and sexual abuse that fall outside Gayford's less inclusive definition.

This broader definition appears well supported by Walker's own research. In explaining this definition, Walker emphasizes that most of the women she studied "describe[d] incidents involving psychological humiliation and verbal harassment as their worst battering experiences, whether or not they had been physically abused."[14] Even where the abuse had been only verbal or psychological, Walker found that "the threat of physical violence was always present: each [woman] believed the batterer was capable of killing her or himself."[15]

Moreover, Walker has made it clear that her definition does not refer to merely isolated instances of minor psychological abuse of the sort common to many relationships. In her study of 435 battered women, Walker found that every one of them reported having been subjected to each of the eight forms of abuse labelled "psychological torture" by Amnesty International: (1) social isolation; (2) exhaustion stemming from deprivation of food and sleep; (3) monopolization of perception manifested in obsessive or possessive behavior; (4) threats (including threats of death) against the woman, her relatives, and friends; (5) humiliation, denial of power, and name calling; (6) administration of drugs and alcohol; (7) induction of altered states of consciousness; and (8) "indulgences" which maintained the woman's hope that the abuse would cease.[16]

These sorts of psychological torture, particularly social isolation, have been amply documented in a number of studies of battered women. For instance, in their study of 60 battered women, Hilberman and Munson found that in nearly all of these cases the batterers had consistently attempted to isolate the women from friends, family, and acquaintances. These women were frequently accused of infidelity, subjected to insults and other forms of verbal degradation in public, and not allowed to work outside the home.[17]

Among the sample of battered women studied by Hoeffler, nearly half reported that their batterers had forbidden them to have personal friends or to have such friends in the home.[18] Kuhl found that 30 percent of the 420 battered women she studied had actually been physically imprisoned by their batterers. These women reported having been locked in closets, locked in or physically confined to their homes, and tied to furniture.[19]

In many cases, it appears that batterers also maintain the social isolation of battered women by limiting or prohibiting their access to financial resources. In Walker's study, for example, she found that 34 percent of the 435 battered women had no access to checking accounts, 51 percent had no access to charge accounts, and 27 percent had no access to cash.[20] Even battered women who are employed outside the home are often denied access to financial resources by their batterers. As one commentator recently observed:

> Batterers frequently demand that they be given total control over their wive's earnings. Battered women, even those with high earnings and successful professional careers, usually accede to this demand. They may do this not only to "keep the peace" at home, but also because they themselves believe that complete command over family finances is a husband's right.[21]

Walker's broader definition of the battered woman is also in keeping with available data regarding rape and other forms of sexual abuse common to battering relationships. In Walker's own study of 435 battered women, 59 percent reported having been forced to have sex with their batterers.[22] Forty-one percent indicated that their batterers had required them to engage in "unusual sex acts" such as "being forced to insert objects in[to] their vaginas, to engage in group sex, have sex with animals and participate in bondage and other sadomasochistic activities."[23]

Other research has confirmed Walker's findings regarding rape and sexual abuse in battering relationships. Among the battered women studied by Kuhl, 30 percent reported having been sexually abused by their batterers.[24] Sexual assaults were also found to be a common occurrence in the lives of the 60 battered women studied by Hilberman and Munson. Indeed, a number of these women reported that their batterers had raped them in the presence of their children.[25]

Finally, Walker's relatively broad definition seems justified in light of the severe consequences of psychological as well as physical abuse. In addition to the already described physical injuries suffered by battered women, most of these women are also left with enduring emotional scars. Indeed, many battered woman have reported that they regard the psychological harm done them as much more significant than the physical harm.[26]

Perhaps the most pervasive emotional consequence of battering, whether physical or psychological, is the development of "learned helplessness."[27] Learned helplessness is a term used by psychologists to describe the response of an organism repeatedly and unpredictably subjected to painful stimuli. The commonly observed response to such treatment includes passivity, feelings of powerlessness, diminished capacity for problem-solving, and a general inability or unwillingness to attempt to avoid the painful stimuli.[28]

Not surprisingly, given the painful abuse to which battered women are repeatedly and unpredictably exposed, such learned helplessness was readily apparent in many of the women Walker studied.[29] As Walker has explained:

> Repeated batterings . . . diminish the woman's motivation to respond. She becomes passive. Secondly, her cognitive ability to perceive success is changed. She does not believe her response will result in a favorable outcome, whether or not it might . . . Next, having generalized her helplessness, the battered woman does not believe anything she does will alter any outcome . . . Finally her sense of emotional well-being becomes precarious. She is more prone to depression and anxiety.[30]

In addition to learned helplessness, battered women do indeed appear to suffer disproportionately from depression, anxiety, and other forms of psychopathology, most of which seem to be the result of being battered, sexually abused, or psychologically tormented.[31] Those who have studied battered woman have almost invariably found them to be depressed, often hopelessly so. For instance, Hilberman and Munson describe their sample of 60 battered women as follows:

> They felt drained, fatigued and numb, often without energy to do more than minimal household chores and child care. There was a pervasive sense of hopelessness and despair about themselves and their lives. They saw themselves as incompetent, unworthy, unlovable and were ridden with guilt and shame. They felt they deserved the abuse, had no vision that there was any other way to live, and were powerless to make changes.[32]

Similarly, two other studies conducted by Rounsaville and colleagues found that more than half of the battered women screened suffered significant symptoms of depression.[33]

As is often the case with those who are seriously depressed, many battered woman contemplate or attempt suicide. Among the 100 battered women studied by Gayford, 42 percent had made suicidal attempts or gestures.[34] Among the 50 battered women studied by Hoeffler, 78 percent reported having suffered, at some time in the battering relationship, from severe depression. Eighteen percent of these women had attempted suicide.[35] Among the 350 battered women studied by Pagelow, almost half had contemplated suicide and 23 percent had attempted suicide.[36] And in one of the studies of battered women conducted by Rounsaville and colleagues, researchers found that 29 percent of the women screened had made at least one suicide attempt.[37]

Not surprisingly, given the constant state of tension in which they live, battered women have also been found to suffer from extreme levels of anxiety and agitation. As Hilberman and Munson describe the psychological turmoil of the battered women they studied:

> The women were a study in paralyzing terror . . . [T]he stress was unending and the threat of the next assault was everpresent . . . Agitation and anxiety bordering on panic were almost always present . . . There was chronic apprehension of imminent doom, of something terrible always about to happen.[38]

In many if not most cases, this chronic psychological distress manifests itself in some form of psychophysiological symptomology. Battered women frequently seek medical treatment, not only for physical injuries, but also for a host of psychosomatic problems, including headaches, asthma, allergies, choking, gastrointestinal upsets, and hyperventilation.[39]

Another common source of psychological abuse for the battered woman is the batterer's physical and/or sexual abuse of her children. Further, it appears that, for a substantial proportion of battered women, one of the psychological consequences of being battered may be that the woman becomes physically abusive to her children. One recent media report on battered women estimated that child abuse is present in 13 percent of all battering relationships.[40] In light of empirical research, however, this estimate seems rather low. In Walker's study, for example, 53 percent of the 435 battered women reported that their batterers had also battered their children[41] and five percent reported that they, themselves, had used physical violence against their children while angry at their batterers.[42]

In Gayford's study of 100 battered women, he found that 37 percent of the women and 54 percent of their batterers had beaten the children.[43] And in Hilberman and Munson's research, they found evidence of physical and/or sexual abuse of children in 20 of the 60 cases they studied. As they concluded: "There seem to be two styles of child abuse: the husband beats the wife who beats the children, and/or the husband beats both his wife and the children."[44]

Barriers to Seeking Help or Terminating the Battering Relationship

Given this extremely bleak portrait of the life of the battered woman, it is often asked, "Why doesn't she leave?" While this question is pertinent to all battered women, it takes on added significance when a battered woman kills her batterer and pleads self-defense. In essence, the woman defendant is claiming that she had no choice but to kill her batterer. Those who sit in judgment of that claim cannot help but ask, "Why didn't she leave?"

Research indicates that battered women remain in battering relationships for a variety of reasons. Any attempt to catalog these reasons or to categorize them seems bound to be both incomplete and somewhat arbitrary. Nevertheless, for purposes of exposition, it may be useful to conceive of these reasons as either environmental or psychological.

Environmental Reasons

Battered women often face formidable, if not insurmountable environmental barriers to leaving their batterers or even seeking help. Perhaps the most significant of these barriers is the batterer himself. Research reports on battered women in general, as well as judicial and media accounts of battered women who kill in particular, are replete with instances in which a batterer has threatened to come after a battered woman, find her, and seriously injure, maim, or kill her if she ever leaves him.[45] Some battered women have also been threatened by their batterers with serious beatings, disfigurement, and death if they ever even discussed the battering relationship with others.[46] The fear engendered by such threats is usually not unfounded. Violence against battered women often escalates any time they attempt to take any control over their lives or the battering relationship.[47]

But even battered women who are not so threatened face major environmental obstacles to leaving their batterers or even seeking help. One obvious barrier is lack of money. For most women, especially for those with children, leaving the batterer is bound to be a costly endeavor. Cut off from financial resources, as so many battered women are,[48] they are likely to find it extremely difficult to set up a new household, which involves finding a new home, paying the first month's rent, and posting a security deposit. Even if they surmount these obstacles, it is likely that they will have to maintain the household and support their children on their own. As one researcher has noted, "[g]iven the well documented failure of divorced men to support their wives, the majority of women know they must support themselves if they leave."[49] Various forms of public assistance may be available, but women may not be eligible for such assistance until they become legally separated or divorced, a process which also costs money and may take weeks or even months.[50]

Of course, the battered woman who leaves might conceivably look, at least temporarily, to friends or family for financial and emotional support. But, in many cases, battered women correctly anticipate that, given the social isolation to which they have been subjected by their batterers, such support is unlikely to be forthcoming.[51] Worst yet, in some cases, the woman might reasonably expect to find her pleas for help met with resistance, if not hostility, from family and friends. Not infrequently, a battered woman's friends and relatives refuse to believe the abuse she has suffered, and even if they do believe her, they blame her and advise her to remain in the relationship and try harder to be a better wife.[52]

In addition to friends and relatives, the battered woman who wants to leave her batterer might look to a battered women's shelter for assistance. A battered women's shelter is an institution, usually privately supported, staffed by volunteers and located in a converted residence, which offers battered women a safe haven from their batterers.[53]

There are now roughly 900 such shelters in the United States.[54] Little if any systematic data has been gathered about these shelters or how they operate, but most of them seem designed to provide only a temporary place of refuge for battered women and, sometimes, their children.[55] It also appears that many of these shelters have very limited capacities, are almost constantly full to—if not beyond—capacity, and cannot possibly accommodate all the battered women who seek admission to them.[56] Moreover, it should be noted that there are many areas of the country where the nearest shelter is hundreds of miles away.[57]

The "shelter movement" appears to be growing. The President recently signed into law legislation allocating a limited amount of federal funds to support shelters for battered women.[58] Nevertheless, even if shelters do become more readily available and capable of offering more than a brief respite from battering relationships, it seems likely that they will be able to assist only a relatively small percentage of battered women: those who seek help. Unfortunately, for many of the internal or psychological reasons explored below, most battered women seem unlikely to turn to shelters or anywhere else for help.[59]

If the battered woman is prevented from leaving by environmental factors, then why not force the batterer to leave? To begin with, even if the battered woman should succeed in getting the batterer out of the home, she is still likely to face many of the same financial hardships already described. But even if she manages to deal with those hardships, forcing the batterer from the home is no guarantee that the relationship or the battering will end. In many cases, battered women have separated from their batterers, either by leaving or forcing the batterer out, only to find that their batterers eventually find them or return to the home and continue to batter them.[60] Even court orders of protection have not stopped some batterers from returning and seriously injuring battered women.[61]

Environmental factors play a major role not only in keeping many battered women from leaving their batterers but also in deterring them from seeking help. Perhaps the most significant deterrent to help-seeking by battered women is the way in which society's helping agents typically respond to them and their batterers.

When a battered woman does look to outsiders for help, it is often the police to whom she turns first. Police officers are frequently called upon to intervene during battering incidents.[62] In some instances, they are called by the woman; in others, they may be summoned by friends, relatives, or neighbors. In either case, the police are likely to be the first of society's helping agents to become aware of the battered woman's plight.

While the police can usually be counted on to put an end to a battering incident in progress, their general failure to do much more than that has been widely documented.[63] As a rule, police officers respond to battering incidents by attempting to calm the batterer and, in some instances, conduct some kind of informal, on-the-spot mediation.[64] Their goal is generally to quiet the situation and then leave as quickly as possible.[65]

While a recent study indicates that arrest may have a significant deterrent effect on future battering,[66] police officers rarely arrest a batterer or even attempt to remove him from the home.[67] A battered women who asks the police to arrest her batterer or remove him from the home is likely to be told that such action cannot be taken unless she goes to the prosecutor's office and files a formal criminal charge against the batterer or goes to court and obtains a restraining order.[68] Worse yet, in some instances, the police may respond to the battered woman's request with disbelief or else appear to sympathize with the batterer.[69]

There are indications that police behavior in response to battering incidents may be changing. Some police departments have begun to initiate special training programs for their officers in how to deal most effectively with such incidents.[70] Legal commentators and influential police organizations have recommended a shift in policy from mediation to arrest.[71] Further, in a recent landmark case, a battered woman won a 2.3 million dollar judgment against a group of police officers whom she claimed had not done enough to protect her from her battering husband.[72] Still, as things now stand in most areas, a battered woman is likely to receive little in the way of significant assistance from the police and may even find police involvement in her situation detrimental.

Of course, some battered women may take the advice of the police and file criminal charges or else seek an order of protection against their batterers. But even then they are unlikely to find the response of the legal system very helpful. Prosecutors may be reluctant to pursue a criminal complaint filed by a battered woman against her batterer.[73] Either they view it as insignificant, or they fear, not unrealistically, that the woman will change her mind and drop the charges before the case goes to court.[74]

But even if a battered woman succeeds in convincing the prosecutor to prosecute her batterer, the result is unlikely to be more than a brief respite from the battering relationship. If the batterer is formally charged and arrested, he will most likely be freed on bail pending further court action and will thus be free to continue to batter the woman. Indeed, the fact that the woman has charged him with a crime and thus caused his arrest may, in some cases, be expected to make him even more likely to batter her.[75] The woman may be able to obtain a restraining order but, as noted earlier, such orders are no guarantee that battering will cease.[76]

Furthermore, obtaining a conviction against a batterer is no easy task. Unless the batterer is willing to plead guilty, the battered woman will be forced to face the trauma of testifying against her batterer in open court. And even if the battered woman succeeds in obtaining a conviction against her batterer, her "victory" may prove to be both bittersweet and short-lived. For the most part, judges are notoriously reluctant to sentence convicted batterers to jail or prison.[77] Most often, a convicted batterer will be placed on probation or ordered to undergo counseling,[78] thus leaving him, in many cases, free to return to the home and resume the battering relationship. Of course, if the batterer is jailed or imprisoned, the woman faces the loss of whatever economic support she and her children have been receiving from the batterer.

The response of prosecutors and the courts to battering, like that of the police, may change with time,[79] but for now battered women are likely to obtain little, if any, lasting protection or assistance from the criminal justice system.

Finally, a battered woman seeking help might be expected to turn to other helping professionals in the community. Here again, however, a number of external or environmental factors make it unlikely that she will receive much, if any, help. For instance, physicians and other health care professionals may see as many battered women as the police do, given the fact that battered women often suffer injuries serious enough to require medical attention. Yet it appears that they lack either the ability or willingness to diagnose these women as victims of battering. Battered women frequently report that they have lied to medical personnel about the cause of their battering injuries and that these lies have gone unquestioned.[80]

Moreover, even where a battered woman is truthful with the medical professional treating her, that professional may not be able to offer her much more than traditional health care. Many health care providers not only lack the training and experience necessary to deal effectively with the non-medical problems of battered women but are unaware of other professionals or agencies in the community to whom they might refer these women for help.[81] The most common medical response to a woman recognized as a battering victim is the prescription of tranquilizing drugs.[82]

Even most mental health and counseling professionals have not been trained to work with battered women and have little understanding of battering relationships.[82] As a result, their clinical response to such women may be clouded, if not shaped, by traditional psychological thought that, contrary to the findings of recent empirical research, regards most battered women as masochistic or emotionally disturbed.[83] Thus, whatever treatment such professionals might be able to provide is likely to focus on the woman and her presumed psychopathology, thereby suggesting, implicitly if not explicitly, that she is somehow to blame for the battering she suffers.

Of course, not all mental health and counseling professionals are un-schooled in the problems of battered women and the dynamics of battering relationships. A variety of psychotherapeutic models for the treatment of these women have been suggested and implemented.[84] Most of these ap-proaches emphasize treating the couple or the family unit rather than just the battered woman. Unfortunately, such approaches require the cooperation of the batterer, which is often difficult to obtain.[85] Furthermore, even where such cooperation is obtained, the likelihood of therapeutic success is rather limited. As Walker recently concluded, "treatment models for a family unit rendered dysfunctional because of the man's violent behavior have had little success in effecting a permanent cessation of the violent behavior."[86]

Psychological Reasons

Until fairly recently, mental health experts assumed that battered women re-mained with their batterers primarily because they were masochists who took some perverse satisfaction in being battered.[87] Such an assumption appears to have its roots in psychoanalytic theory dating back to the early work of Freud on masochism in women.[88] In the past decade, however, research on battered women has not only refuted this assumption but has demonstrated that the battered woman's inability to leave her batterer is generally the result of a complex combination of environmental and psychological forces.[89]

Among the psychological forces which appear to tie battered women to their batterers are: (1) their rigid stereotypic images of marriage, family, and male-female roles and relations; (2) their predictable response to the cyclical nature of the battering relationship; (3) the traumatic bond they develop with their batterers; (4) their learned helplessness; and (5) the depression they suffer.

Sex Role Stereotypes and Expectations. Those who have worked with or studied battered women almost invariably report that these women tend to have rigidly stereotypic images of marriage, family, and the respective roles of men and women in these social institutions.[90] Many battered women feel that family life centers around the man, who has the right to control both them and the children and to make all important family decisions.[91] Their own role, as these women perceive it, is to do what the man tells them, to please him and fulfill their wifely and motherly obligations, and to strive to keep the family intact.[92]

As a result, many battered women accept, at least to some extent, the abuse they suffer as an expression of the man's right to control or discipline them and as deserved punishment for failure to live up to their own and their batterers' expectations.[93] They feel that if only they could somehow be better wives or lovers, their batterers would be less inclined to batter them.[94] Since they believe that the battering is their fault, they are often embarrassed or ashamed to reveal it to others.[95]

It also appears that for many battered women, their unrealistic expectations regarding family life leads them to overestimate the benefits of keeping the family intact. Many battered women report that they have remained with their batterers, despite the repeated infliction of severe abuse, to avoid breaking up the family and denying their children a home with two parents.[96]

Given attitudes such as these, it is not difficult to see why many battered women fail to seek help from others, much less attempt to leave their batterers.

The Predictable Response to the Battering Cycle. In Walker's extensive studies of battered women, she has found that battering relationships have a clearly discernible cyclical pattern to which battered women respond in a predictable fashion. Battering relationships generally involve repetition of a three-phase cycle of violence.[97] Indeed, according to Walker, a woman is a battered woman only if she and her batterer have gone through this cycle at least twice.[98]

In the initial phase of the cycle, called the "tension reduction" phase, the batterer inflicts upon the woman verbal and/or minor physical abuse, to which the woman responds with "anger reduction techniques" aimed at placating the batterer.[99]

The second phase, which involves an "acute battering incident," results from the growing and unresolved tension characteristic of the initial phase. In this phase, the woman is subjected to severe physical and verbal abuse and often seriously injured. When the incident is over, there is a predictable "sharp physiological reduction in tension."[100]

This reduction in tension, in turn, leads to the third phase, "loving contrition," in which the batterer becomes remorseful, apologetic, and loving and assures the woman that the battering incident will not be repeated. Such contrite behavior on the part of the batterer reinforces the woman's commitment to the relationship and her hopes for change.[101]

In some relationships, this third phase may last for an extended period of time, but in the battering relationship it invariably fades, tension mounts anew, and the woman is subjected again to an acute battering incident.[102]

As the cycle is repeated, the level of violence and accompanying psychological abuse escalates. Yet with the completion of each succeeding cycle, the woman is again encouraged to believe that the batterer will change and that the battering will cease; she receives "positive reinforcement for remaining in the relationship."[103]

The "Traumatic Bond" Between Battered Woman and Batterer. An alternative, but clearly related, psychological explanation of why battered women fail to leave their batterers lies in the concept of "traumatic bonding."[104] Traumatic bonding refers to "the strong emotional ties [which develop] between two persons where one person intermittently harasses, beats, threatens, abuses or intimidates the other."[105] Such ties, which "manifest themselves in positive feelings and attitudes by the subjugated party for the intermittently maltreating or abusive party," have been observed between hostages and their captors, battered children and their abusive parents, cult members and their oppressive leaders, and concentration camp prisoners and their guards.[106]

In demonstrating the relevance of the traumatic bonding concept to battered women, Dutton and Painter have observed that "There are two common features of social structure in such apparently diverse relationships as battered spouse-battering spouse, hostage-captor, abused child-abusive parent, cult follow-leader, prisoner-guard."[107]

The first of these common features is an imbalance of power "wherein the maltreated person perceives himself or herself to be subjugated or dominated by the other."[108] The less powerful person in the relationship—whether battered woman, hostage, abused child, cult follower, or prisoner—becomes extremely dependent upon, and may even come to identify with, the more powerful person. In many cases, the result of such dependency and identification is that the less powerful, subjugated persons become "more negative in their self-appraisal, more incapable of fending for themselves, and thus more in need of the high power person."[109] As this "cycle of dependency and lowered self-esteem" is repeated over time, the less powerful person develops a "strong affective bond" to the more powerful person in the abusive relationship.[110]

The second feature common to the relationships between battered woman and batterer, hostage and captor, battered child and abusive parent, cult follower and leader, and prisoner and guard is the periodic nature of the abuse. In each relationship, the less powerful person is subjected to intermittent periods of abuse, which alternate with periods during which the more powerful, abusive person treats the less powerful person in a "more normal and acceptable" fashion.[111] As Dutton and Painter correctly observe,

> The situation of alternating aversive and pleasant conditions is an experimental paradigm within learning theory known as partial or intermittent reinforcement, which is highly effective in producing persistent patterns of behavior that are difficult to extinguish or terminate. Such intermittent mal-

treatment has been found to produce strong emotional bonding effects in both animals and humans.[112]

Given the clear power differential between battered women and their batterers and the intermittent nature of physical and psychological abuse common to battering relationships, it seems fair to conclude, as do Dutton and Painter, that many battered women are psychologically unable to leave their batterers because they have developed a traumatic bond with them.[113]

Learned Helplessness. As noted earlier in this chapter, many battered women appear to suffer from what psychologists call learned helplessness.[114] The concept of learned helplessness has been used by many to explain the failure of battered women to leave their batterers or even to seek help.[115] To understand why, it is helpful to explore the broader psychological meaning of this concept.

According to Seligman, who developed the concept of learned helplessness,[116]

> [O]rganisms, when exposed to uncontrollable events, learn that responding is futile. Such learning undermines the incentive to respond, and so it produces a profound interference with the motivation of instrumental behavior. It also proactively interferes with learning that responding works when events become controllable, and so produces cognitive distortions.[117]

Animal and human research, conducted by Seligman and others, demonstrates that those "who have experienced uncontrollability show reduced initiation of voluntary responses [and] have difficulty learning that responses produce outcomes."[118] Such research also indicates that this learned helplessness becomes generalized to other aspects of the individual's experience. As Seligman puts it,

> Men and animals are born generalizers . . . The learning of helplessness is no exception; when an organism learns that it is helpless in one situation, much of its behavioral repertoire may be undermined.[119]

In Seligman's own research, for example dogs subjected to inescapable electric shocks continued to behave in a passive, helpless manner even when given opportunities to avoid being shocked. Other dogs, who had not experienced inescapable shocks, quickly learned to avoid being shocked, but the "helpless" dogs never did so.[120] Experiments with human subjects, using a loud noise instead of electric shocks, have achieved the same results.[121]

Like Seligman's "helpless" dogs and the human subjects exposed to inescapable loud noise, battered women find themselves in life situations where they are repeatedly exposed to painful stimuli (beatings, psychological torment, or sexual abuse) over which they have no control and from which there is no readily apparent avenue of escape. Not surprisingly, these women respond to such "uncontrollability" with classic symptoms of learned helplessness. As Walker has observed, they become passive, lose their motivation to respond, and come to believe that nothing they do will alter or affect any outcome.[122] As a result, like Seligman's dogs and the human research subjects, they eventually cease trying to avoid the painful stimuli and fail to recognize or take advantage of available opportunities for escape.

Depression. In addition to learned helplessness, many battered women suffer from serious depression.[123] Learned helplessness and depression are closely related and many if not most of the symptoms of learned helplessness have direct parallels in depression.[124] For instance, depressed individuals tend to experience, among other debilitating symptoms, decreased motivation, loss of emotional and physical energy, and lowered initiation of voluntary responses.[125] As Beck, a leading psychiatric authority on depression, has observed,

> In severe cases, there is often a complete paralysis of the will. The patient has no desire to do anything, even those things which are essential to life. Consequently, he may be relatively immobile unless prodded or pushed into activity by others. It is sometimes necessary to pull the patient out of bed, wash, dress and feed him. In extreme cases, even communication may be blocked by the patient's inertia.[126]

Depressive reactions obviously vary in their intensity, and few battered women are completely immobilized by depression. Nevertheless, as noted earlier in this chapter, one group of researchers found that the battered women they studied all "felt drained, fatigued and numb, often without energy to do more than minimal household chores and child care."[127] If a battered woman is so depressed that she is barely able to care for her home and children, it is difficult to see how she can have the energy to surmount the serious environmental barriers which prevent her from leaving her batterer or seeking outside help.

3
Battered Women Who Kill

Men are the perpetrators as well as the victims in the vast majority of homicides in the United States. In 1984, for example, of the 13,856 individuals arrested for murder or non-negligent manslaughter, more than 86 percent were men.[1] During the same year, men comprised over 74 percent of murder victims.[2]

While women are less likely to kill, when they do their victims are most often male intimates: husbands, boyfriends, or cohabitants.[3] There are no definitive data as to how many of these homicides are committed by battered women against their batterers, but there is good reason to believe that many females who kill are, in fact, battered women who kill their battering mates.

For example, in one survey of women jailed on homicide charges, it was found that 40 percent stood accused of killing a husband or boyfriend who had battered them.[4] Another study conducted in a women's prison found that of the 114 inmates in custody for murder or manslaughter, 36 had killed their legal or common-law husbands.[5] Of these 36 women, 28 reported having been subjected to "unreasonable amounts" of physical or psychological abuse by the men they killed.[6]

In recent years, battered women who kill their batterers have generated significant legal controversy and media attention[7] but very little, if any, systematic research. Systematic research could lead to a better understanding of these women, their life situations, and the dynamics of their homicidal acts. But such research would be extremely difficult and costly. Researchers would have to identify and gain access to a large sample of these women and be able to demonstrate that this sample was generally representative of the larger population of battered women who kill their batterers.

Given the tremendous practical obstacles entailed by such requirements, the lack of systematic research in this area is not surprising. There are, however, other ways in which a rich though less than scientific body of data might be gathered regarding battered women who kill their batterers.

Walker's Fifty Women

One way to gather such data is illustrated by the work of Walker, who has frequently conducted psychological examinations of battered women homicide defendants and has testified as an expert in many of their trials.[8]

Recently, Walker has provided brief accounts of her evaluations of 50 of these women.[9] While Walker makes no claim that these women are representative of all battered women who kill their batterers, her study is, to date, one of the closest approximations to systematic research in this area. It is difficult to disagree with her assertion that her interviews with these women provide a "rare glimpse" into battering relationships which culminate in homicide.[10]

Like battered women in general, these 50 women had all been subjected to repeated, often brutal, physical attacks by their batterers.[11] Three-quarters of them also reported having been raped by their batterers.[12] Reports of extreme psychological abuse were also pervasive among the women in this sample.[13]

Nearly all of these women had been threatened with weapons. They reported that their batterers seemed fascinated with weapons and frequently used them to make threats during battering incidents.[14] Thirty-eight of the women killed their batterers with a gun. In 29 of these cases, the homicide was committed with the very same gun the batterer had previously used to threaten the woman.[15]

Most of these 50 women had also been subjected to other threats of serious injury, disfigurement, and death, especially when they made any attempt to leave their batterers. Among the non-lethal threats reported were "cutting up her face, sewing up her vagina, breaking her kneecaps, and knocking her unconscious."[16] Like the 435 subjects in Walker's larger study of battered women in general, all of these 50 women believed that the batterer would or could kill them. Moreover, many felt that leaving the batterer would provide no escape from this danger.[17]

Apparently such beliefs were not unfounded:

> Many of these women had tried to leave and had been badly beaten for it. Some actually had gotten away but their husbands traced and followed them, even to another state. Some . . . had been separated or divorced for up to two years before the final incident, and yet still experienced life-threatening harassment and abuse.[18]

Other forms of psychological abuse reported by these women who killed included social isolation enforced by threats against family and friends, the flaunting of extra-marital affairs, administration of mind-altering drugs, and the physical or sexual abuse of the woman's children.[19] More than 75 percent of these women reported that their children had been physically or sexually abused by their batterers.[20]

The emotional consequences of such physical and psychological abuse were predictable. These women reported feeling that they were "trapped in a deadly situation," that they were not being taken seriously by others, and that they could not rely upon anyone but themselves for protection.[21] They all struggled to "keep control of their own minds, recognizing that the batterer had the ability to control their bodies."[22]

Not surprisingly, many of these women became suicidal. Indeed, more than a third of them reported having attempted suicide.[23] Moreover, some of them had been in the process of killing themselves when, at the last minute, they changed their minds and killed their batterers instead.[24]

Walker's published accounts of the actual homicides are sparse in detail. She has reported, however, that in a number of these cases the batterer had threatened to kill the woman unless she killed him first.[25] Furthermore, her reports suggest that several of these homicides appear to have been precipitated by the woman's discovery that the batterer had been sexually molesting an adolescent daughter or by situations in which the batterer set himself up to be "caught" in a sexual liaison with another woman.[26] Walker also reports that several of these 50 women killed their batterers in efforts to prevent the physical or sexual abuse of their children.[27]

While Walker notes that the women in her sample killed for a variety of reasons, her data indicate that all 50 "resorted to using such violence as their last attempt at protecting themselves from further physical and mental harm."[28]

Browne's Forty-Two Women

Browne, one of Walker's former associates, has recently reported the results of a similar study of battered women who have killed.[29] Browne interviewed 42 battered women. Thirty-three of these women were charged with murdering their batterers, six with attempted murder and three with conspiracy to commit murder.[30]

Like Walker, Browne gained access to these women through her role as psychological consultant to their attorneys and makes no claim that these women are representative of the larger population of battered women who kill their batterers.[31] Nevertheless, the results of Browne's extensive interviews provide a good deal of insight into the predicament of the battered woman who kills her batterer.

All 42 of the women Browne interviewed reported having been physically and psychologically abused by the men they eventually killed, attempted to kill, or conspired to kill.[32] All 42 claimed to have been physically battered at least twice and most reported four or more battering incidents, including being slapped, punched, thrown, choked, smothered, bitten, beaten with an object, assaulted with a weapon, scalded, or held underwater.[33] Nearly 40 percent of these women reported being battered more than once a week.[34] Injuries suffered as a result of these batterings included bruises, cuts, black eyes, concussions, fractures, joint damage, partial loss of vision and hearing, miscarriages, and scars from stab wounds, burns and bites.[35]

Psychological abuse, which the women reported generally accompanied the physical batterings, included "extreme verbal harassment," surveillance, restriction of activity, sleep deprivation, and threats of injury and death.[36] Eighty-three percent reported that their batterers had threatened to kill them or others.[37] The specific effects of such psychological abuse are not reported, but Browne does note that almost half of these women had threatened to commit suicide.[38]

In addition to such physical and psychological abuse, most of the women in Browne's sample reported having been sexually abused by the men they ultimately killed or tried to kill. More than 75 percent of these women reported having been raped (that is, forced to have sexual intercourse) at least once by their batterers. Twenty-two percent said they had been raped three or more times and 39 percent claimed to have been raped "often" in the course of the battering relationship.[39]

Additionally, nearly 62 percent of these 42 women said that their batterers had either forced or urged them to participate in sexual acts other than ordinary intercourse:

> These acts included the insertion of objects into the woman's vagina, forced oral or anal sex, bondage, forced sex with others and sex with animals. One woman reported being raped with her husband's service revolver, a broom handle, and a wire brush.[40]

While such incidents are described as "sexual" abuse, it seems clear that many were, in fact, instances of extreme physical and psychological assault:

> Some . . . were quite severe and involved a combination of sexual and other physical abuse and threats. Often they lasted for hours and resulted in the woman being severely injured and psychologically devastated.[41]

Browne seems to imply that many if not most of the women in her sample acted in self-defense when they killed, attempted to kill, or conspired to kill their batterers.[42] Unfortunately, she provides no description or analysis of the actual incidents in which these women resorted to such action against their batterers.

Jones's Thirty-Seven Women

Another rich but anecdotal source of data regarding battered women who kill their batterers lies in the various published reports of such cases. In 1980, Jones devoted a portion of her book *Women Who Kill* to a review of media reports on 37 battered women who had killed their batterers.[43] Like Walker and Browne, Jones makes no claim that this limited sample of cases is representative of the universe of such cases. Some of the cases in Jones's review are portrayed in great detail, but most are described only briefly. Yet overall, her portrait of the battered woman who kills is strikingly similar to the picture of such women provided by Walker and Browne.

The physical abuse suffered by these women was often severe. One woman had been beaten with a dog chain, pistol-whipped, and shot at by her batterer. She had been hospitalized seven times as a result of injuries she suffered in these batterings.[44] Another woman, beaten for 10 years, had been stabbed with a knife and clubbed with a baseball bat.[45] Still another had been beaten, raped, scalded with boiling water, and thrown down a flight of stairs. While she was hospitalized for injuries from the latter incident, her batterer came to the hospital and tried to assault her there.[46]

The injuries suffered as a result of these batterings were often serious. For example, over the course of 15 years of beatings, one woman had suffered broken vertebrae and ribs, lost sight in one eye, and experienced a premature childbirth brought on by beatings while she was pregnant.[47]

Most of these 37 women had also been subjected to severe psychological abuse as well. For instance, one had been forced by her batterer to watch while he dug her grave, killed the family cat and decapitated a pet horse.[48] At least two of the women had been sexually abused by their batterers.[49] In one case, the batterer had sexually abused the woman's daughter as well.[50] In two others, the batterer had physically abused the women's children.[51]

In many of the cases reviewed by Jones, the batterer had threatened to kill the woman or members of her family. Most of these threats appear to have been made in an effort by the batterer to keep the woman from leaving or to force her back after she had left.[52] In other cases, the women appeared to have been restrained from leaving by deliberate techniques of control and isolation.[53]

These women were cut off from contact with family and friends or denied access to cash. In one case, the battering husband ripped the phone wires out of the wall whenever he suspected that his wife had made a call.[54] Another responded to his wife's telephone use by smashing the telephone to bits.[55] Some of these women were locked in their homes by their batterers. In one case, a battering husband refused to let his wife out of his sight during their five-month marriage "except for some 'monitored trips to the bathroom.'"[56]

Despite threats, physical control, and isolation, nearly a third of these 37 women had managed to leave their batterers, but in each case the batterers forced them back. Two of these women were forced back home at gunpoint, and another returned when the batterer put a gun to her child's head and ordered her back.[57] Two women were forced to return by threats to kill their loved ones.[58] In two cases, the batterers tracked the women across state lines to get them to return.[59] One batterer found his wife seven years after she left him and "cut her up."[60]

In 13 of the 37 cases, Jones described details of the actual homicides. In four of these cases, the women killed their batterers during a battering incident.[61] Two women killed their batterers after the batterers threatened their children.[62] One woman killed her batterer after an argument, and one while the batterer was attempting to break into her home.[63] Four of these 13 women killed their batterers as the batterers slept.[64]

Other Women Who Have Killed Their Husbands

A third source of data regarding battered women who kill their batterers is the study of more general samples of women who have killed their husbands. Two such studies have been reported in recent years and, not surprisingly, both include a substantial number of what appear to be battered women.

Totman's "Murderesses"

Totman has reported on interviews she conducted with 50 women prison inmates who had been convicted of killing either their legal or common-law husbands or their children. Thirty-six of these women had killed their spouses and 28 of this number reported that the men they killed had subjected them to "what they defined as undeserved and unreasonable amounts of physical and/or verbal humiliation."[65]

While it is not entirely clear that each of these 28 women would be classified as a battered woman as that term is currently defined[66], excerpts from Totman's interviews make it clear that many were subjected to repeated beatings and extreme psychological abuse by the men they ultimately killed.

Excerpts from interviews with these women include statements such as: "He had beaten me lots of times"; "He'd cuss me out and knock me and the kids (from another marriage) around"; "It's the story of my life. The same fighting, drinking, beating"; "My doctor talked to me . . . after one of my beatings"; "If he didn't like what I was saying, he'd punch me in the mouth"; "He kept on hitting me and threatening me."[67]

Other women in Totman's sample described instances of gross psychological abuse. For example:

He was on some kind of drugs. He did terrible things. He knew I loved my kitten so he killed it. He would wake me up and hold a gun to my head and threaten to kill me.[68]

Many of these women also described the social isolation they felt in the abusive relationship. For example, several women noted that they had no one they could have talked to about the abuse they were suffering from their husbands: "The only people I knew seemed like they had as many—even more—problems than I did . . . They were all drunks." "What's the point of telling your family about it? My family couldn't help me." "My family was all in Hawaii. We had just moved . . . and I didn't have any friends . . . You can't just talk to anyone about that." "What did I have? I only had him."[69]

Other women told Totman why they did not leave their abusive mates before killing them:

I'd get mad and tell him I was going to leave. He'd tell me I was going to leave when he wanted me to leave and not before. He'd knock me up along side of the head.[70]

I was afraid to [leave]. He said he was having the Mafia watch me, and I better not talk to anyone—or else.[71]

I'd tell him things were going to have to change. I'd tell him and tell him. And he'd say "Sure, you're right," and then go out and do the same thing.[72]

You keep thinking things will get better. You look for signs that he's happier or you're getting along better. And sometimes things are better for a little while. Mostly you're just kidding yourself, but you want it to work.[73]

Have you ever asked the police for help when you're getting knocked around by your old man? You know what they do? They talk to him and then they put him in their car and they drive him around the block and they let him out. And he comes right back and starts that same old mess again.[74]

I went to the Army chaplain one time. He told me to try to work it out. He said a divorce would be bad for my husband's career.[75]

Some of the women Totman interviewed also described the actual homicidal incident. Self-defense was a theme in many of the women's explanations:

He had beaten me lots of times. That wasn't different. But this time, it seemed worse. I thought he was going to kill me. It seemed like him or me . . .[76]

He never threatened me with a weapon before . . . But like I told you, he was acting crazy. He was walking around the property at night with a gun in his belt . . . Then he came in and we went to bed. We even made love. Then he woke up and left the bedroom, and I heard one of the kids crying like he was scared. I called to my husband, and he came back into the bedroom with a meatcleaver. It took me five seconds to get a gun. I fired it until it was empty.[77]

I had left him after four years of abuse and gone to my mother's . . . he followed me up there a couple of days later . . . He got mad and hit my mother . . . he picked up the baby and threw him against the wall . . . We were scuffling and fighting. He said he was going to kill me. I picked up the rifle . . . I aimed it at him.[78]

In several cases, however, the killing took place outside of a direct physical confrontation between the woman and her husband:

It wasn't the hitting. After five years, you can get used to that. And after it's over, it's over. It's the words. They hurt more. He found out exactly what to say to really get me the most . . . [T]hat day . . . he started in on my kids and how I'd ruined them and what kind of a terrible mother I was. He told me I should blow my head off. I told him he should show me how to do it if he wanted me to, and I went and got the rifle.[79]

They tell me, and I have to believe it, that I took my pistol and went looking for [him]. I went to two bars before I found him. I went up to him and started firing . . .[80]

I just wanted to frighten him. I didn't go over to his house to kill him. He wouldn't let me see the kids, and I was going to scare him. I didn't even realize that I had pulled the trigger until I saw him lying on the floor . . .[81]

Twenty-two of the 36 women in Totman's sample killed with guns, nine with knives, three with other instruments, and two by setting the man afire.[82]

Barnard's Study of "Spouse Murder"

More recently, Barnard and his colleagues have reported on a sample of men and women who killed their spouses. Eleven of the 34 subjects in their sample were women.[83] In eight of these 11 cases, there was evidence that the women had been battered previously by the men they killed.[84]

Barnard's report provides no details regarding the batterings these women suffered or the incidents in which they killed their batterers. The report does, however, indicate that five of these women had attempted suicide at some time prior to killing their husbands.[85] Furthermore, the report notes that nine of the 11 women killed with guns and that six of the 11 women admitted to alcohol use on the day of the killing.[86] Finally, the report states that eight of the 11 male victims had histories of alcohol abuse.[87]

One Hundred Battered Women Who Killed

In an effort to supplement the picture provided by Walker, Browne, Jones, Totman and Barnard, the present author examined American wire service reports, articles in major newspapers and magazines, scholarly articles, books, and trial and appellate court opinions published between 1978 and 1986, describing cases in which battered women had killed their batterers.[88] One hundred cases were found in which females identified or readily identifiable as battered women had killed men who had allegedly battered them. The details of each of these cases are summarized in the appendix to this volume.

Clearly, no claim can be made that these 100 cases are representative of the larger population of battered women who kill their batterers. Nevertheless, these 100 cases do help shed further light on a phenomenon that has proven difficult to study in any truly systematic fashion. Furthermore, if nothing else, an analysis of the published accounts of these cases helps flesh out the limited picture of battered women who kill presented in Jones's similar (but less extensive and less detailed) review and the empirical studies conducted by Walker, Browne, Totman, and Barnard.

Physical Abuse

Like the 50 women in Walker's study and the 42 interviewed by Browne, these 100 woman all claimed to have been subjected to repeated, often severe, physical abuse by the men they killed. These women were beaten with fists, clubs, baseball bats, mallets, tire irons, belts, and a variety of other objects. Several were battered while pregnant, resulting in at least three miscarriages. A number of these women were also pistol-whipped, stabbed, shot at with guns, or assaulted with other lethal weapons. Three were choked into unconsciousness, and one was thrown from a moving car and then run over.

Injuries suffered by these women included lacerations, black eyes, bruises, concussions, broken bones, dislocations, and the loss of teeth. In many of these cases, the women had to be hospitalized for treatment of their injuries. Perhaps the most vivid account of such physical abuse and its medical consequences was provided by an appellate court in its published decision affirming the manslaughter conviction of a battered women who shot and killed her batterer after he threatened to whip her:

Defendant also testified that she worked until 1974 when the deceased broke her ankle. She had been wearing a cast on her arm as a result of an altercation with deceased during which he had twisted her hand. She had a scar on her right arm some 2½ or 3 inches long resulting from surgery in connection with this injury. After this incident, the deceased kicked her elbow and dislocated it. This required a cast. At that time the deceased struck her face so that her eyes and mouth were swollen shut and she could neither see nor eat. On another occasion deceased struck her on the head with a car jack which scarred her. He struck her on the breast which ultimately required a surgical procedure for removal of a knot. He threw her forcibly across a chair and caused four fractured ribs. During May 1976 [at the time of the killing] she was taking medication for her "nervous" condition and headaches.[89]

Psychological Abuse

Nearly all of these 100 women had also been subjected to severe psychological abuse by the men they killed. Among the indignities to which these women were subjected by their batterers were the killing of family pets, beatings in front of the children, the keeping of a miscarried fetus in the family freezer, forced prostitution, forcible drug injection, and the physical and sexual abuse of their children. In one case, the batterer forced the woman's face into a mound of red ants.

Threats of physical injury, mutilation, or death were also common among these 100 cases. In 41 cases, it was reported that the batterer had threatened to kill the woman. Thirty-nine women had been threatened or assaulted at least once with a weapon. In several cases, the batterer had also threatened to kill the woman's children. Significantly, in many cases, threats against the woman or her children were made by the batterer whenever the woman gave any indication of leaving.

Sexual Abuse

Eighteen of these 100 women reported having been subjected to various forms of sexual abuse including rape, forced sodomy, and the insertion of objects (such as a wooden dildo, an electric immersion coil, a cucumber, and a roll-on deodorant bottle) into their vaginas. Two woman had been forced into prostitution and one had been compelled to act in pornographic movies. One of these women was raped and tortured with a lighted cigarette while pregnant. Three women reported that their children had been sexually abused by their batterers.

In one case, the sexual abuse was described by an appellate court in some detail.[90] The court gave the following account of the testimony of Jeanette Minnis, who was convicted of killing her husband, Movina:

She commenced by describing her marital problems with Movina which had their origin in her failure to bring enough women home to have sexual encounters with him. She claimed that he had repeatedly subjected her to beatings on account of this. She stated that he wanted other partners because she was not pleasing him enough and that they were to teach her how. She approached other women regularly for this purpose and when they declined, Movina beat her again because he felt she was not trying hard enough.

She then recounted her version of the events commencing with Movina's return from work about midnight on Friday, October 9 through Saturday, October 10 as follows: she was asleep but he awakened her and told her that he had company. She got up, dressed and went into the living room where Movina introduced her to his friend, Duane, who, he said, was a male prostitute. She sat on the floor watching television while Movina and Duane went to Movina's weight room. They returned shortly thereafter and placed a heavy set of barbells across her legs which were outstretched on the floor. She was unable to move. They then engaged in homosexual intercourse. Movina stated to her, "If you just do what you're supposed to do, I wouldn't have to do this." After the unnatural act was completed, Movina removed the barbells and she fled to the bathroom to vomit. When she came out, she attempted to leave the house but was restrained by Movina. Both he and Duane then attacked her sexually and later Movina beat her and again sexually assaulted her. He then tied her to the knob on the bedroom door and left the house. He assigned as his reason that he was concerned that she would tell someone about the homosexual intercourse.

She was uncertain when he returned home, but when he did, he was still ranting and raving that she might tell someone about what had happened. He untied her and she went to the bathroom to bathe. He followed and pushed her head into the toilet and repeatedly threatened her with death. He then forced her to perform fellatio on the bathroom floor and next dragged her to the waterbed where he commenced having intercourse with her . . .[91]

Why They Didn't Leave

As noted above, in many cases the batterers threatened to injure, mutilate, or kill the women or their children if they left. In other cases, the women were cut off from social contacts and financial resources in apparent efforts to isolate them. In one case, the battering husband had refused to allow the woman to work. Each morning, when he left home, he put marks under the car tires so that he could tell if she had driven the car while he was gone.[92] In the Leslie Emick case, described in Chapter 1, the batterer reportedly glued shut the door to the couple's mobile home when he left for the day.[93]

Despite threats and attempts at social and financial isolation, a number of these 100 women had managed to leave their batterers. One women left several times but each time was persuaded to return by the batterer's promises to reform.[94] Another left her batterer for 10 months and filed for divorce before being persuaded to return by her need for money, the batterer's improved behavior toward her, and his reasoning that the children would have fewer problems at home and school if he were around to care for them.[95] Yet another woman and her children moved three times to escape from the woman's battering boyfriend. Each time, the boyfriend found them and continued to inflict both physical and psychological abuse, including beatings, threats with a gun and a knife, and destruction of the woman's property.[96]

In several of these 100 cases, the women managed to force their batterers out of the home, in some cases by means of a court order. Yet in each of these cases, the batterer returned to threaten or physically abuse the woman. In one case, the woman had her husband removed from the home under the state Protection from Abuse Act. After being evicted, he called her several hundred times a day. When she took the telephone off the hook to prevent this harassment, he would come to the house and threaten her in person.[97]

The Homicidal Incidents

In 87 of these 100 cases, published reports included details of the actual homicidal incidents. Significantly, in view of the current legal doctrine of self-defense, which justifies the use of deadly force only to protect oneself from an *imminent* threat of death or serious bodily injury,[98] only one-third of these killings (29 out of 87) took place during the course of a battering incident.

In 34 of these 87 cases, the killing occurred sometime after either a battering incident or a threat to injure or kill the woman. In only five of these cases was the threat made with a weapon. Two killings occurred after the batterer had beaten the woman's child.

In 10 of these 87 cases, the woman killed her batterer after what might best be described as an argument. In 18 cases, the killing took place while the batterer was asleep or nearly asleep. Five women arranged to have their batterers killed by others.

Battered Women Who Kill and Those Who Do Not

Are battered women who kill any different than those who do not? Based on available data, there can be no clearcut answer to that question. It does appear, however, that there may be some major differences between these two groups of battered women.

Physical Abuse

To date, only two studies (those of Walker and Browne) appear to have compared battered women in general and those who kill. Both studies suggest that there may be important differences between these two groups in terms of the physical abuse they have suffered at the hands of their batterers.

Browne compared her sample of 42 battered women homicide defendants with a "control" group of 42 battered women who had not killed, attempted to kill, or conspired to kill their batterers.[99] This control group was drawn from Walker's earlier study of battered women in general.[100]

Browne found no significant difference in the overall number of violent acts reported by women in these two groups, but observed that women in the "homicide" group had suffered much more serious physical injuries.[101] Moreover, Browne found that while 40 percent of the women in the "homicide" group reported being battered more than once a week, only 13 percent of those in the "control" group reported such a high frequency of battering.[102]

Walker's reports provide no specific comparative statistical data, but her comparison of battered women in general to those who kill also suggests that there may be major differences between these two groups of women in terms of physical abuse. Based upon her studies of women in both groups, Walker has concluded that there is a "higher lethality risk"—that is, a greater likelihood that the woman will eventually kill her batterer—when the first battering incident involves "life-threatening or severe violent acts or injuries."[103] These same studies have led Walker to conclude that rapid, as opposed to gradual, escalation in the severity of battering incidents is also a good predictor of eventual homicide.[104]

Psychological Abuse

Though it is difficult to generalize in the absence of fully comparable data, it appears that at least three aspects of psychological abuse may help differentiate battered women who kill from those who do not.

Death Threats. In Browne's study, 83 percent of the women in the "homicide" group reported that their batterers had threatened to kill them or others. Only 59 percent of those in the "control" group (battered women who had not killed) reported such threats.[105] Similarly, over 61 percent of the women in the "homicide" group, but only 51 percent of those in the "control" group, reported that their batterers had threatened to kill themselves.[106]

Threats With a Weapon. Walker's research suggests that threats with a weapon may also distinguish battered women who kill from those who do not. Among Walker's general sample of battered women, only 10 percent reported that their batterers had threatened them with a weapon.[107] Yet among her sample of 50 battered women who had killed their batterers, 58 percent reported having been threatened with a weapon.[108]

Walker's findings with regard to this latter group are largely substantiated by analysis of the 100 homicide cases reviewed earlier in this chapter. Among these cases, 39 percent of the battered women who killed reported that their batterers had threatened or assaulted them at least once with a weapon.

Child Abuse. As noted in Chapter 2, a common source of psychological abuse for the battered woman is the batterer's physical or sexual abuse of her children. Fifty-three percent of the battered women in Walker's general sample,[109] 54 percent of those in Gayford's sample,[110] and 51 percent of those in Browne's nonhomicidal "control" group[111] reported that their batterers had physically or sexually abused their children. By contrast, 71 percent of the battered women homicide defendants interviewed by Browne reported incidents of such abuse.[112]

Sexual Abuse

It appears that battered women who kill are significantly more likely than battered women in general to have been sexually abused by their batterers. Moreover, the frequency of such abuse seems to be greater in battering relationships which culminate in homicide.

In Browne's study of battered women who killed or tried to kill their batterers, she found that 79 percent reported having been forced, at least once, to have sex with their batterers.[113] This compares to only 59 percent of the battered women in her nonhomicidal "control" group[114] and 59 percent of those in Walker's general sample of battered women.[115] Browne also found that while 39 percent of the battered women in her "homicide" sample said they had been raped "often," only 13 percent of those in her "control" group reported such a high frequency of sexual assault.[116]

Finally, 62 percent of the battered women in Browne's "homicide" sample reported having been compelled or urged against their will to engage in other "sexual" acts, including the insertion of objects into their vaginas, anal and oral intercourse, bondage, sex with others, and bestiality.[117] Only 37 percent of the women in Browne's "control" sample[118] and 41 percent of those in Walker's general sample[119] reported having been compelled or urged to engage in such acts.

Why They Don't Leave

Battered women in general as well as those who kill in particular report facing the same kinds of obstacles to leaving their batterers: social isolation, lack of access to financial resources, and threats of retaliation. There is reason to believe, however, that battered women who kill might be distinguished from those who do not by the degree to which they are threatened with retaliation and socially isolated by their batterers.

According to Walker's research, threats of retaliation bear a direct, positive correlation to the "risk of lethality" in battering relationships.[120] Walker's studies also indicate that the greater the extent to which the batterer socially isolates the woman, "the higher the risk for a lethal incident."[121]

Demographic Factors

Do battered women who kill differ from other battered women in terms of demographic factors such as age, race, education, or social class? Here, too, generalization is difficult, given the limits of available data. These data do suggest, however, that some significant demographic differences may exist.

Age. Available data suggest that battered women who kill tend to be somewhat older than those who do not. The mean age of battered women in Walker's general sample and Browne's "control" group (a subset of Walker's general sample) were 32 and 31 years, respectively.[122] By contrast, the mean ages of women in Browne's homicidal group and those in Totman's sample of "murderesses" were 36 and 34 years, respectively.[123]

Browne's research suggest that these age differences are not solely a function of the duration of the battering relationship. Women in her non-homicidal "control" group had, in fact, been married to or involved with their abusers longer than those in the "homicide" group. This difference, 7.7 years vs. 6.9 years, is, however, not statistically significant.[124]

Race. The available data regarding race are intriguing but difficult to interpret. Perhaps the only clear inference to be drawn from these data is that the majority of battered women, whether they kill or not, are white:

Study	Sample	Percent White	Percent Non-white
Jones[125]	Homicidal	75.7	24.3
Browne[126]	Homicidal	66.0	34.0
Totman[127]	Homicidal	55.5	44.5
Barnard[128]	Homicidal	89.9	10.1
Walker[129]	General	81.0	19.0
Browne[130]	General	76.0	24.0

At first glance, these data might appear to reflect major racial difference between battered women who kill (the homicidal samples) and those who do not (the general samples). There are, indeed, substantially more non-white women in the homicidal samples than in the general samples of battered women. This difference, however, seems more likely the result of differing sampling procedures used in the various studies than of any actual racial differences between the two categories of battered women.

The battered women in the homicidal samples had all been charged with or convicted of homicide. If, as Jones asserts, the criminal justice system is inherently biased against "women of color,"[131] it should come as no surprise that non-white women are overrepresented in these samples.

On the other hand, the battered women in Walker's general (nonhomicidal) sample, and thus those in Browne's "control" group (a subset of Walker's general sample), were selected through a process in which special efforts were made to insure that the racial and ethnic composition of the sample closely approximated that of the overall population in the region from which the sample was drawn.[132]

Education. Battered women in Walker's general sample and those in Browne's "control" group had, on the average, 12.7 and 12.2 years of formal education, respectively.[133] Over 60 percent of the women in Walker's general sample had at least some college education.[134]

Overall, battered women in the various homicidal samples had somewhat less formal education. Women in Browne's sample had an average of 11.8 years of formal schooling[135] and those in Totman's sample had a mean of only 9.8 years.[136] Barnard and his colleagues did not report the average number of years of formal education for the women in their homicidal sample, but only one of these 12 women had been educated beyond high school.[137]

Here, again, differing sampling procedures may limit the meaningfulness of comparisons among the various studies, but these data do at least suggest the possibility that battered women who kill may be somewhat less well educated than battered women who do not kill.

Social Class. Battering is a phenomenon present in all social classes.[138] And it appears that the same may be said of battered women who kill their batterers.[139] Unfortunately, however, current data do not provide an adequate basis for comparing the social class status of battered women who kill and those who do not.

Browne compared the battered women in her "control" group and those in her "homicide" group in terms of their social class of origin (the social class in which they were raised as opposed to the social class in which they were living at the time of the battering relationship). She found that those battered women who had killed their batterers "came from slightly higher class backgrounds."[140] A similar comparison of the batterers in each group revealed the same nonsignificant pattern.[141]

*Substance Abuse and Availability
of Deadly Weapons*

Two other possible distinguishing factors worth noting are substance abuse and the presence of weapons, particularly guns, in the home.

Substance Abuse. Alcohol abuse seems to be more common in battering relationships which result in homicide. In Walker's study of 50 women who killed their batterers, 48 percent of the women and 88 percent of the batterers were "frequently intoxicated."[142] Similarly, Browne found that 80 percent of the batterers in her "homicide" sample (batterers whose victims either killed or attempted to kill them) "reportedly became intoxicated every day or almost every day."[143]

In contrast, in Walker's study of battered women in general, she found that just 20 percent of the women and 67 percent of the batterers were frequently intoxicated.[144] Similarly, only 40 percent of the battered women in Browne's nonhomicidal "control" group reported that their batterers became intoxicated nearly every day.[145]

The conclusion that alcohol abuse by either or both parties to a battering relationship may increase the risk of homicide is supported by the facts in the 100 homicide cases reviewed by the present author. As noted earlier, in 87 of these cases, published reports provide details of the events surrounding the actual homicides. In 24 (more than one-quarter) of these 87 cases, it was reported that the batterer had been drinking or was intoxicated at the time of the killing. This conclusion regarding alcohol abuse is further supported by Barnard's finding that eight of the 11 husbands killed by their wives had histories of alcohol abuse and that six of the 11 homicidal wives had been drinking on the day of the killing.[146]

Like alcohol abuse, drug abuse may also differentiate battering relationships that culminate in homicide and those that do not. Twenty-nine percent of the women in Browne's "homicide" sample reported that their batterers had been using "street" (presumably non-prescription) drugs every day or almost every day by the end of the relationship. By contrast, only 7.5 percent of the battered women in Browne's nonhomicidal "control" group reported such a frequency of drug use by their batterers.[147]

Presence of Weapons. As mentioned earlier, threats with weapons appear to be associated with an increased risk of homicide in battering relationships. Walker has further concluded that the mere "presence of weapons in the home also seems to increase the risk for a lethal incident to occur."[148] The mode of death in the 100 cases reviewed by the present author seems to support this conclusion. Among the 95 cases in which the woman killed the batterer herself, a gun was used in 69 (73 percent) of the cases. Moreover, the reported facts in most of these cases suggest that the gun was probably present in the home before the killing.

Walker's conclusion regarding the presence of weapons also draws some support from Barnard's data. Among the 11 cases he and his colleagues studied, nine of the women killed with guns.[149] These findings regarding choice of weapon by battered women who kill are especially intriguing because earlier research has suggested that women who kill generally do so by stabbing their victims.[150]

In light of these data, it might be speculated that one major difference between battered women in general and those who kill is ready access to a firearm.

Summary

As emphasized at several points above, any comparison of battered women who kill and battered women in general based on currently available data must be approached with caution. The various "data sets" reviewed in this chapter and the preceding one are all based on samples of convenience and none is claimed to be truly representative of battered women in general or battered women who kill. Moreover, the sampling methods employed in deriving these sets of data vary considerably from one set to another, both within and between the two contexts.

Nevertheless, it seems possible to offer an educated guess as to some of the ways in which battered women who kill differ from those who do not. While this analysis is admittedly speculative, it suggests that battered women who kill not only face greater adversity in their relationships with their batterers but also have fewer resources with which to cope with that adversity.

Overall, it seems that the battered woman who kills her batterer has been battered more frequently and has suffered more serious injuries in the course of more rapidly escalating physical abuse. She is more likely to have been raped and sexually abused, threatened with death, and menaced with weapons. Her children are more likely to have been abused by her batterer. She is more likely to live in an environment where a gun is present, and her batterer is more likely to be an alcohol or drug abuser.

In addition, it seems that the battered woman who kills may be somewhat older, somewhat less well educated, and more socially isolated than the battered woman who does not kill—characteristics which, coupled with more frequent threats of reprisal for leaving, make it more difficult for her to leave her batterer.

4

The Legal Response to Battered Women Who Kill

A number of popular and scholarly articles convey the impression that battered women who kill their batterers are generally acquitted of criminal charges. That is, that they "walk away unpunished after killing their husbands."[1] The fact is, however, that many battered women who kill their batterers plead guilty to or are convicted of serious criminal charges—usually murder or manslaughter—and are often sentenced to lengthy prison terms.

For example, Schneider, an attorney who has helped defend a number of these women, has reported the legal results in 15 of their cases. Seven of these women were acquitted on grounds of self-defense. One was found not guilty by reason of insanity. The remaining seven were convicted of, or pleaded guilty to, either murder or manslaughter.[2]

Walker has reported the legal outcomes in 28 of the 50 cases in her study of battered women who killed.[3] At the time of Walker's report, four of the 28 cases were awaiting trial. Charges against one woman had been dropped. In seven cases, the women had pleaded guilty to reduced homicide charges. Four of these seven women had been sentenced to probation while three had received sentences ranging from one to eight years in prison. In one case, the charges against the woman had been reduced, but apparently no plea had been entered at the time of the report.

Fifteen of these 28 cases had gone to trial. Eight of these 15 women were convicted and seven acquitted. Those convicted received a remarkably wide range of sentences: 10 years probation; one year in prison; six months in county jail; 15 years in prison; two years in prison; 15 years in prison; and 25 years in prison. The duration of the prison sentence given one convicted woman was not reported.

Browne has reported the legal dispositions in 41 of the 42 battered woman homicide cases she studied.[4] Thirty-three of these women had been charged with murder, six with attempted murder, and three with conspiracy to commit murder. Making no distinction between those women in her sample charged with murder and those charged with attempt or conspiracy,

Browne reports that nine women were acquitted, 31 were convicted and one had the charges against her dropped by the district attorney before trial. In one case, for which no disposition was reported, the battered woman defendant was awaiting trial at the time of Browne's report. Among the 31 women convicted, 11 were placed on probation or given suspended sentences, but the remaining 20 were sentenced to prison for terms ranging from six months to 50 years.

Jones has reported the legal results in 33 of the cases she reviewed.[5] Among these battered women who had killed their batterers, eight were acquitted, three had the charges against them dropped, one was found not guilty by reason of insanity, and 21 either pleaded guilty to or were convicted of homicide charges. In addition, Jones reported the sentences given 12 of the 21 women who were convicted by guilty plea or at trial. Two of these women received life sentences and the other 10 were sentenced to prison terms ranging from five to 25 years.

Among the 100 battered woman homicide cases reviewed in the appendix, nine women pleaded guilty to murder, manslaughter, or criminally negligent homicide and received sentences ranging from conditional discharge or probation to 20 years in prison, three entered pleas of not guilty by reason of insanity and were acquitted on that basis, and three had the charges against them dropped before trial. The remaining 85 all went to trial on homicide charges, and claimed self-defense. Twenty-two were acquitted. The other 63 were convicted of various forms of criminal homicide:

Charge	*Number Convicted*
First degree murder	7
Second degree murder	15
Third degree murder	1
Unspecified murder	12
Voluntary manslaughter	11
Involuntary manslaughter	5
Unspecified manslaughter	8
Manslaughter with firearm	1
Reckless homicide	3
TOTAL CONVICTIONS	63

Twelve of these women, all convicted of murder, received sentences of life in prison, one without parole for 50 years. Sentences for the others convicted after trial ranged from four years probation (with the first year to include periodic incarceration) to 25 years in prison. Seventeen of these women received prison sentences potentially in excess of ten years.

Among these 63 women convicted at trial, 55 have appealed and have now had their appeals decided. The appellate courts have affirmed 29 of these convictions, reversed and remanded for new trials 22 of them, and dismissed four of them for insufficient evidence to support a conviction. The four women in these latter cases cannot be retried. In nine of the 22 cases remanded for new trials, the verdict was reversed on appeal because the trial court erroneously excluded expert testimony regarding the battered woman syndrome. Four of the women whose convictions were reversed on appeal waived new trials and pleaded guilty to the original charge or some lesser form of criminal homicide.

Among the 11 spouse killers studied by Barnard, most of whom appear to have been battered women, seven were charged with first degree murder and four with second degree murder. Two of these charges were eventually reduced to manslaughter. Six of the 11 women were convicted and four others pleaded guilty or no contest to the charges against them. In one case, the result was not known.[6]

Since Totman studied only women in prison for killing their spouses or children, all of the women in her sample had either pleaded guilty or been convicted. Among the 36 women who had killed their husbands, five had been convicted of first degree murder, nine of second degree murder, 16 of voluntary manslaughter, five of involuntary manslaughter, and one of an unspecified form of manslaughter.[7]

To understand why so many battered women who kill their batterers plead guilty to or are convicted of murder or manslaughter requires a brief examination of both the law of homicide and the primary legal defenses available these women—namely, insanity and self-defense.

The Law of Homicide

Criminal homicide is the taking of the life of another without justification or excuse. In common law and modern statutes, criminal homicide is divided into two classes of crime, murder and manslaughter. In most jurisdictions, each of these crimes is further divided on the basis of the actor's mental state at the time of the homicide.[8]

Murder

The law recognizes several forms of murder. The form most consistent with the common understanding of the crime is the so-called "intent to kill" murder. In this form of murder, "A, with an intent to kill B, by his conduct succeeds in killing B."[9] Thus, a battered woman who intends to kill her batterer and does so without lawful excuse or justification may be charged with murder.

Proof of intent to kill, however, is not necessary to sustain a conviction for murder. Conduct intended not to kill but rather only to inflict serious bodily injury is also recognized as murder where such conduct results in the death of another.[10] Thus, a battered woman who claims, as many do, that she did not intend to kill her batterer, may be convicted of murder upon proof that she did intend to seriously injure him and that her actions toward that end resulted in his death.

Furthermore, conduct may constitute murder, despite a lack of intent to kill or seriously injure, where it is extremely negligent, creates a very high risk of death or serious bodily injury, and causes death—the so-called "depraved heart murder."[11] Thus, for example, the battered woman who points a loaded gun at her batterer, intending only to frighten him, may be convicted of murder if the gun discharges and the batterer is killed.[12]

In most jurisdictions, murder is divided into two degrees. First degree murder, which is punished more harshly, generally includes deliberate killings committed with premeditation.[13] Premeditation has been taken to mean "thought of beforehand for some length of time, however short."[14] Thus, a battered woman who deliberately kills her batterer with any form of prior planning may be convicted of first degree murder. Examples include women who kill sleeping batterers and those who commission others to kill the batterer.

Second degree murder generally encompasses intentional killings without premeditation, killings resulting from an intent to seriously injure, and "depraved heart murder."[15]

Manslaughter

At common law and in most modern statutes, manslaughter is divided into two separate crimes: involuntary and voluntary manslaughter. Involuntary manslaughter generally refers to killings which result from recklessness or extreme negligence.[16] Voluntary manslaughter, the more serious of the two offenses, refers to an intentional killing committed in the heat of passion resulting from serious provocation by the person killed.[17] In some jurisdictions, the definition of voluntary manslaughter has been expanded to cover intentional killings committed under the influence of "extreme emotional disturbance" for which there is a reasonable excuse or explanation.[18]

Given that most battered women kill only in response to extreme provocation by their batterers—extended physical, psychological, or sexual abuse—one might expect to find few of them prosecuted on charges higher than voluntary manslaughter (that is, seldom for murder). Although many battered women are indeed charged with and convicted of voluntary manslaughter, many others are charged with and convicted of murder. When this occurs, the verdict often seems to be the result of the so-called "cooling time" rule.[19]

Even when a person kills in response to adequate provocation, the killing may still be treated as a murder if there is a time lag between the provocation and the killing.[20] The theory behind this rule is that such a lag gives the actor "cooling time"—time to regain the self-control that presumably was lost as a result of the provocation.[21] It is left to the jury to decide how much of a time lag is required to negate a claim that the killing was provoked and, therefore, manslaughter rather than murder.[22] Thus, the battered woman who is provoked by a beating or a threat of death, but waits until her batterer is asleep before killing him, may be found guilty of murder rather than voluntary manslaughter.

Legal Defenses to Homicide Charges

There are a number of legal defenses to a charge of homicide.[23] As a practical matter, however, the legal defenses available to battered women who kill are generally quite limited. As a rule, there is no question that the woman killed her batterer—most of these women admit to the killing.[24] Furthermore, in most cases, there is little question that the killing was intentional. The result is that most battered women who kill must either raise an insanity defense or plead self-defense.[25]

Insanity

A very small percentage of battered women who kill their batterers plead not guilty by reason of insanity and are acquitted on that basis.[26] Legal definitions of insanity vary, but most jurisdictions adhere to a variation of one of two common standards.

Under the *M'Naughten* standard, a battered woman homicide defendant may be acquitted by reason of insanity if, at the time of the killing, she was, by reason of mental disease or defect, unable to know the nature and quality of her act *or* unable to realize that it was wrong.[27] Under the Model Penal Code standard, the woman could be found not guilty by reason of insanity if, at the time she killed, she suffered a mental disease or defect and as a result lacked the substantial capacity either to appreciate the wrongfulness of the killing *or* to conform her behavior to legal requirements.[28]

The fact that few battered women homicide defendants raise an insanity defense is not surprising. First of all, it seems clear that most such defendants, though perhaps emotionally distraught or on the verge of mental illness, were well aware of what they were doing when they killed their batterers and knew that killing was morally and legally wrong.[29] For the most part, when battered women kill their batterers, they do so for a rational reason: namely, to protect themselves from further physical or mental suffering.[30] Moreover, while most of these women claim to have believed that the killing was necessary, there is generally little reason to surmise that they were substantially unable to control their conduct at the time they killed.

Second, few battered women homicide defendants claim insanity, probably because this defense is so rarely successful.[31] As Schneider has observed, "juries not only generally mistrust psychiatric defenses, but may . . . apply a different standard to women."[32] As Schneider further explains,

> The jury may require a woman who asserts an impaired mental state defense to sound truly insane. A woman who sounds too angry or too calm may not fulfill the jurors' role expectations. The jury may then feel punitive toward her for not conforming to the stereotype.[33]

Finally, and perhaps most importantly, battered women homicide defendants may be discouraged from pleading insanity by the consequences of an acquittal by reason of insanity. Defendants found not guilty by reason of insanity are generally committed to state mental institutions for indeterminate periods[34] and often end up in state custody much longer than they would have if they had been convicted.[35] And, even when released from custody, they must forever bear the stigma of having been declared legally insane and having been committed to a state institution for the criminally insane.

Not surprisingly, attorneys who have defended battered women who kill conclude that the insanity defense "should be considered only as a last resort, with full awareness of its social implications."[36]

Self-Defense

It appears that the vast majority of battered women who kill their batterers claim to have done so in self-defense. Walker describes all 50 of the women she studied as having killed their batterers in self-defense.[37] Among the 100 cases reviewed by the present author, 87 included formal claims by the women defendants that they had killed in self-defense. Schneider, advising other attorneys faced with defending battered women who kill, has suggested that "a self-defense approach should be thoroughly explored as a first step" in every such case.[38]

While that is undoubtedly good advice, the fact is that many battered women who kill and plead self-defense are convicted of murder or manslaughter despite abundant evidence that they were severely abused, both physically and psychologically, by the men they eventually killed. A brief review of the current legal doctrine of self-defense will explain why.

The Basic Doctrine. In general, the doctrine of self-defense permits the use of reasonable force against another person when one reasonably believes that person is threatening him or her with imminent and unlawful bodily harm and that such force is necessary to prevent the threatened harm.[39] This general statement of self-defense law is, however, qualified when the force used is deadly force—force calculated to bring about death. Generally, a person is privileged to use deadly force against another in self-defense only in the reasonable belief that the other is threatening him or her with imminent death or serious bodily injury and that deadly force is necessary to avert the infliction of such harm.[40]

Unlike insanity, which is regarded as an "excuse" for criminal conduct, self-defense is generally viewed as a "justification"[41]—the difference apparently being that "[a] justification speaks to the rightness of the act; an excuse to whether the actor is accountable for a concededly wicked act."[42] While the theoretical boundaries between excuse and justification have never been delineated precisely,[43] a killing in self-defense, whether regarded as justified or merely excused, is not a crime.[44] Thus, a legal judgment that a battered woman killed her batterer in self-defense means that she is completely exonerated.

In some jurisdictions, the defendant has the burden of proving that he or she acted in self-defense.[45] But in most states, once the defendant produces evidence of having acted in self-defense, the prosecution must assume the burden of disproving the defendant's claim.[46]

Barriers to Acquittal. Regardless of which party has the burden of proof, many battered women who kill their batterers find that their claims of self-defense simply do not accord with the narrow limits of self-defense doctrine. In many if not most cases, one or more essential elements of self-defense are not met.

The major barriers to successful self-defense claims in these cases lie in the requirements that, at the time of the killing, the defendant *reasonably* believed (1) she was in imminent danger of death or serious bodily injury; and (2) it was necessary to resort to deadly force to avert that danger. Often, either or both of these requirements make the battered woman's self-defense plea untenable.

Consider, for example, those cases in which women have killed their batterers as the batterers slept. Several such women have testified that they honestly believed that the batterer would kill them when he awoke.[47] Unfortunately for these women, in most jurisdictions, an honest belief in the imminence of danger is not sufficient. Self-defense doctrine generally requires also that a reasonable person, faced with the same circumstances, would have believed that death or serious bodily injury was imminent.[48]

Would a reasonable person believe that someone asleep posed an imminent threat of death or serious bodily injury? Even in a jurisdiction which requires only an honest belief, it is easy to see how a self-defense claim could fail where the battered woman has killed a sleeping batterer. The jurors must still ask themselves, "Did this woman really believe that her sleeping victim was about to kill or seriously injure her?" Not surprisingly, women who have killed sleeping batterers have generally been convicted.[49]

Similar reasoning helps explain the high conviction rate among women who kill (or have others kill) their batterers *after* arguments or acute battering incidents.[50] At the time of such killings, these women are not objectively threatened by their batterers, except perhaps to the extent that the batterer's very presence may be perceived as an imminent threat of death or serious bodily injury to the battered woman. Would a reasonable person believe (or did this particular woman honestly believe) that at the time of the killing—some hours or even days after the incident had ended—she was in imminent danger of death or serious bodily injury?

While the bulk of homicides by battered women seem to take place outside of direct confrontations between these women and their batterers, some battered women do kill their batterers during the course of an acute battering incident. In these cases, one might well expect a woman reasonably to conclude that being severely beaten, choked, or attacked with a weapon constituted an imminent threat of death or serious bodily injury. Nevertheless, a number of women who have killed their batterers under such circumstances have been convicted despite their pleas of self-defense.

To cite just a few examples: Jennifer Patri, who claimed that she shot her battering husband as he came at her with a knife, was convicted of second degree murder and sentenced to 10 years in prison;[51] Joyce Hawthorne, who claimed she shot her battering husband as he was choking her, was convicted of manslaughter and sentenced to 15 years in prison;[52] and Betty Ann Harrison, who claimed she stabbed her batterer as he was dragging her back into a trailer where he had just beaten and attempted to rape her, was convicted of murder and sentenced to life in prison.[53]

In cases such as these (as in most homicides by battered women), there is, of course, the question of the woman's credibility: were the circumstances surrounding the killing in fact as she recounted them?[54] But probably an even greater barrier to acceptance of self-defense as a justification in these confrontational cases is the question of whether the defendant actually and reasonably perceived an imminent threat of death or serious bodily harm at the moment she killed.

In many if not most of these cases, the women have been subjected repeatedly to similar treatment by their batterers in the past and yet have never before attempted to kill their batterers in response. Given that, and the fact that none of these women have ever managed to leave their batters for good, jurors reasonably wonder whether the incident that culminated in the batterer's death was really all that much different from the many previous battering incidents that both the woman and her batterer had survived. Thus, ironically, the woman's status as a battered woman might be a factor that detracts from rather than supports her plea of self-defense.

In many cases, the success of a battered woman's claim of justification may also be limited by the legal requirement that the degree of force used in self-defense be reasonable. Even if a battered woman reasonably believes that she is faced with imminent danger of death or serious bodily injury, her killing the batterer will not be justified as self-defense unless it reasonably appeared necessary to use deadly force to avert that danger. This additional requirement may thwart the self-defense claim of a battered woman who kills because circumstances which reasonably explain her fear of death or serious bodily injury do not necessarily explain why she found it necessary to use deadly force to protect herself.

Perhaps the classic example of this problem is the battered woman who kills her sleeping batterer. Among the 100 cases reviewed in the appendix, at least 18 involved battered woman who killed their batterers as the batterers slept. Having been beaten or threatened with death by the batterer before he went to sleep, these women may have honestly, even reasonably, believed that their lives were in danger. But if that were the case, why didn't they telephone the police or simply flee? Is it reasonably necessary to kill someone who is sound asleep in order to keep that person from killing or seriously injuring you?

Again, similar reasoning applies to cases where the killing takes place *after* an altercation between the woman and her batterer. Even if the woman honestly and reasonably fears for her life or bodily safety, is it reasonably necessary to kill to prevent the possibility of further injury or death *sometime in the future*? Again, why doesn't the woman leave or seek help from the authorities? Is it sufficient that her batterer had threatened to kill her if she ever left him or told others about the way he treated her?

Even battered women who kill their batterers during a battering incident may find that the rule of reasonable necessity thwarts their claims of self-defense. This problem arises, for example, when a batterer attacks a woman with nothing but his bare hands and she responds by drawing a gun and shooting him.[55] Even if jurors believe that the woman honestly or reasonably feared for her life or bodily integrity, will they accept as reasonably necessary the use of a gun against a man who is unarmed and using only his bare hands? That question becomes even more critical where, as is often the case, the woman has armed herself in anticipation of an attack by the batterer.[56]

Perhaps some astute jurors will recognize, as many legal commentators have, that by virtue of their socialization and life experience, few women have the strength, skills, or determination to engage in hand-to-hand combat and defend themselves without using a weapon.[57] But the numerous convictions of battered women who have used deadly weapons to kill unarmed batterers, even during a brutal battering, suggest that such sensitivity is unlikely to be found in a contemporary jury.

In trying to overcome the barriers to acquittal posed by the reasonableness and imminence requirements of current self-defense law, many battered women homicide defendants have turned to psychological and psychiatric experts. These experts have been called upon at trial to testify on the battered woman syndrome—essentially those characteristics of battered women and battering relationships described in Chapter 2. Expert testimony on the battered woman syndrome in these cases has met with mixed success, both in terms of its admissibility and its apparent benefits to battered women defendants. The use of such testimony and the controversy it has engendered is explored in detail in the next chapter.

5

Expert Testimony Regarding the Battered Woman Syndrome

As the preceding chapter suggests, the battered woman who kills her batterer and pleads self-defense faces an uphill battle in court. The State ordinarily bears the burden of proving that the defendant's homicidal act was not reasonable—specifically, that she did not act in self-defense.[1] But as a practical matter, to be acquitted on grounds of self-defense, the battered woman defendant has to convince the jury that what, in some cases, may seem patently unreasonable is, in fact, reasonable. As Schneider has explained:

> A woman who kills her husband is viewed as inherently unreasonable because she is violating the norm of appropriate behavior for women. A battered woman who kills her batterer has to overcome special myths and misconceptions about battered women. She must explain particularly why she stayed in the relationship and did not leave her home; why she didn't call the police or get other assistance before acting; and why she believed that at the time she responded the danger she was facing was imminent, posed a threat to her life, and was therefore different and more serious than other times when she had been beaten, had not acted, and survived.[2]

In efforts to meet this burden, many battered women homicide defendants have sought the assistance of psychologists, psychiatrists, or other mental health professionals. These experts have been called upon at trial to testify regarding the battered woman syndrome. Typically, the expert's testimony has two components.

First, the expert describes the battered woman syndrome. Generally, the expert explains the three-stage cycle of violence posited by Walker: the "tension building" stage, where the abuse is relatively minor; the "acute battering" stage, where the woman is severely beaten; and the stage of "loving contrition," where the batterer temporarily stops abusing the woman, seeks forgiveness, and promises to reform.[3] The expert then describes (1) how the physical and psychological abuse escalates as the cycle repeats itself; and (2) the psychological consequences for the battered woman: learned helplessness, depression, incapacitation, and false hope that the batterer will change.[4] Finally, the expert usually explains how these consequences, combined with economic and social factors (for instance, lack of financial resources, sex-role stereotypes, social and familial pressures to remain with the batterer, inadequate response from the police and the courts, and lack of safe living alternatives for battered women and their children) prevent battered women from leaving their batterers.[5]

Second, the expert generally testifies that the battered woman defendant suffered from the syndrome and, in some cases, explains how the defendant's status as a battered woman affected her perceptions and behavior at the time of the killing.[6]

Expert testimony regarding the battered woman syndrome is thought to be especially helpful to women who have killed their batterers outside of acute battering incidents. Such testimony is said to answer the "instinctive" questions of lay jurors as to why the woman endured such serious abuse for so long, why she did not leave the batterer, and why she believed it was necessary to use deadly force at a time when she was not being battered.[7]

Logically, where the killing has taken place *during* a battering incident, expert testimony on the battered woman syndrome would not seem necessary, since the defendant's homicidal act conforms to traditional legal notions of self-defense: the use of deadly force to repel an attack which objectively threatens death or serious bodily injury.[8] Yet even in these cases, attorneys for many battered women homicide defendants have felt it necessary to present such testimony.[9] Crocker has explained why:

> [T]he defendants have found it necessary to introduce evidence of prior severe or life-threatening attacks by the victim to counter the cultural assumption that women are unable to perceive danger reasonably. Ironically, the same evidence may be used against the defendant to cast doubt on the severity of the attack in question because she did not respond similarly to prior beatings. This could lead the jury to conclude that her perception of danger at the moment she acted in self-defense was unreasonable and that the degree of force used was excessive. Because of this twisted line of reasoning, the defendant must offer battered woman syndrome testimony to put the evidence of prior abuse into perspective.[10]

As a legal matter, expert testimony regarding the battered woman syndrome is said to be relevant to the battered woman's claim of self-defense in at least two ways. First, such testimony is said to bolster the woman's credibility at trial. In *State v. Kelly* (1984), for example, the New Jersey Supreme Court upheld the admissibility of expert testimony on the battered woman syndrome, in part, because such testimony, by showing that [the defendant's] experience, although concededly difficult to comprehend, was common to that of other women who have been in similarly abusive relationships, [helps] the jury understand that [she] could have honestly feared that she would suffer serious bodily harm from her husband's attacks, and yet still remain with him.[11]

As the Court then went on to explain:

[E]xperts point out that one of the common myths, apparently believed by most people, is that battered wives are free to leave. To some, this misconception is followed by the observation that the battered wife is masochistic, proven by her refusal to leave despite the severe beatings; to others, however, the fact that the battered wife stays on unquestionably suggests that the "beatings" could not have been too bad for if they had been, she certainly would have left. The expert could clear up these myths, by explaining that one of the common characteristics of a battered wife is her *inability* to leave despite such constant beatings; her "learned helplessness"; her lack of anywhere to go; her feeling that if she tried to leave, she would be subjected to even more merciless treatment; her belief in the omnipotence of her battering husband; and sometimes her hope that her husband will change his ways.[12]

Second, expert testimony regarding the battered woman syndrome is believed by some courts to be directly relevant to the reasonableness of the woman's belief that she was threatened with death or serious bodily injury at the time of the killing. As the Court explained in *Kelly*,

Depending on its content, the expert's testimony might also enable the jury to find that the battered wife, because of the prior beatings . . . is particularly able to predict accurately the likely extent of violence in any attack on her. That conclusion could significantly affect the jury's evaluation of the reasonableness of [the] defendant's fear for her life.[13]

To the contrary, several courts have concluded that battered woman syndrome testimony is irrelevant to the self-defense claims of women who kill their batterers.[14] For example, in *People v. White* (1980), an Illinois appellate court rejected the battered woman defendant's contention that such expert testimony should have been admitted at trial because the testimony "had a direct bearing on the credibility of the defendant as regards her claim of self-defense."[15] In rejecting this contention, the Court concluded that expert testimony regarding the battered woman syndrome was "neither relevant nor material" because "the issue of self-defense should be determined . . . upon evidence of what transpired during the 'particular instant' in which the death was caused."[16]

Similarly, in *State v. Thomas* (1981), the Ohio Supreme Court held that expert testimony regarding the battered woman syndrome was inadmissible because

> [t]he jury is well able to understand and determine whether self-defense has been proven in a murder case without expert testimony . . . The jury will base its decision upon the material and relevant evidence concerning the participant's words and actions before, at and following the murder, including defendant's explanation of the surrounding circumstances.[17]

This conclusion that the jury is capable of understanding the plight of the battered woman without the aid of expert testimony has been echoed by a number of other courts.[18] For example, the Idaho Supreme Court, in upholding the exclusion of such testimony in a battered woman homicide case, observed that:

> Fear is a common human emotion within the understanding of a jury and hence expert psychiatric explanation is not necessary. A jury is as capable as a psychiatrist in determining the ultimate fact in this case—whether appellant acted under fear when she shot her husband.[19]

Other reasons given by the courts for excluding expert testimony on the battered woman syndrome have included: (1) the syndrome is not sufficiently well established within the scientific community (that is, among psychologists and psychiatrists) to make it the subject of expert testimony;[20] (2) such testimony would invade the province of the jury;[21] and (3) the probative value of such testimony is outweighed by its prejudicial impact on the jury.[22]

While the judicial response to expert testimony regarding the battered woman syndrome obviously has been mixed, the clear trend seems to be toward admissibility of such testimony. For instance, among the 100 cases reviewed in the appendix, such testimony was offered in 44 of the 88 cases that went to trial. The testimony was admitted in 26 cases and excluded in 18. All 18 cases in which the testimony was excluded resulted in convictions, but eight of these 18 convictions were reversed on appeal and the cases remanded for new trials because the testimony had been excluded.

Recently, citing 37 trial court cases involving battered women who had assaulted or killed their batterers, attorneys for the American Psychological Association informed a Florida appeals court that:

> The admissibility of expert testimony on the battered woman syndrome has been so clear to most courts that they have routinely admitted it without even issuing an opinion—including courts in Alaska, California, Colorado, Indiana, Iowa, Kansas, Michigan, Minnesota, Montana, Nevada, New Jer-

sey, Oregon, Pennsylvania, South Carolina, Texas, Virginia, Washington, Wisconsin, and Wyoming.[23]

While expert testimony regarding the battered woman syndrome appears generally admissible in many jurisdictions, there remains the question of whether such testimony is as helpful to battered woman homicide defendants as some have maintained.[24] To date, there is no clear-cut answer to that question. It does seem quite clear, however, that this sort of testimony, whatever its relevance in any given case, is far from a guarantee of acquittal on grounds of self-defense.

For instance, as noted earlier, among the 100 cases examined in the appendix, 88 of which went to trial, expert testimony on the battered woman syndrome was admitted in 26 cases. The fact that this testimony was proffered at all indicates that defense counsel believed that it might be helpful. The fact that it was admitted means that the trial court clearly found it relevant to the defendant's claim of self-defense. Nevertheless, in 17 of these 26 cases, roughly two out of three, the battered woman defendant was convicted of murder, manslaughter, or reckless homicide. It is worth noting that in only three of these 17 cases did the killing occur during a battering incident; all 14 of the others were either committed by a third party hired by the woman or occurred after batterings or while the batterer slept.

The fact that expert testimony on the battered woman syndrome has not proved to be a legal panacea for battered women who kill their batterers and claim self-defense should come as no surprise. As explained in the preceding chapter, under current self-defense doctrine, the ultimate and dispositive test of the battered woman's claim of self-defense is the reasonableness of her homicidal act: whether she acted to avert what reasonably appeared to be an imminent threat of death or serious bodily injury.[25] Expert testimony regarding the battered woman syndrome helps explain why, despite frequent and severe beatings, the defendant did not leave her batterer. But what does such testimony offer in the way of an explanation of the reasonableness of the woman's ultimate homicidal act?

Such testimony may, as some courts and commentators suggest, help the jury understand why, because of the beatings she had suffered previously, the battered woman is better able to predict the likely degree of violence in any particular battering incident.[26] But, of course, even to the extent that expert testimony serves this function, it does so primarily, if not exclusively, in the minority of cases—those in which battered women kill during the course of a battering incident.[27]

In most cases, expert testimony regarding the battered woman syndrome—if admitted—probably does little if anything to illuminate the ultimate legal question of whether it was reasonable for the woman to take her batterer's life. Since in most cases the killing takes place *after* a battering incident or while the batterer is asleep or otherwise preoccupied,[28] the defendant's ability to predict the likely extent of the violence involved in any given battering incident is not immediately relevant to her legal claim of self-defense.[29]

In any event, by emphasizing the battered woman defendant's helplessness, weakness, and victimization, expert testimony on the battered woman syndrome may explain why the woman did not leave her batterer, but "it does not address the crucial issue of the woman's action, or her agency, in a prosecution for homicide—namely, why the battered woman acted" as she did.[30]

Indeed, there is good reason to believe that, in many cases, expert testimony on the battered woman syndrome may undermine rather than support the defendant's claim of reasonableness. The goal of the battered woman defendant who claims self-defense is to have the jury conclude that she acted reasonably in killing her batterer. Yet expert testimony on the battered woman syndrome often paints a stereotyped picture of battered women inconsistent with that conclusion. As Schneider has explained:

> From the standpoint of the jury's determination of whether the woman acted reasonably in self-defense the explanation of "battered woman syndrome" is only partial. Giving commonality to an individual woman's experience can make it seem less aberrational and more reasonable. Yet, to the degree that the explanation is perceived to focus on her suffering from a "syndrome," a term which suggests a loss of control and passivity, the testimony seems to be inconsistent with the notion of reasonableness, and the substance of the testimony appears to focus on incapacity.[31]

As Schneider also points out, by emphasizing the helplessness and passivity of the battered woman, and thus explaining why she was unable to leave her batterer before killing him, expert testimony "highlights a contradiction implicit in the message of 'battered woman syndrome'—if the battered woman was so helpless and passive why did she kill the batterer?"[32]

Finally, as Schneider and other legal commentators have concluded, expert testimony on the battered woman syndrome may "backfire" for one or both of two other reasons.

First, such testimony may be heard by the jury as supporting not a claim of self-defense but rather one of mental disturbance or incapacity:

> Regardless of its more complex meaning, the term "battered woman syndrome" has been heard to communicate an implicit but powerful view that

battered women are all the same, that they are suffering from a psychological disability and that this disability prevents them from acting "normally."[33]

Under current law, where the woman is charged with murder, a jury conclusion that she was acting under extreme emotional disturbance when she killed may (and in many cases probably does) result in a verdict of guilty—not of murder, but voluntary manslaughter, which is defined in some jurisdictions as an intentional killing under the influence of extreme emotional disturbance.[34] Indeed, Walker, who has provided expert testimony on behalf of many battered women homicide defendants, concedes that in many cases the "success" of such testimony lies in its ability to convince the jury that the defendant is guilty of "only" voluntary manslaughter rather than murder.[35]

Second, expert testimony on the battered woman syndrome might elicit a negative reaction from the jury if the testimony is heard as somehow implying that there is a separate "battered woman's defense": that battered women in general have a right or license to kill their batterers, whether or not their acts meet the ordinary legal requirements of self-defense.[36]

This analysis, of course, should not be read as suggesting that expert testimony has no value to any battered women homicide defendants who plead self-defense. At a minimum, as noted earlier, such testimony helps explain why the battered woman defendant did not simply leave her batterer before killing him. Additionally, such testimony can, and probably often does, serve to counter attempts by the prosecution to paint the woman as a masochist who enjoyed or provoked the abuse she suffered.[37] To the extent that expert testimony serves either or both of these functions, it may increase jury sympathy for the battered woman defendant.

The point of this analysis, however, is that the presentation (and judicial acceptance) of battered woman syndrome testimony is not without substantial risks for battered women who kill. By stereotyping battered women as weak, passive, helpless, and disturbed, such testimony may well undermine an individual battered woman defendant's claim of reasonableness, thus helping to defeat her claim of self-defense. Moreover, ironically, as such testimony becomes more generally accepted by the courts, at least some battered women who kill are likely to find it more rather than less difficult to be acquitted on grounds of self-defense.

In accepting expert testimony on the battered woman syndrome, the courts have not created a separate "battered woman's defense." Battered women who kill are still subject to the existing law of self-defense. What the courts seem to have done, however, is to accept a stereotyped view of the battered woman, one which may well lead (if it has not already) to "a separate standard of reasonableness for battered women."[38]

The problem for battered women who kill their batterers is that many of them do not conform to either this "separate standard" or the traditional "reasonable man" standard. As Crocker has observed:

> Some courts seem to treat battered women syndrome as a standard to which all battered women must conform rather than as evidence that illuminates the defendant's behavior and perceptions. As a result, a defendant may be considered a battered woman only if she never left her husband, never sought assistance, never fought back. Unless she fits this rigidly-defined and narrowly-applied definition, she is prevented from benefiting from battered woman syndrome testimony. Simultaneously, the prosecution characterizes her actions as unreasonable under the rubric of the reasonable man. Under that standard, the defendant must explain why her act of self-defense does not resemble a man's. The result is that the claims of the individual woman get caught between two conflicting stereotypes: the judicial construct of the battered woman based on the syndrome testimony, and the prosecutorial model that uses myths about battered women to prove their unreasonableness. Neither of these stereotypes allows a battered woman to portray the reasonableness of her actions accurately to the jury.[39]

As some legal commentators see it, this problem is a function not only of the way expert testimony on the battered woman syndrome is heard but also the way it is presented. Schneider, for instance, concludes that:

> [A]lthough the rationale for admission of expert testimony on "battered woman syndrome" was to counteract stereotypes of battered women as solely responsible for the violence, testimony is being presented, heard and sometimes misheard, that goes to the other extreme, depicting battered women as helpless victims and failing to describe the complexity and reasonableness of why battered women act. Courts are reflecting these perspectives in opinions on expert testimony on "battered woman syndrome" that resonate with familiar stereotypes of female incapacity.[40]

Schneider may be correct. But how else can expert testimony on the battered woman syndrome be presented or heard? It seems abundantly clear that most battered women (particularly those who end up killing their batterers) are, as the expert testimony suggests, victims—frequently helpless victims. The expert can, of course, as Schneider suggests, "describe the particular experiences of the individual woman,"[41] but cannot stop there.

The battered woman, herself, and other lay witnesses can (and ordinarily do) describe these "particular experiences." By law, the function of *expert* testimony is to provide evidence which cannot be provided by lay witnesses—evidence whose subject matter "must be so distinctively related to some science, profession, business or occupation as to be beyond the ken of the average layman."[42] As the courts have emphasized repeatedly, expert testimony on the battered woman syndrome is admissible primarily because, by tying the battered woman defendant's experience to scientific understanding of the battered woman syndrome, such testimony addresses issues "beyond the ken" of the average juror.[43]

Given the nature of the syndrome as it has thus far come to be understood through scientific and clinical study of women physically, sexually, or psychologically abused by their mates, battered woman syndrome testimony must, if it is to be accurate and admissible, address the general victimization and helplessness of battered women.

Though often it does stereotype battered women, expert testimony on the battered woman syndrome generally provides an honest description of what is known about the victimization experience and psychological functioning of these women. If such testimony fails to address adequately the reasonableness of the battered woman defendant's homicidal act, that failure is more a function of the limits of current self-defense law than of the testimony itself or the way it is presented or heard.

The testimony, as it must, paints a rather graphic and compelling picture of the psychological state of the battered woman. That psychological state—while not "normal" in the statistical sense—is not necessarily inconsistent with reasonable behavior. It only appears inconsistent with reasonable behavior because of the narrow way in which self-defense law defines what is reasonable.

Under existing self-defense doctrine, it is "reasonable" (and thus justifiable) to use deadly force only to protect oneself from an imminent threat of death or serious bodily injury. Viewed from this limited legal perspective, the battered woman's act of killing her batterer (particularly where the homicide occurs outside of an acute battering incident) often seems *per se* "unreasonable," and expert testimony on the battered woman syndrome probably does little more than help explain why the woman acted "unreasonably."

The failure of expert testimony on the battered woman syndrome to provide direct affirmation of the battered woman's claim of reasonableness suggests not that such testimony needs to be presented or heard in a different fashion, nor that the law should establish a separate standard of reasonableness for battered women. Instead, this failure suggests that the current law of self-defense—with its narrow emphasis on averting only bodily harm or death—does not give adequate consideration to the awful psychological plight of the battered woman or to the possibility that, under certain circumstances, killing her batterer to escape that plight may be an entirely reasonable and justifiable act.

The remainder of this volume is devoted to laying the groundwork for, proposing, and describing the implementation of a new standard of self-defense which would respond directly to the battered woman's psychological plight and give it the legal recognition it properly deserves.

6
Why Battered Women Kill:
A Theory of Psychological Self-Defense

Why do some battered women kill their batterers? As suggested in Chapter 3, part of the explanation may lie in the degree of abuse to which these women are subjected and their relative lack of resources. As was noted, it may be that these women are more frequently and more seriously beaten, more often raped and sexually abused, more often faced with threats of reprisal for leaving, and more likely to be threatened with death and menaced with weapons than battered women who do not kill. As was also noted in Chapter 3, it may be that battered women who kill are generally somewhat older, less educated, more socially isolated, and thus perhaps even less likely than other battered women to be able to leave their batterers.

Whatever the dynamics of battering relationships that culminate in homicide, almost all battered women who kill claim to have done so to protect themselves from imminent death or serious bodily injury at the hands of their batterers. For some of these women, this claim—which not surprisingly coincides with the legal definition of self-defense[1]—is undoubtedly accurate. For instance, a woman who kills her batterer in direct and immediate response to his attack upon her with a deadly weapon clearly does so to save herself from imminent death or serious bodily injury. While the batterer may, in fact, intend neither death nor serious harm, the law does not require the woman to stand by idly until he makes his intentions absolutely clear; the woman is entitled to act upon a reasonable perception that she is about to be killed or seriously injured.[2]

On the other hand, as the cases reviewed in the preceding chapters indicate, for many if not most battered women who kill, this legal claim of self-defense is open to serious doubt. In most cases, it is difficult to argue persuasively that battered women who kill (or have others kill) their batterers sometime *after* battering incidents (or well *before* anticipated battering incidents) do so to protect themselves from what is reasonably perceived to be an imminent threat of death or serious bodily harm.

While some of these cases do result in acquittals, such verdicts often seem more the result of jury sympathy for the battered women defendants and/or antipathy toward their deceased batterers than any legal conclusion that these women killed in self-defense. In their classic studies of jury decision-making in actual criminal cases, for example, Kalven and Zeisel found that jurors were influenced by sympathy for wives who had killed their abusive husbands and sometimes acquitted such women where judges, hearing the same evidence, said they would have found the women guilty.[3] Alternatively, as Acker and Toch point out, jurors may acquit some battered women defendants not so much because they sympathize with these women or conclude that these killings were committed in self-defense, but because they believe the deceased batterer deserved to die:

> The killing of a battering husband could be "justified" in the jurors' minds not because it was necessary that a battered woman act with responsive deadly force when she was threatened with death or serious bodily injury by her mate but because it was a fitting act of retribution directed at a member of a sadistic fraternity who had finally reaped his just deserts.[4]

Yet to conclude that a battered woman did not kill her batterer in response to what reasonbly appeared to be an imminent threat of death or serious bodily injury is not necessarily to conclude that she did not kill in self-defense. Many battered women who kill their batterers—including those who kill outside of direct confrontations with the batterers—undoubtedly do so in self-defense, although not in the unduly narrow legal sense of that term.

As indicated in the preceding chapters, the law of self-defense equates "self" with only the corporeal aspects of human existence—physical life and bodily integrity. This simple equation has proven convenient and, in many ways, functional for legal standards, which reflect the law's need for reasonable certainty and society's generally preeminent concern for the preservation of physical life. Yet this equation, however convenient or functional, denies what psychologists, philosophers, theologians, and people in general have long realized: namely, that there is more to "self" than mere physical being or bodily integrity.[5]

As commonly understood outside the law, "self" encompasses not only the physical aspects of being but also those psychological functions, attributes, processes, and dimensions of experience that give meaning and value to physical existence.[6] If "self" is viewed from this broader and more commonly accepted perspective, it would seem that many, perhaps even most, battered women who kill their batterers do so in self-defense. They kill to prevent their batterers from seriously damaging, if not destroying, psychological aspects of the self which give meaning and value to their lives. In short, they kill in *psychological self-defense*.

At first glance, this theory of psychological self-defense may seem rather abstract, overly speculative, and perhaps even radical, particularly to those accustomed to thinking of self-defense in traditional legal terms. But the utility of this theory in explaining why many battered women kill becomes clear once the experiences of these women are examined in light of contemporary thinking and knowledge in the fields of self psychology, psychopathology, victimology, and the psychology of terrorism.

Self Psychology: Ontological Insecurity, Disintegration Anxiety, and the Victimized Self

While there is no universally accepted definition or theory of self, self psychologists and others generally regard this construct as a constellation of attributes and processes, both physical and psychological, which distinguish one from others and the environment and give meaning and value to individual existence—that is, one's physical appearance, mannerisms, character, beliefs, attitudes, values, identity, perception, cognition, memory, etc.[7] As William James, the great psychologist, put it nearly a century ago, one's self is "the sum total of all that he can call his."[8]

As conceived by many, especially existential theorists, the self is continually evolving and being shaped by one's life experiences.[9] In the widely shared view of these theorists, one's psychological adjustment or mental health is largely a function of the extent to which one feels secure in one's self. Experiences which validate one's sense of individuality, autonomy, and personal worth contribute to one's self-security and thus to one's psychological adjustment. Experiences which invalidate the sense of individuality, autonomy, and worth undermine self-security, contribute to psychological maladjustment, and may lead to serious forms of psychopathology.[10]

The effect of life experience on self-security and the relationship of self-security to psychological adjustment have been described perhaps most trenchantly by Laing, an existential psychiatrist, and Kohut, a psychoanalyst. Equating self and being, Laing and other existential analysts speak of ontological security and insecurity.[11] In a similar vein, Kohut speaks of "self integration" and "disintegration anxiety."[12]

According to Laing, the individual whose experiences with others are largely self-validating is "basically ontologically secure"; that is, secure in his or her being. Ontologically secure people experience themselves in life as "real, alive, whole, and, in a temporal sense, continuous."[13] They experience themselves as clearly differentiated, autonomous, and worthwhile individuals, capable of relating to others in self-gratifying ways.[14]

On the other hand, the person whose interpersonal experiences are primarily self-invalidating risks becoming ontologically insecure. Ontologically insecure people "feel more unreal than real . . . more dead than alive."[15] Their "identity and autonomy are always in question," they are unable to perceive themselves as "genuine, good [or] valuable," and they become "preoccupied with preserving rather than gratifying themselves."[16]

For the ontologically insecure individual, "the ordinary circumstances of everyday life constitute a continual and deadly threat" to self.[17] Unable to take his or her realness, aliveness, and identity for granted, the ontologically insecure person becomes obsessed with "contriving ways of keeping himself or others alive, of preserving his identity, in efforts, as he will often put it, to prevent himself from losing himself."[18] Unchecked, ontological insecurity leads to an increasingly withdrawn, schizoid existence in which the individual becomes unable to relate to others in any meaningful fashion.[19]

As Kohut sees it, the individual whose experience is largely what Laing and others would call self-validating maintains a functioning and integrated self, one in which "ambitions, skills, and ideals form an unbroken continuum that permits joyful creative activity."[20] On the other hand, the individual whose experience is continually self-invalidating develops what Kohut calls "disintegration anxiety."[21]

Disintegration anxiety, a psychological state remarkably similar to what Laing calls ontological insecurity, is "an intense and pervasive anxiety [t]he core [of which] is the anticipation of the breakup of the self."[22] Such anxiety is manifested in a variety of symptoms, including "severe fragmentation, serious loss of initiative, profound drop in self-esteem, [and a] sense of utter meaningless."[23] Unchecked, this disintegration anxiety poses "the danger of regression to psychosis."[24]

While Laing and Kohut have used ontological insecurity and disintegration anxiety to explain the development of severe psychopathology, these concepts also help explain why many battered woman homicides are best conceived of as instances of psychological self-defense. To understand how ontological insecurity and disintegration anxiety relate to battered women, particularly those who kill their batterers, it is helpful to consider the relationship of these concepts to what Johnson and Ferraro have called the battered woman's "victimized self."[25]

In their extensive work with battered women, Johnson and Ferraro observed that these women do not experience themselves as victims solely as a result of being physically and psychologically abused. Initially, at least, battered women avoid defining themselves as victims by denying or rationalizing the abuse they suffer. For instance, some battered women deny that they are being abused while others admit (to themselves) that they are being abused but blame the abuse not on the batterer but rather on external circumstances (the batterer's drinking, emotional problems, unemployment, etc.) or on themselves and their own inadequacies.[26]

For some battered women, such denial or rationalization can "sustain a marriage through a lifetime of violence or abuse," but most battered women eventually "experience a turning point when the violence or abuse done to them comes to be felt as a basic threat, whether to their physical or social self, or both."[27] This "turning point," which leads to the emergence of the victimized self, may be the result of any one of several catalysts.

In some cases, the turning point comes when there is a marked increase in the severity of the abuse and the woman is forced to realize that she is in grave danger. In other cases, the turning point occurs when the abuse becomes visible to others outside the relationship, who then question the woman's denial or rationalizations. Finally, in still other cases, the turning point comes in response to a significant change in the battering relationship—for instance, when the stage of "loving contrition" (the time in the battering cycle when the batterer is apologetic and loving) grows shorter or disappears altogether.[28]

Whatever the catalyst, the victimized self—a "new sense of self [which] emerges [at the] turning point"—is "all consuming" and "overrides other aspects of the self."[29] The self becomes organized around what the woman now regards as a fundamental threat to self; past events are reinterpreted and reconstructed as life-threatening; the woman is left in a state of pervasive fear which consumes all of her thoughts and energies. As Johnson and Ferraro put it: "The self is left without a reality base, in a crisis of ambiguity."[30]

This crisis, these authors note, forces the battered woman to take "practical actions to see that the victimization stops or does not reoccur."[31] As they put it: "Since victimization represents a primordial threat to the self, individuals are highly motivated to change [their] circumstances."[32]

Not surprisingly, given the overwhelming kind of self invalidation battered women suffer at the hands of their batterers (often the most significant people in their lives), the victimized self described by Johnson and Ferraro (although they do not draw the analogy) represents a psychological state in many ways similar to what Laing calls ontological insecurity and what Kohut refers to as disintegration anxiety.

The victimized self is clearly akin to ontological insecurity; the two states may, in fact, be one in the same. By the time the battered woman reaches the turning point, she may have already experienced such extreme self invalidation that conscious recognition of her victimization (assumption of the victimized self) means little more than accepting what Laing would call her basic ontological insecurity. In that event, the psychological injury suffered by the woman is so severe that she is quite unlikely to be able to take any effective practical actions to end her victimization.

In most cases, however, the turning point directly results not in the kind of end state that might be called basic ontological insecurity but rather in the sort of conscious anticipation or dread that is best described as disintegration anxiety. To use Kohut's terms, the "fundamental threat" perceived by the battered woman at this point is the "anticipated breakup of the self." In short, what the battered woman recognizes at the turning point is that she must assert her self or risk losing her self.

Some battered women are able to assert themselves and avert this primordial threat to self by leaving their batterers. For most battered women, however, leaving is not a viable alternative. Not only do these women face tremendous environmental and psychological obstacles to leaving, but many—especially those who ultimately kill—face a more pressing barrier: their batterers threaten them (and, in some cases, their children) with physical destruction if they ever try to leave.[33]

Under these circumstances, the battered woman's options for practical action, though not entirely absent, are extremely limited. To attempt to leave is to run the risk of physical death or the death of loved ones. Yet to remain with the batterer is to risk what amounts to psychological death, what Laing aptly describes as "life without feeling alive."[34]

Many, perhaps most, battered women who reach the turning point in their battering relationships "choose" to remain and assume this latter risk. As Walker and others have documented, the psychological consequences are both predictable and devastating.[35] On the other hand, at least some battered women avoid that fate by taking what they perceive to be the only avenue of self-assertion open to them. They kill their batterers.

Of course, killing the batterer is, in many ways, self-defeating. The battered woman who kills her batterer pays a heavy price both emotionally and practically. Emotionally, taking the life of another human being, under any circumstances, is likely to leave one psychologically scarred for life. And, as a practical matter, the battered woman who kills her batterer not only destroys the family unit, orphans her children, and cuts off whatever economic support the batterer provided the family, but also runs the risk of being convicted of homicide and sent to prison.

Yet while the emotional and practical costs of killing the batterer are great, so too are the benefits. Obviously, the battered woman who kills averts the threat of future physical harm or even death at the hands of the batterer. But, probably more importantly in most cases, she also puts an end to the kind of abuse which, if allowed to continue, ultimately would have reduced her to a state of virtual nothingness tantamount to psychological death. To put it another way, she averts what she reasonably perceives as the threatened annihilation of her psychological self.

Psychopathology: Learned Helplessness, Depression, and Suicide

As indicated in Chapter 2, a common psychological result of the battered woman's experience is the development of "learned helplessness." Such helplessness is a psychological state which develops when, as a result of being repeatedly exposed to outcomes beyond one's control, one "learns" that nothing one does will affect or alter any outcome.[36]

Walker has found that battered women tend to suffer from learned helplessness.[37] Such a finding is not surprising given the nature of most battering relationships. Battered women are repeatedly and unpredictably subjected to severe physical or psychological abuse over which they have no control and from which they generally cannot escape. Moreover, they usually find that there is little, if anything, they can do to alter the relationship or prevent further abuse.

Walker and others have used the concept of learned helplessness to explain why batterd women do not leave their batterers. As Walker sees it, the battered woman's lack of control in the battering relationship—her inability to prevent the batterer from abusing her no matter how she responds—diminishes her motivation to respond at all. The woman becomes passive, fails to see how any response might prove helpful, and ultimately comes to believe that nothing she does will be of any avail.[38]

While learned helplessness is certainly a plausible explanation for why many battered women fail to leave their batterers, it may also help explain why some of these women eventually kill their batterers and why many of these homicides should be regarded as instances of psychological self-defense. To understand the relationship of learned helplessness to homicides by battered women, it is necessary to explore the relationship between learned helplessness and depression and that between depression and self-destructive impulses and behavior.

The relationship between learned helplessness and depression has been thoroughly developed by Seligman, who suggests that "cognitions of helplessness are the core cause of depression."[39] Not only do all of the symptoms of learned helplessness have direct parallels in depression,[40] but, as Seligman also explains,

> [T]he depressed patient believes or has learned that he cannot control those elements of his life that relieve suffering, bring gratification, or provide nurture—in short, he believes that he is helpless.[41]

Seligman is not alone in regarding helplessness as the primary cause of depression. The other psychopathologists he cites as sharing this thesis are worth quoting in some detail. Bibring, for example, describes the relationship of helplessness to depression as follows:

> What has been described as the basic mechanism of depression, the ego's shocking awareness of its helplessness in regard to its aspirations, is the core of normal, neurotic, and probably also psychotic depression.[42]

Melges and Bowlby view depression from a very similar perspective:

> Our thesis is that while a depressed patient's goals remain relatively un-
> changed his estimate of the likelihood of achieving them and his confidence
> in the efficacy of his skilled actions in achieving them are both diminished
> . . . [T]he depressed person believes that his plans of action are no longer
> effective in reaching his continuing and long range goals . . . From this state
> of mind is derived, we believe, much depressive symptomology, including
> indecisiveness, inability to act, making increased demands on others and
> feelings of worthlessness and guilt about not discharging duties.[43]

And Lichtenberg defines depression as "a manifestation of felt hopelessness regarding the attainment of goals when responsibility for the hopelessness is attributed to one's personal defects."[44]

Seligman's "learned helplessness model of depression" helps account for
the mental state of battered women—women who have been the victims of
repeated and uncontrollable abuse from which there is no apparent escape.
As Seligman's model predicts, these women are typically depressed. Moreover, their depressive symptoms—lack of energy and motivation, feelings of
incompetence and powerlessness, and inability to perceive of alternatives[45]—
closely parallel the symptoms of learned helplessness.

In many cases, it seems likely that the combination of learned helplessness and depression immobilizes the battered woman, making it psychologically difficult, if not impossible, for her to initiate responses which might
bring about an end to the abuse she is suffering. How then does the learned
helplessness model of depression help explain the fact that some battered
women do respond by killing their batterers? The answer to that question
lies in the relationship between depression and suicide and in how that relationship is mediated by learned helplessness.

Psychologists, psychiatrists, and other mental health experts have long
recognized that there is a crucial link between depression and suicidal
thoughts and actions.[46] Summing up the literature on this relationship, Silverman has asserted that "depression prior to suicide is probably universal."[47]

Certainly the risk of suicide is extremely high among individuals who are
depressed. While suicide accounts for only one out of every 10,000 deaths in
this country, it has been estimated that one out of every 200 depressed individuals will die by their own hands.[48] Not only does this estimate probably
err on the conservative side, but it says nothing of the clearly much higher
percentage of depressed people who are plagued with suicidal ideation and/
or attempt unsuccessfully to kill themselves.[49]

Although the relationship between depression and suicidal thought and
behavior makes sense intuitively as well as statistically, it is a relationship just
beginning to be understood.[50] In recent years, however, various lines of re-

search on this relationship have converged on a single significant finding: hopelessness of the sort inherent in learned helplessness is one of the best predictors, if not the best predictor, of suicidal behavior.[51] As Beck put it recently,

> During the last 25 years, hopelessness has emerged as an important psychological construct for understanding suicide. [W]hen depressed patients believe there is no solution to serious life problems, they view suicide as a way out of an intolerable situation. [H]opelessness is a core characteristic of depression and serves as the link between depression and suicide.[52]

One study, for example, found that the seriousness of suicidal intent expressed by depressed patients was most highly correlated with one particular feature of depression—negative expectations about the individual's future. Even subjects who were only mildly depressed demonstrated high suicidal intent when their expectations for the future were slight.[53] Another study resulted in the conclusion that "hopelessness accounts for 96% of the association between depression and suicidal intent."[54] Other research has led to similar conclusions.[55]

Given that learned helplessness appears to be both a cause of depression and a major mediating variable between depression and suicidal thought and behavior, it is hardly surprising that battered women have inordinately high rates of self-destructive ideation and conduct. In Gayford's study of 100 battered women, for example, he found that 42 had made suicidal gestures or attempts.[56]

The overall incidence of suicidal ideation and acting-out among battered women who eventually kill is not known, but is probably quite high. For instance, among Walker's sample of 50 battered women who killed, more than a third had attempted suicide.[57] And among the 42 battered women Browne interviewed, all of whom had killed, attempted to kill, or conspired to kill their batterers, nearly half had at least considered suicide.[58]

When a battered woman's helplessness and depression lead her to the brink of suicide, she has, in the words used by Johnson and Ferraro to describe the victimized self, "hit bottom."[59] Realization of her victimization impels her toward positive action to end her suffering, but learned helplessness inhibits her from responding and prevents her from appreciating the full range of behavioral alternatives.

At this point in the victimization process—unable to leave the battering relationship but threatened with psychological destruction if she stays—the battered woman may well come to believe that the only way to end her victimization is to take her own life. Undoubtedly many battered women do.[60] But as the cases reviewed in Chapter 3 suggest, at least some suicidal battered women are able to see, albeit at the last minute, at least one alternative to self-destruction: killing the batterer who is the source of their victimization, helplessness, and depression. For example, a number of the battered women studied by Walker had been in the process of killing themselves when, at the last moment, they suddenly changed their minds and killed their batterers instead.[61]

For the battered woman whose helplessness and depression have led her to see no viable alternatives other than suicide and homicide, the choice is between killing and dying. Since the threat of imminent death comes "only" indirectly from the batterer, the woman's decision to kill him instead of herself is unlikely to be regarded as self-defense under current law. Yet, from a psychological perspective, it is difficult to view a killing under these circumstances an anything other than an act of self-defense.

Victimology: The Psychological Effects and Aftereffects of Violent Crime

Over the past two decades, there has developed a new interdisciplinary behavioral science known as victimology, the study of the interaction between victim and criminal.[62] While, to date, most victimologists have focused on the role that victims play in stimulating or precipitating the crimes by which they are victimized, at least some have begun recently to explore the psychological effects and aftereffects of criminal victimization.

Victimological research of this latter sort is still in its infancy. What little is known about the psychological impact of criminal victimization has been deprived primarily from clinical observations and retrospective studies of the victimization experiences of individuals who are emotionally disturbed.[63] Nevertheless, there is a growing consensus among victimologists and other social scientists that, for most people, being the victim of a crime, particularly a violent crime, has serious immediate and long-term psychological consequences.[64]

Battered women, at least those who are physically battered, are, of course, victims of violent crime. Their victimization is peculiar, if not unique, in that the criminal is known to them (indeed intimately related to them) and the crime is repeated over time. Still, it seems likely that much of what is known about the effects of violent crime on victims in general will be applicable to battered women as well. Moreover, it appears that at least some of what is known about these effects supports the theory that many battered women who kill do so in psychological self-defense.

Research suggests that being the victim of any crime, even a nonpersonal and nonviolent crime such as burglary, may have traumatic psychological effects.[65] Most research on the psychological effects of crime, however, has been directed toward violent crimes against the person, where such effects are more readily apparent. Furthermore, much of this research may be classified according to the nature of the crime involved—for example, crimes where there is only brief contact between criminal and victim versus those in which such contact is more prolonged.[66] While research indicates that the psychological effects of both types of violent crime may be similar,[67] studies of this latter sort of violent crime are clearly more relevant to the victimization experience of the battered woman.

Prolonged contact between victim and criminal in crimes of violence is unusual but occurs frequently in crimes such as rape and kidnapping and occasionally in armed robbery. The psychological effects of exposure to "prolonged contact" crimes have been described in detail by Symonds, a psychiatrist who has studied them for many years.[68] Based on his extensive research and clinical practice with victims of violent crime, Symonds has concluded that the psychological responses of these victims follow "certain sequential phases regardless of what type of crime was involved" and that "only the duration and intensity of each phase [is] influenced by the nature and quality of contact with the criminal."[69]

In phase one, all violent crime victims "initially respond with shock and disbelief."[70] This phase, which Symonds characterizes as "denial," rapidly gives way to phase two, in which "denial is overwhelmed by reality" and the victim becomes terrified.[71] Phase three, which the victim generally enters *after* the crime has been completed, is characterized by "circular bouts of apathy, anger, resignation, irritability, 'constipated' rage, insomnia, startle reactions, and replay of the traumatic events through dreams, fantasies and nightmares."[72]

In Symonds' experience, victims are rather unlikely to engage in any phase three responses while still in contact with the criminal. As he puts it, these victims, "in the presence of criminal terror, still respond as if they were in stage two."[73] In fact, if contact with the criminal is especially protracted, as in kidnapping or hostage-taking, victims come to fear for their lives, become frozen with fright, and begin to demonstrate what Symonds calls "traumatic psychological infantilism"—a regressive psychological defense mechanism which "causes adults to set aside recently learned experience and to respond instead with the early adaptive behavior of childhood for survival[,] compels victims to cling to the very person who is endangering their lives [and] accounts for the obedient, placid, compliant and submissive behavior seen in frozen fright."[74]

Symonds and others have also studied the psychological effects of criminal victimization which develop *after* the traumatic incident is over, that is, the psychological aftereffects of violent crime. In addition to the overwhelming psychological symptoms of Symonds' "phase three," violent crime victims have been found to suffer from persistent paralyzing fear, anxiety, depression, feelings of hopelessness and helplessness, and a host of painful psychophysiological disorders.[75]

It should be noted that when Symonds and other victimologists speak of violent crime victimization, they are speaking generally about exposure to a *single episode* of violent crime, however protracted it may be. The battered woman, on the other hand, is exposed to *repeated episodes* of criminal violence in the context of a relationship with the criminal which endures over a long period of time.

If the findings of Symonds and other victimologists are applied to battered women, it becomes apparent that these particular victims of violent crime suffer what might be termed the worst of both worlds. Battered women, who are physically abused time and time again, repeatedly experience the terrifying aspects of Symonds' phase two—frozen fear and traumatic infantilism. Yet because the battering they suffer tends to be cyclical, battered women also suffer repeatedly, if not continuously, the symptoms of phase three and the other psychological aftereffects of violent crime victimization.

When a battered woman, faced with the never-ending prospect or such compounded and continuous suffering, kills her batterer (the one directly responsible for that suffering), some might be inclined to view her act as revenge of the sort occasionally engaged in by other victims of violent crime—a mere release of her "constipated rage." In some—perhaps many—of these cases, there is an element of vengeance underlying the woman's homicidal act. But even in those cases, the fact that the woman is motivated in part by a desire for revenge does not necessarily negate the inference that she killed in defense of self.

To begin with, acting vengefully implies a judgment on the part of the actor not only that he or she has been injured but that the injury suffered was both wrongful and undeserved. Thus, to the extent that a battered woman kills to avenge the abuse she has suffered, her homicidal act represents, at least in part, an assertion of her own self-worth. In seeking revenge, she is, in effect, asserting that she was neither fully to blame for nor deserving of such abuse. Viewed in this light, even what appears to be largely a vengeful act might reasonably be viewed as an act of psychological self-defense.

But vengeance provides only a partial explanation for homicides by battered women. The violent criminal victimization of the battered women is unique not simply because it is repeated over time by a single perpetrator who is intimately related to the woman and often results in more severe psychological injury, but also because in many cases the woman has no viable means of escape. Unlike the ordinary victim of violent crime, she is often effectively trapped in a continuing relationship with the perpetrator, a relationship which holds only the promise of more victimization and even greater psychological injury. Thus, while she may share with other crime victims the natural impulse to avenge her victimization, she also has a more powerful and understandable motive for striking back at the perpetrator: killing her batterer may be the only effective way she perceives to end her victimization and minimize the dire psychological consequences of that victimization.

The Psychology of Terrorism: The Effects of "Conjugal Terrorism"

A final line of theoretical and empirical support for the claim that many battered women kill their batterers in psychological self-defense comes from the evolving psychology of terrorism.

Terrorism is generally regarded as describing the actions of people who "plant bombs, blow up buildings, hijack planes, take people hostage, harm them physically and emotionally, and in other ways bully the Establishment for political ends."[76] Consistent with this popular stereotype, most of the psychology of terrorism has been devoted to the study of these people, their actions, and the effects of those actions on their immediate victims and the world at large.[77]

Recently, however, at least some behavioral scientists have suggested that the abuse of women by their conjugal mates is also a form of terrorism, even a form of "political terrorism." As noted in Chapter 2, Walker has pointed out the similarities between the abuse suffered by battered women and the kinds of abuse Amnesty International has defined as torture.[78] Further, Dutton and Painter have used the concept of "traumatic bonding" to explain why battered women do not leave their batterers. They have also observed that such bonding is characteristic of hostage-captor relationships.[79]

Martin, who, like Walker, has written extensively about the plight of battered women, has specifically identified battering as a form of political terrorism:

> Battering men wield guns or knives or fists to terrorize "their" women. Many literally hold their wives hostage—controlling their every move, isolating them, raping them and holding them captive in the home—by the use or threat of violence. Battered women are political prisoners. Male dominance and protection of the patriarchal system are the political issues at stake.[80]

Martin's notion of the battered woman as terrorist captive is quite consistent with the concept of "captivity stress situation" used in the psychology of terrorism.[81] As Eitenger has explained, there is a wide range of such situations, but "[a]ll share certain features, including loss or limitation of freedom, loss of power over one's fate, some kind of relationship to one's incarcerator, and usually some effort to relate to one's family and/or society."[82]

Finally, Morgan, in his book *Conjugal Terrorism*, has explained that:

> Conjugal terrorism is a term describing the behavior of the violent husband, whose atttides and behavior bear a remarkable resemblance to those of the political terrorist. Conjugal terrorism is the use or threatened use of violence in order to break down the resistance of the victim to the will of the terrorist. It is "the use of coercive intimidation for political motives." Ultimately the terrorist uses violence to further his political cause and for the conjugal terrorist, the violent husband, his political cause is the maintenance of his idealized self-image.[83]

The political imagery used by Martin and Morgan might be questioned by some, and neither author has developed this notion of conjugal terrorism in any systematic fashion. Yet their description of battering as terrorism is clearly in keeping with current psychological conceptions of that term. As Fields has observed in delineating the psychological parameters of terrorism:

> The actual process of terrorization is the exertion of irresistible strength with the threat of annihilation. It is accompanied by unpredictability and received with the physical and psychological shock of any severe trauma. Terrorization is the application of this force, overwhelming the victims' capacity for willing their own behavior. The fear of imminent destruction is accompanied by a sense of powerlessness and unpredictability. There are four basic threats that induce the stress response and they are all present in terrorization: threat to life, threat to bodily integrity, threat to security, and threat to self-image. The consensus among laboratory and field researchers is that appraisal of a stimulus as one or more of these kinds of threats brings about a stress reaction with both physical and psychological proportions.[84]

Here, as in the case of violent crime victimization, the analogy to the experience of the battered woman is close but not exact. There is little doubt that battered women are terrorized by their batterers or that many of them are literally held captive by their batterers. The major differences between the battered woman's relationship to her batterer and that between the typical hostage and political terrorist lie in the nature and duration of the relationship. Terrorist and hostage are generally strangers whose relationship is limited to the duration of the siege. Battered woman and batterer are intimates engaged in what is often a long-term relationship.

These differences, however, may not be all that significant when it comes to the psychological effects of terrorization. Both hostage and battered

woman are in a form of captivity, subjected to severe physical and psychological threats if not torture, and helpless to end the traumatic situation in
which they find themselves. Furthermore, both show marked tendencies toward the development of psychological ties to their captors. For the hostage,
this phenomenon has been identified as the "Stockholm Syndrome."[85] For the
battered woman it has been called "traumatic bonding."[86]

The stranger versus intimate dichotomy may have some significance, but
it is not clear which way that difference cuts. Given what is known about the
psychological and social dynamics of close interpersonal relationships, it may
well be more traumatic to be terrorized by an intimate than by a stranger.[87]
Likewise, duration of terrorization, generally longer for the battered woman,
may have significance. But, if anything, this difference suggests that the battered woman may incur more psychological damage than the typical terrorist
hostage.

Currently there is little in the way of hard data (data which are not anecdotal or clinical) on the psychological effects of terrorist victimization, but
what data there are all indicate that these effects are often devastating.[88] Frozen fright and traumatic psychological infantilism, as described by Symonds
in his studies of violent crime victims, appear to be common reactions among
terrorist victims as well.[89] Not surprisingly, many terrorist victims seem also
to respond with overwhelming anxiety, panic, depression, helplessness, suicidal ideation and behavior, loss of self-esteem, paranoia, disturbances of
sleep and appetite, and psychophysiological symptoms such as recurring
acute gastrointestinal upsets[90]—virtually all of the same kinds of psychological problems generally reported by battered women.[91]

Whether the battered woman is a victim of terrorism or "merely" the
repeated victim of violent crime, it seems clear that the psychological effects
and aftereffects of her victimization/terrorization are often truly extreme. The
analogy to terrorist victim, though not exact, is useful in explaining why
some battered women kill, because it places the woman's homicidal act in a
context people seem better able to understand.

Recent world events, and the tremendous publicity generated by them,
have forced us all to become sensitive to terrorism, its consequences, and the
threat it poses to our national and personal security. Extensive media coverage of recent terrorist incidents, including hijackings, kidnappings, and other
hostage situations, has left little to the imagination. As a result, we have all
come to see ourselves as not only potential victims but, in many ways, actual
victims of terrorism.

Once battering is recognized as a form of domestic or conjugal terrorism,
it becomes easier to identify with the psychological plight of the battered
woman and to understand why the use of deadly force to escape that plight
is, in many cases, a form of self-defense.

Summary

No single theory, whether derived from self psychology, psychopathology, victimology, or the psychology of terrorism, fully explains why battered women kill. Yet when the experiences of battered women are examined in light of theory and research from all of these disciplines, it becomes clear that many of these women are faced with an extreme threat to their psychological as well as physical selves. Indeed, it becomes clear that for some of these women the threat to their psychological selves is so grave that failure to avert it would likely result in what could fairly be characterized as self-disintegration.

Certainly not all battered women are so seriously threatened, and some who are find ways other than homicide to avert such a threat. But many battered women do face what amounts to a threatened annihilation of their psychological selves. And, for reasons beyond their control, many of these women reasonably perceive no viable alternative other than killing their batterers. Under those circumstances, their homicidal acts are clearly instances of self-defense.

7
Psychological Self-Defense as Legal Justification

Most battered women who kill their batterers are convicted of murder or manslaughter and many receive substantial prison sentences despite their claims of self-defense and despite abundant evidence of the extreme physical, psychological, and/or sexual abuse inflicted upon them by the men they have killed. Indeed, even where such claims are supported by expert testimony regarding the battered woman syndrome, most of these women are still convicted.

As observed in Chapter 4, this result comes as little surprise, given the current law of self-defense. No matter how severely a batterer has injured a woman in the past, be it physically, psychologically, or sexually, her use of deadly force in response is not justified as self-defense unless it reasonably appeared necessary to protect herself from *imminent death or serious bodily injury*. Evidence, including expert testimony, that she is a battered woman undoubtedly evokes considerable sympathy for her and may, in some cases, even lead a jury to acquit her regardless of the law. But unless the facts surrounding the woman's lethal act fit within the narrow confines of current deadly force doctrine, a jury unwilling to forsake its sworn duty has no alternative but to reject her claim of self-defense.

In some cases, this result may be entirely appropriate. Not all battered women who kill their batterers do so in self-defense, however that term is defined. Those who kill under circumstances which fall within the narrow confines of current deadly force doctrine are, of course, entitled to be acquitted on grounds of self-defense. But what of those, perhaps the majority of battered homicide defendants, who kill not to avert an imminent threat of death or serious physical injury but rather to protect themselves from the infliction of extremely serious psychological injury—those who kill in what has been called psychological self-defense?

While these women may not be faced with a choice of killing or being killed, many are confronted with a dilemma nearly as dreadful. Unable to escape from the battering relationship, they face the "choice" of killing (either their batterers or themselves) or being reduced to a psychological state in which their continued physical existence will have little if any meaning or value. Whatever one chooses to call this state—"life without feeling alive," "partial death," utter hopelessness, chronic pathological depression, or "psychological infantilism"—the net result for the battered woman is a life hardly worth living.

This chapter argues that the use of force, even deadly force, to avoid such a dire fate is a legitimate form of self-defense and should be recognized as such by the criminal law. In short, this chapter presents the case for psychological self-defense as legal justification for homicide. The argument for a legal doctrine of psychological self-defense will be developed in three parts.

Part one briefly spells out the parameters of the proposed doctrine of psychological self-defense, differentiating it from the so-called "battered woman syndrome defense." Part two explains why the proposed doctrine is not inconsistent with, but rather a logical and warranted extension of, current law justifying the use of deadly force in self-defense. Finally, part three examines anticipated practical objections to the proposed doctrine and explains why such objections do not preclude legal acceptance and implementation of a carefully circumscribed doctrine of psychological self-defense.

The Proposed Doctrine

In recent years, a number of commentators have described what they call the "battered woman syndrome defense" to homicide charges.[1] In fact, as should be clear by now, there is no such defense. What these commentators have called the "battered woman syndrome defense" is nothing more than the admissibility of expert testimony regarding the syndrome in support of a battered woman homicide defendant's self-defense claim.[2] As was demonstrated in earlier chapters, whatever its merits, such testimony is clearly no guarantee of acquittal.

The doctrine proposed here is *not* a battered woman syndrome defense. A battered woman syndrome defense would not only arguably violate constitutional guarantees of equal protection[3] but would be unsound as a matter of public policy. Attaining the status of "battered woman," or even "battered person," is not and should not be a justification by itself for homicide.

Consider, for example, Walker's expansive definition of a battered woman: "one who is repeatedly subjected to *any* forceful physical or psychological behavior by a man in order to coerce her to do something he wants her to do without concern for her rights."[4] Such a definition certainly seems appropriate for clinical and research purposes but, by itself, provides no compelling basis for a defense to a charge of homicide.

The legal doctrine of psychological self-defense to be proposed here is both broader and narrower than a battered woman syndrome defense would be. The proposed doctrine is broader because it would not be limited to battered women or, for that matter, to battered spouses. While it is likely that battered women who kill their batterers would be the primary beneficiaries of such a doctrine, the doctrine would provide a possible justification for other homicide defendants as well; for example, battered children who kill their battering parents.[5]

At the same time, however, the doctrine proposed here is much narrower than a battered woman syndrome defense because it would justify only those killings committed to protect oneself from the most extreme forms of psychological injury. It would justify the use of deadly force only where such force appeared reasonably necessary to prevent the infliction of extremely serious psychological injury. Under this doctrine, extremely serious psychological injury would be defined as gross and enduring impairment of one's psychological functioning which significantly limits the meaning and value of one's physical existence.

The Legal Basis for a Doctrine of Psychological Self-Defense

The criminal law operates on the assumption of free will; it assumes that normal people choose to behave the way they do. This assumption provides much of the moral authority for punishing people who engage in conduct proscribed by law. Having *chosen* to behave in an unlawful fashion, these people are viewed as personally responsible, and thus criminally responsible, for their actions.

In some instances, however, the criminal law recognizes that the choices made by normal individuals are not fully the product of free will and thus should not subject them to criminal responsibility. The deadly force doctrine of current self-defense law is perhaps one of the clearest examples of the law's recognition of what some have called "partial determinism."[6] In large measure, this doctrine reflects "the common-sense view that a person sometimes has 'no choice' but to kill his adversary. If his back is to the wall, if it is his life or his adversary's, the human response is to kill rather than be killed."[7]

In fact, however, one who kills in such a situation is not entirely without choice:

> In a weak sense, the defender does "choose" to kill his adversary. Stressing the element of involuntariness is but our way of making the moral claim that he is not to be blamed for the kind of choice that other people would make under the same circumstances.[8]

In a similar sense, the battered woman who kills her batterer in psychological self-defense "chooses" to do so. For the most part, however, her "choice" is dictated by external and internal forces beyond her conscious control. The batterer has, in effect, pushed the woman's "back to the wall." Unable to escape the battering relationship, her options are extremely limited: she can kill herself, kill the batterer, or resign herself to a fate sometimes not much better than physical death. Under such extreme circumstances—which admittedly do not occur in every battering relationship—the "instinct of self-preservation"[9] leaves the battered woman with little in the way of true choice. To the extent that the woman "chooses" to kill her batterer, her "choice" is basically the "choice that other people would make under the same circumstances."[10]

Even under this analysis, however, there remains the troubling fact that the battered woman who kills in psychological self-defense has, in effect, sacrificed the life of another, not to prevent her own physical destruction but rather to preserve her psychological integrity. At first glance, this imbalance or lack of proportionality, however slight it might be perceived to be, suggests that such a killing should not be regarded as legally justified. As a general principle, one's interest in continued physical existence outweighs all other interests.[11] Legal recognition of psychological self-defense as a justification for the use of deadly force would seem contrary to that principle and might be regarded by some as denigrating the value of human life.

But neither law nor society gives absolute priority to the preservation of physical life.[12] The current law of self-defense readily acknowledges as much. For instance, even the currently narrow deadly force doctrine does not require complete proportionality (that is, taking a life only to save a life). To be justified as self-defense, a killing need not be in response to a clear threat of *death*; a reasonable belief in imminent serious physical injury is sufficient.[13] Thus, under existing law, one may justifiably take the life of another not only to prevent one's own death but also to spare oneself serious bodily harm which falls short of death.

More importantly, other aspects of the current law of justification make it clear that even a reasonable belief in imminent serious bodily injury is not always required to render a killing justifiable homicide. A number of well-established criminal law doctrines justify the use of deadly force to protect what are clearly psychological interests. Consider, for example, the legal rules regarding "retreat," defense of habitation, and the use of deadly force to repel or resist rape and kidnapping—all of which may be seen as protecting essentially psychological interests at the expense of human life.

"Retreat"

If self-defense law gave absolute priority to the preservation of life, one would expect to find in such law a requirement that, if possible, one retreat from an attack or threatened attack rather than resort to deadly force. In some jurisdictions, this is indeed the law: even in the face of an imminent threat of death or serious bodily injury, a person may not resort to deadly force in self-defense "if he knows that he can with complete safety as to himself and others avoid the necessity of doing so by retreating."[14]

The "retreat" doctrine is, however, by no means universal. Indeed, in the majority of American jurisdictions, one is not required to retreat from an imminent threat of death or serious bodily injury, even if such retreat can be accomplished with complete safety, but one may stand one's ground and justifiably kill the attacker.[15] This "no retreat" doctrine, known at common law as the "true man" rule,[16] has a clear psychological basis: "There is a strong policy against the unnecessary taking of a human life [but] there is [also] a policy against making one act a cowardly or humiliating role."[17] As one early legal commentator explained, "no one should be forced by a wrongdoer to the ignomy, dishonor and disgrace of a cowardly retreat."[18]

Even in jurisdictions where retreat is required, there remains an exception which also has a clear psychological basis: one need never retreat when attacked or threatened with attack in one's own home.[19] This so-called "castle" doctrine derives from the ancient principle that "a man's home is his castle"—the one place, if no other, where he can feel secure.[20] The "castle" doctrine, like the "true man" rule, clearly places greater value on a defender's psychological security and well-being than on an attacker's life or bodily integrity.

Defense of Habitation

Related to the "castle" doctrine is the law of defense of habitation. While it is generally, if not universally, recognized that deadly force may not be used justifiably to protect mere property interests, the vast majority of American jurisdictions regard the use of deadly force to prevent unlawful entry into one's home as legally justifiable.[21] Here, as with the "true man" rule and the "castle" doctrine, the law is obviously concerned with protecting distinctly psychological interests, even at the expense of human life:

> This rule . . . attaches . . . special importance to the dwelling as a place of security, for it permits the use of deadly force even when the anticipated attack would not result in the killing or serious injury of someone within.[22]

Likewise, there has long been a common law recognition of a right to use deadly force to resist being wrongfully dispossessed of one's dwelling place.[23] Again, concerns for the dweller's psychological interest in security are placed above the physical interests, even the life, of the intruder:

> On the one hand, it is desirable to reduce to a minimum the cases where

fatal force may be used by way of self-help. To kill a man is, on a dispassionate view, an evil both more serious and more irrevocable than the loss of possession of a dwelling house for a period while a court order is being obtained to recover it . . . On the other hand, to be illegally ousted from one's dwelling is a provocation that is not to be depreciated.[24]

Rape and Kidnapping

An overwhelming majority of American jurisdictions have justified the use of deadly force not only to prevent death or serious bodily injury but also to resist kidnapping or rape (sexual intercourse compelled by force or threat of force).[25]

Rape, of course, is generally a violent crime. Some rape victims are indeed threatened with death or serious bodily injury. But in some cases, rape is accomplished without the threat of death or serious bodily harm, and the most serious injury to the victim is psychological.[26] Nevertheless, as the law now stands in most jurisdictions, the use of deadly force to resist sexual intercourse compelled by force or threat *of any kind* will be regarded as justifiable self-defense.[27] Ironically, however, this particular justification for the use of deadly force is unavailable to many battered women since, in most jurisdictions, forced sexual intercourse by a spouse is not regarded as rape.[28]

Kidnapping may also be a crime of violence as, for instance, when threats of death are made in order to secure payment of ransom. In some kidnappings, however, the major harm to the victim appears to be the temporary denial of liberty and autonomy. The kidnap victim who resists or attempts to escape by use of deadly force may be acting to prevent death or serious bodily injury, but in some cases may resort to such force largely out of concern for fundamental psychological interests such as liberty and autonomy—that is, from a desire to escape captivity. Regardless of motive, however, the kidnapping victim's use of deadly force to resist or escape captivity will, in most jurisdictions, be regarded as justified.[29]

In a sense, the continued existence of rules such as these might be regarded as a strong argument for the doctrine of psychological self-defense proposed here. After all, if the law is willing to justify the sacrifice of human life to prevent the humiliation of a "true man," or to protect the sanctity and security of his "castle," why should it not offer similar justification when—as seems to be the case in many battered woman homicides—life is sacrificed to protect other more vital psychological interests?   A more powerful argument for the proposed doctrine, however, lies not in the existence of these rules *per se* but rather in the principles behind them, principles which help explain why such rules exist and why they are not inconsistent with respect for human life. What lies behind these rules—and what underlies, to a large extent, the doctrine of psychological self-defense proposed here—are the principles of autonomy and lesser evils.

The Principle of Autonomy

In large measure, the above described legal justifications for the use of deadly force, all of which appear to protect distinctly psychological values even at the expense of human life, may be viewed as expressions of the principle of autonomy. As Kadish has observed,

> The strong current of sentiment behind such rules can be understood best as a reflection of the autonomy principle, which extends the right to resist aggression broadly to cover threats to the personality of the victim. It is hard to see where the force behind the elevation of these distinctly lesser interests can come other than from *the moral claim of the person to autonomy over his life.*[30]

Kadish's conclusion is well supported by the history of self-defense doctrine and the law of justification. As Fletcher has demonstrated, the principle of autonomy has "taken hold at various stages of history" and has informed self-defense doctrine at least since the time of Biblical and early Roman law.[31] Perhaps the most cogent account of this principle was given by Locke in 1697:

> [H]e who attempts to get another Man into his Absolute Power, does thereby put himself into a State of War with him; It being to be understood as a Declaration of a Design upon his Life. For I have reason to conclude, that he who would get me into his Power without my consent, would use me as he pleased, when he got me there, and destroy me too when he had a fancy to it; for no body can desire to have me in his Absolute Power, unless it be to compel me by force to that, which is against the Right of my Freedom, i.e., make me a slave. To be free from such force is the only security of my preservation . . .
>
> This makes it Lawful for a Man to kill a Thief, who has not in the least hurt him, nor declared any design upon his Life, any farther than by the use of Force, so to get him in his Power, as to take away his Money, or what he pleases from him; because using force, where he has no Right, to get me into his power, let his pretense be what it will, I have no reason to suppose, that he, who would take away my Liberty, would not when he had me in his Power, take away everything else. And therefore it is Lawful for me to treat him, as one who has put himself into a State of War with me, i.e., kill him if I can; for to that hazard does he justly expose himself, whoever introduces a State of War, and is aggressor in it.[32]

Locke's formulation of the autonomy principle and its relationship to justifiable homicide is, of course, extreme by contemporary moral and legal standards. Even the "true man" rule, the "castle" doctrine and the rules regarding rape and kidnapping do not go as far as Locke would have the law go in justifying the use of deadly force to protect one's autonomy. Nevertheless, the essence of Locke's view remains informative and continues to be reflected in these and other modern rules of justification.[33]

Implicit in these rules—as well as in the proposed doctrine of psychological self-defense—is the well-grounded recognition that the value of human life lies not in mere physical existence but rather in the capacity to experience that existence in a psychologically meaningful and rewarding fashion. When, as in the experience of some battered women, victimization becomes so severe that the capacity to function as an autonomous—psychologically integrated and self-directed—individual is lost, severely impaired, or threatened with loss or severe impairment, physical existence ("life") loses much, if not most, of its meaning and value.

To justify the taking of a life to prevent such loss or severe impairment of one's essential selfhood in no way denigrates respect for life. Indeed, such justification expresses a respect for human life even greater than that implicit in current self-defense doctrine. Unlike current self-defense law, which generally gives priority only to mere physical existence, the proposed doctrine of psychological self-defense would give equal priority to those vital aspects of human functioning which give meaning and value to such existence—in other words, those psychological attributes which make life worth living.

The Principle of Lesser Evils

Also reflected in the above-described rules, which protect psychological interests even at the expense of human life, is the principle of lesser evils. Fletcher has argued that self-defense law as a whole may be viewed, at least in part, as an expression of this principle.[34] He observes that the principle of lesser evils explains not only why the law of self-defense favors the life of a defender over that of an aggressor but also why the life of an aggressor may justifiably be sacrificed to protect interests ordinarily regarded as "less valuable than life."[35]

Fletcher sees the principle of lesser evils as requiring not only a balancing of interests (for instance, those of the defender against those of the aggressor) but also consideration of the culpability of the aggressor:

> The culpability of the aggressor is used as a rationale for diminishing the interests of the aggressor relative to those of the victim . . . The more significantly one regards the culpability of the aggressor, the less significant the

victim's interest has to be for the victim to have the right to use deadly force.[36]

Fletcher's explication of the principle of lesser evils and its relationship to self-defense law not only helps explain many of the various rules described above, but also provides an additional and significant counter argument to the proportionality criticism that might be raised against the proposed doctrine of psychological self-defense.

To see why, consider the prototypical case of psychological self-defense: the battered woman who kills her batterer to protect herself from extreme psychological harm. Even if the batterer's interest in his physical life initially outweighs the battered woman's interest in preserving her psychological self, the ultimate balance need not favor the batterer's interest if the batterer's culpability is taken into account.

Acquittal by reason of psychological self-defense under the proposed doctrine would require a finding that the battered woman killed her batterer to prevent him from inflicting extremely serious psychological harm—harm so serious that it would significantly limit the meaning and value of her physical existence. In such a case, the batterer's culpability would, of course, be extremely significant. Accordingly, under the principle of lesser evils, the battered woman's interest in psychological integrity may reasonably be seen as outweighing the batterer's interest in remaining alive—an interest which, though admittedly great, has been "discounted" or "partially waived" by his gross culpability.[37]

Practical Objections to a Legal Doctrine of Psychological Self-Defense

Even though it makes sense intuitively, empirically, and legally, the proposed doctrine of psychological self-defense seems bound to generate considerable controversy. Even those who accept the basic premises of such a doctrine may still resist legal recognition of the doctrine on practical grounds. Specifically, skeptics may be expected to argue that legal acceptance of the proposed doctrine would: (1) undermine the deterrent effects of the criminal law of homicide and result in an increase in lethal domestic violence; (2) inevitably lead to spurious claims of self-defense, some of which might prove to be successful; and (3) be exceedingly difficult, if not impossible, to implement fairly.

These are, of course, all serious arguments which, taken at face value, might seem to rule out any expansion in self-defense doctrine of the sort proposed here. Careful analysis of these arguments, however, suggests that none of them poses an insurmountable practical barrier to legal recognition of a carefully circumscribed doctrine of psychological self-defense.

Deterrence

In 1984, according to the most recent FBI Uniform Crime Reports, "[e]ighteen percent of all killings [in the United States] involved family relationships, 48 percent of which involved spouse killing spouse."[38] In view of these data, which are consistent with those for other recent years,[39] and which probably underestimate the true incidence of lethal domestic violence,[40] it is not difficult to understand why any legal effort to expand the scope of justification for intrafamilial homicide might be met with serious doubt, if not outright resistance.

In criminal law, one of the basic justifications for punishment is the deterrence of criminal conduct:

> Punishment acts as a *general deterrent* insofar as the threat of punishment deters potential offenders in the general community. It acts as a *special deterrent* insofar as the infliction of punishment on convicted defendants leaves them less likely to engage in crime.[41]

Putting these theories of deterrence into the present context, it might be argued that punishing battered women who kill their batterers will not only deter other battered women from killing but also make it less likely that battered women, having killed once, will do so again. Furthermore, it might be argued that any law—such as the proposed doctrine of psychological self-defense—that decreases the probability of such punishment will increase the likelihood that battered women will kill.

There has long been serious doubt as to whether criminal punishment actually serves the purposes of either general or special deterrence.[42] But for purposes of argument, assume that it does. Does this necessarily imply that a doctrine of psychological self-defense, such as that proposed here, would lead to an increase in lethal domestic violence, especially that committed by battered women? To answer that question, consider first general and then special deterrence.

General Deterrence. According to the theory of general deterrence, a battered woman will be deterred from using deadly force against her batterer out of fear of arrest, conviction,and imprisonment. According to this same theory, if the battered woman is aware that she is unlikely or less likely to be punished for killing her batterer, she will have less incentive to avoid using deadly force against him. While this application of general deterrence theory to the problem of battered women homicides may seem intuitively sensible, even a cursory examination of the dynamics of such homicides will demonstrate its fallacy.

To begin with, this application of general deterrence theory, like any other, presupposes an actor who reflects upon the consequences of his or her intended criminal act before committing that act. Moreover, it presupposes a situation in which the likely consequences of the intended act outweigh the benefits of that act. In cases of battered women who kill their batterers in psychological self-defense, only rarely are either of these presuppositions met.

As the cases reviewed in Chapter 3 clearly indicate, homicides by battered women though generally intentional and often premeditated, are rarely the result of careful reflection, let alone cost-benefit analysis. By far, the majority of these killings occur during or not long after an incident in which the woman has been battered and/or threatened with death by the batterer. Moreover, many if not most of these killings give every appearance of being the result of a sudden impulse, often coupled with ready access to a firearm. Given these circumstances, it strains the imagination to suggest that any sizable proportion of battered women decide whether or not to kill their batterers only after reflecting upon the criminal consequences of their decision.

But suppose—as must occasionally be the case—a battered woman, on the brink of using deadly force against her batterer, does stop to weigh costs and benefits. What will she conclude? On the one hand, if she kills the batterer, she will undoubtedly be arrested, probably convicted of a serious crime, and quite possibly sentenced to a lengthy period of incarceration. On the other hand, given the nature of battering relationships, if she does not kill the batterer, she will most certainly continue to be exposed to severe physical, psychological, or sexual abuse, often far more devastating than the stigma of criminal conviction and the trauma of imprisonment, however lengthy. In many cases, especially those which might fall under the proposed doctrine of psychological self-defense, it would seem clear that the benefits of killing the batterer not only outweigh the costs but effectively render unnecessary any careful assessment of such costs.

A general deterrence argument against the proposed legal doctrine of psychological self-defense also fails because it presupposes that a battered woman considering the use of deadly force will (1) be aware of such a potential defense and (2) be able to assume, with some degree of confidence, that this defense will justify her lethal actions.

Legal acceptance of the proposed doctrine would almost certainly generate significant attention from the mass media. As a result, some, perhaps many, battered women (*as well as their batterers*) would become at least vaguely aware of the doctrine, just as most people are at least vaguely aware of the contours of current self-defense law. But awareness of a potential legal defense is a far cry from understanding its legal technicalities or being able to assume confidently that a jury will find it applicable to the circumstances surrounding one's own conduct.[43]

Legal rules of justification, including self-defense, are necessarily somewhat vague and open-ended.[44] Their application depends largely upon the precise facts of the particular case in question and the result is rarely fully predictable. A few cases are clear, but most are open to argument. Some defendants who claim justification are acquitted, others are convicted. The proposed doctrine of psychological self-defense, with its reliance upon the necessarily vague and open-ended standard of "extremely serious emotional harm" is no exception.

If the doctrine of psychological self-defense has any appreciable effect upon the general deterrence of lethal domestic violence, that effect is likely to be a positive one. Just as a battered woman could never be certain that the doctrine would justify her particular actions if she killed her batterer, her batterer could never be sure that it would not. Thus, common knowledge of the doctrine, generated by media reports and word-of-mouth, might well create a disincentive for battering in at least some cases. In short, some batterers might be deterred from seriously abusing women by the threat of legally justified homicide. And for every batterer so deterred, there may well be one less battered woman who ultimately perceives the need to resort to deadly force against her batterer.

Special Deterrence. According to the theory of special deterrence, criminal punishment of a battered woman who kills her batterer will reduce the likelihood of recidivism. There are two general explanations for this purported effect. First, at least while she is incarcerated, the battered woman will be in no position to engage in spousal homicide.[45] Second, as a result of having been severely punished for killing her batterer, the battered woman will learn that spousal homicide is counterproductive.[46]

Both of these explanations rest upon the assumption that, having killed once, the battered woman poses a heightened risk of lethal violence to the community or at least to other men with whom she may develop close relationships. Undoubtedly, this assumption is fueled in large measure by the commonly held beliefs that battered women are masochistic and that they somehow provoke violence from the men with whom they share close emotional ties.[47] If such beliefs were valid, it would not be unreasonable to assume that, absent powerful state intervention, a battered woman who kills might well end up in another battering relationship where she might again perceive the need to resort to deadly force.

In fact, research on battered women has demonstrated consistently that such beliefs are myths. There is simply no evidence that battered women are masochists or that they provoke the abuse inflicted upon them by their batterers.[48] On the contrary, there is a growing body of empirical data which indicate that battering is primarily a function of the personality characteristics of the batterer.[49]

There is, of course, always the possibility that a battered woman who has killed her batterer will subsequently become involved in yet another battering relationship. Even then, however, there is little reason to believe that the battered woman who has been severely punished for killing her batterer will be significantly less likely to resort to deadly force in her new relationship. Ironically, the woman who has been stigmatized by a felony conviction and incarcerated may be even more likely to perceive the need for lethal violence in a subsequent battering relationship.

As was observed in earlier chapters, social isolation, lack of financial independence, and absence of a social support network are all factors which contribute to a battered woman's inability to leave her batterer and ultimately, in some cases, to her perceived need to resort to deadly force. A battered woman who has been convicted of murder or manslaughter and incarcerated for any period of time is likely to find that she has lost whatever social support network and financial independence she may have had prior to the killing and that it is now exceptionally difficult, if not impossible, to establish supportive relationships or to secure gainful employment.

Thus, should the woman once again become entangled in a battering relationship, she is likely to find it all the more difficult to leave her batterer. To the extent that she thus feels trapped in the relationship, she will be all the more likely to perceive lethal violence as a potential, if not necessary, means of escape.

Spurious Claims of Psychological Self-Defense

There can be little doubt that the doctrine of psychological self-defense, like all legal defenses, would have the potential for at least some abuse. Spurious claims of psychological self-defense might be raised not only by battered women who kill but by other homicide defendants as well. On rare occasions, such claims might even prove to be successful.

Here, however, as in other areas of excuse and justification, the potential for abuse is minimized by the legal procedures utilized in criminal trials and may be even further minimized by careful circumscription of the doctrine itself.

For instance, as is the case in current self-defense law, merely raising a claim of psychological self-defense would not necessarily carry that claim to the jury. As with the current doctrine of self-defense, the defendant would first have to meet what is known as the burden of production.[50] He or she would have to present at least some evidence that the use of deadly force was in response to a threat of extremely serious emotional harm. Unless the court finds that the defendant has met this burden, he or she would not be entitled to a jury instruction on psychological self-defense. Thus all claims of psychological self-defense would initially be screened by a judge, who would have the authority to dismiss them summarily.

The amount of evidence necessary to meet the burden of production on a claim of self-defense varies among jurisdictions:

> The quantum of evidence required has been expressed in a variety of ways: "some evidence," "more than a scintilla," "slight evidence," "evidence to support," "evidence supporting," "evidence sufficient to raise a reasonable doubt," "evidence which would justify a reasonable jury in finding the existence or non-existence of the fact," and evidence that would allow a rational factfinder to conclude that "there is a sufficiently high probability that the relevant issue will be proved."[51]

One obvious and simple way to circumscribe the doctrine of psychological self-defense and thus further minimize the potential for its abuse is to require that the burden of production be met by a rather high quantum of evidence: namely, "evidence which would justify a reasonable jury in finding" that the defendant used deadly force to protect himself or herself from a threat of extremely serious emotional harm. A defendant unable to produce such a quantum of evidence would not be entitled to a jury instruction as to psychological self-defense and thus could not be acquitted on that basis.

Another potential procedural safeguard against the success of spurious claims of psychological self-defense lies in the burden of persuasion, sometimes referred to as the burden of proof.[52] As was noted in Chapter 4, under current self-defense law in most jurisdictions, once the defendant meets the burden of production, the burden falls on the prosecution to prove beyond a reasonable doubt that the defendant did *not* act in self-defense.[53] In some jurisdictions, however, the burden of persuasion with regard to self-defense falls upon the defendant.[54]

There has been some controversy over the constitutionality of allocating the burden of persuasion on self-defense to the defendant. Lower courts, however, have generally concluded that a state may require the defendant to bear the burden of persuasion on this issue[55] and the United States Supreme Court has never clearly ruled otherwise.[56] In any event, under current constitutional doctrine, enunciated by the Supreme Court in *Patterson v. New York*,[57] it seems clear that in the case of an *expanded* defense such as that offered by the proposed doctrine of psychological self-defense, there would be no constitutional barrier to placing the burden of persuasion on the defendant.[58]

Allocating the burden of persuasion or proof on psychological self-defense to the defendant would be yet another way of minimizing the risk that this expanded doctrine might successfully be misused by battered women or other homicide defendants. Generally, where the defendant in a criminal case bears the burden of persuasion on a given claim, he or she must prove the facts supporting that claim by a preponderance of the evidence.[59] Thus, in the case of a claim of psychological self-defense, the defendant would have to demonstrate to the jury's satisfaction that, *more likely than not*, he or she used deadly force to protect against the infliction of extremely serious emotional harm.

Requiring defendants to meet the burden of production by a high quantum of evidence and forcing them to bear the burden of persuasion should make it extremely unlikely that a spurious claim of psychological self-defense would succeed. However, even this minimal risk might be reduced by placing one further limitation on the doctrine of psychological self-defense. The law could require the defendant to prove not only that the use of deadly force was in response to a threat of extremely serious emotional harm, but that at some point, at or near the time of the killing, he or she had been physically battered or threatened with battery (or death) by the individual killed.

This additional limitation is similar to the way in which tort law deals with certain claims of psychological injury. In some jurisdictions, plaintiffs may not recover for psychological injury unless they prove that they also sustained some physical impact as a result of the defendant's actions.[60] In most jurisdictions, however, this "impact" rule has been superseded by the so-called "zone-of-danger" rule, which allows recovery for purely psychological harm if, at the time of the defendant's tortious actions, the plaintiff was thereby exposed to the risk or threat of actual physical injury.[61]

The additional limitation suggested here, analogous to the "impact" and "zone-of-danger" rules in tort law, would bring the doctrine of psychological self-defense closer to current self-defense law by making it clear that mere verbal abuse, no matter how severe, is insufficient to justify the use of deadly force. Such a limitation would not affect the psychological self-defense claims of most battered woman homicide defendants, but would rule out the psychological self-defense claims of those defendants unable to prove that they had been, at some point, subjected to or threatened with physical injury by the person killed.

This limitation, combined with the limitations imposed by the burdens of production and persuasion, should be sufficient to preclude success in all but the rarest of spurious claims of psychological self-defense.

Problems of Implementation

The proposed doctrine of psychological self-defense would justify the use of deadly force to protect oneself from what reasonably appears to be a threat of extremely serious emotional harm. Thus, in resolving claims of psychological self-defense, the trier of fact (usually a lay jury) would be faced with two general questions: Did the defendant, at the time of the killing, honestly believe that the individual killed was threatening him or her with extremely serious emotional harm? And, if so, was that belief reasonable under the circumstances?

There can be little doubt that in many cases these questions would be difficult to answer. They would require the trier of fact to reconstruct the defendant's mental state at the time of the killing and to assess, ex post facto, the reasonableness of that reconstructed state of mind. Given the abstract, intangible nature of the psychological factors involved, such inquiries seem bound to be not only difficult but also at least somewhat speculative. Thus, it might be argued that the proposed doctrine simply could not be implemented fairly, at least by the typical lay jury unfamiliar with sophisticated psychological analyses.

In the abstract, this argument has a certain logic, but it loses most of its persuasive force when considered in light of the wide variety of existing legal doctrines, including current self-defense law, the application of which requires lay jurors to undertake similarly difficult and speculative psychological inquiries. In criminal law, for example, similar reconstructive inquiries are clearly required in cases involving claims of insanity, diminished responsibility, and automatism, where the issue is the defendant's state of mind at the time of the alleged offense.[62] Indeed, given the *mens rea* requirements inherent in all but strict liability offenses, difficult, reconstructive, and often speculative inquiries into the defendant's mental state are required in almost all criminal prosecutions.[63]

Moreover, a number of well-established criminal law doctrines require not only a reconstruction of the defendant's mental state at the time of the alleged offense but also an assessment of the reasonableness of that mental state. For example, the criminal law has long recognized that under certain circumstances, provocation may reduce to manslaughter a killing which would otherwise be murder. For such a reduction to occur, however, the trier of fact must conclude that two conditions have been met: (1) that the defendant was so carried away by passion that he or she experienced a temporary loss of normal self-control; and (2) that the circumstances which aroused that passion were such that a reasonable person would have been similarly affected.[64]

Likewise, in a number of jurisdictions, a killing which would otherwise be murder may be reduced to manslaughter if the trier of fact finds that the defendant acted under the influence of "extreme emotional disturbance."[65] Ordinarily, however, the trier of fact must also find that, under the circumstances as the defendant believed them to be, there was a "reasonable explanation or excuse" for the emotional disturbance under which the defendant acted.[66]

Outside the criminal law, similarly difficult and speculative psychological inquiries are also required in tort law (where the intentional infliction of emotional harm is a recognized cause of action);[67] workers' compensation law (under which a worker may be compensated for solely psychological injuries occurring as a result of and in the course of employment);[68] civil commitment law (which requires the trier of fact to decide whether the individual to be committed is mentally ill, dangerous to self and others, and in need of psychiatric care and treatment);[69] and even probate law (where a testator's capacity to make a legally valid will may be challenged long after he or she is dead).[70]

Additionally, and most significantly in the present context, the kinds of difficult and often speculative inquiries required by the proposed doctrine of psychological self-defense are remarkably similar to those demanded by current self-defense law. Whether evaluating a typical claim of self-defense (under current doctrine) or a claim of psychological self-defense (under the proposed doctrine), the trier of fact would be required to reconstruct the defendant's mental state at the time of the alleged offense and to assess the reasonableness of that mental state.

The mental state involved would, of course, be different. Current law requires a reasonable fear of death or serious bodily injury, while the proposed doctrine would require a reasonable fear of extremely serious psychological injury. But in the typical case, where the reasonableness of the defendant's claimed fear is arguable, the process of inference employed by the trier of fact would be the same. Under either doctrine, current or proposed, the trier would assess the defendant's claimed fear and the reasonableness of that fear by examining the circumstances surrounding the alleged offense and asking: Would a reasonable person, under these circumstances, have responded with the kind of fear claimed by the defendant?

There is, of course, no denying that in some cases the assessment required by current self-defense law would be less difficult than that required by the proposed doctrine. For example, where an aggressor has put a loaded gun to the defendant's head and threatened to pull the trigger immediately, the process of inferring that the defendant's fear of death (or serious bodily injury) and the defendant's lethal response to that fear (killing the aggressor) were reasonable presents little if any difficulty. Such clear cases, however, rarely go to trial. Typically, under current self-defense law, the trier of fact is confronted with an ambiguous situation in which the threat is much more subtle and the defender's response much less predictable. Obvious examples are the many cases in which battered women kill their batterers, purportedly in self-defense, hours or even days after the last battering incident or verbal threat to their lives.[71]

The subtle nature of the threatening stimulus and the lack of a clearly predictable response to that stimulus complicate the process of inference in these more typical cases, just as they would in cases litigated under the proposed doctrine of psychological self-defense. But the fact that the process of inference may be rather complicated has never stopped the law from requiring jurors to engage in that process where a defendant has an arguable claim of traditional self-defense. Nor should it when a defendant has an arguable claim of psychological self-defense.

Just as in cases of self-defense litigated under current doctrine, jurors weighing a claim of psychological self-defense may be expected to deal with such complications sensibly and fairly. To begin with, as they would in assessing claims of traditional self-defense, jurors may be expected to use their common sense and everyday experience, both direct and vicarious. Just as people ordinarily have a good sense of what it means to be threatened with and fear physical injury or death, they also have a good sense of what it means to be threatened with and fear extremely serious psychological injury.

Furthermore, where certain issues are "beyond the ken" of the lay jurors (as in the case of self-defense claims raised by battered women homicide defendants under current doctrine) they may be expected to rely, at least to some extent, upon expert testimony. Expert testimony regarding the battered woman syndrome, for example, is said to be admissible under current self-defense doctrine because it helps the trier of fact to understand why a battered woman may reasonably have feared for her life at the time she killed her batterer. To the extent that such testimony accomplishes that purpose, it does so by explaining how and why the defendant's psychological predicament—the fact that she was slowly but surely being destroyed psychologically—was similar to that of the typical battered woman.

It takes no great stretch of the imagination to see how that very same sort of expert testimony would assist the trier of fact in resolving a battered woman defendant's claim of psychological self-defense. In fact, such testimony would seem much more directly relevant and useful in assessing claims of psychological self-defense than it is in assessing self-defense claims under current doctrine.

In cases not involving battered woman, psychologists, psychiatrists, and other mental health professionals might be expected to provide the trier of fact with similarly useful expert testimony. Such experts, for example, might testify as to the nature, seriousness, and long-term consequences of the psychological threat to which the defendant purportedly responded with deadly force. While some might regard this sort of expert testimony with skepticism, there is no reason to believe that it would be any less valid, reliable, or useful in this legal context than it is in the many others—including current self-defense law—in which it is generally accepted.

8
Conclusion

The battering of women is a serious social and legal problem in modern society. No one knows the true extent of the problem, but it has been estimated that, during any given year, as many as six million American women will be beaten by the men with whom they share intimate relationships.[1] The individual, familial, and social costs of this national tragedy are staggering.

In recent years, growing awareness of the nature and magnitude of this problem has sparked numerous efforts to reduce the incidence and severity of battering. Mental health and medical professionals have been alerted to the problem and provided with methods for diagnosing and treating battered women.[2] Research has begun to suggest possible ways of treating batterers as well.[3] Shelters for battered women have grown in number and, where available, now provide a temporary safe haven for some battered women and their children.[4] Additionally, the police and other legal authorities have begun to treat battering as a crime.[5] Further, there is now evidence to suggest that treating battering as a crime may serve to deter at least some batterers.[6]

All of these efforts are, of course, laudable. Unfortunately, all remain in a state of relative infancy. Thus far, relatively few battered women have been diagnosed or treated by mental health or medical professionals;[7] mental health professionals have had little success in treating batterers;[8] shelters are extremely limited in number and capacity compared to the population of women and children who need their services;[9] and criminal justice strategies for deterring batterers have just begun to be implemented.[10]

Naturally, these efforts as well as others can and must continue if society ever hopes to eradicate or even significantly reduce the incidence of battering. But meanwhile, both society and its legal institutions have to recognize that the problem is far from being solved. Despite the best of efforts, there are and will continue to be, at least in the foreseeable future, millions of battered women in this country. Furthermore, it seems all too likely that a small percentage of these women will continue to view homicide as their only viable means of escaping the battering relationships in which they find themselves trapped.

The major purpose of this book has been to address the plight of this small but increasingly visible minority of battered women who are, in many cases, doubly victimized: once by the men who have battered them and again by a system of criminal justice which holds them to an unrealistic standard of accountability. Efforts to reduce the former sort of victimization—the battering which leads these women to kill—obviously should continue. Any appreciable reduction in the incidence and/or severity of battering seems bound to be reflected in a reduction in the number of battered women who kill. Meanwhile, the latter sort of victimization—that inflicted by our system of justice—must also be addressed.

Thus far, many courts have held that expert psychological or psychiatric testimony regarding the battered woman syndrome is admissible in support of the self-defense claims of battered women who kill their batterers. This judicial response to the problem clearly reflects a growing societal and legal recognition of the psychological plight of battered women. In admitting such testimony, the courts are acknowledging that the legal culpability of battered women homicide defendants can be assessed fairly only in light of the psychological harm they have suffered at the hands of the men they have killed.

On its face, this judicial response might seem to be a significant step in the direction of fairer legal treatment of these women. In some cases, perhaps it is. But, as was demonstrated in Chapter 5, even where such testimony is presented and admitted into evidence, the majority of battered women homicide defendants are still convicted of murder or manslaughter. Where the killing has taken place outside of a direct confrontation between the woman and her batterer (as is common), such testimony simply is not adequate to outweigh the circumstances of the killing and convince a jury that the woman's lethal act fell within the narrow confines of current self-defense law.

The additional reform proposed in this volume—legal recognition of a carefully circumscribed doctrine of psychological self-defense—likewise would not exculpate all battered women who kill. The justification offered by the proposed doctrine is necessarily narrow and would apply only where the battered woman defendant could prove that her lethal act was reasonably necessary to protect herself from the infliction of extremely serious psychological harm. Nevertheless, the proposed doctrine would have significant impact, both practical and symbolic.

As a practical matter, recognition of the doctrine would provide jurors with a legitimate legal basis for acquitting battered women homicide defendants who, by virtue of their psychological plight, do not deserve to be convicted or punished but would not be acquitted under current self-defense law. Under current self-defense law, such women may be acquitted only through jury nullification. Under the proposed doctrine, the legal fate of these women would be determined by an honest application of the law rather than the unpredictable willingness of some jurors to ignore the law.

Symbolically, legal recognition of the proposed doctrine of psychological self-defense would benefit not only those few battered women who killed their batterers but also the vast majority who do not. In recognizing this doctrine, which would have its primary application in cases of homicide by battered women, the law would fully and unequivocally acknowledge the dreadful psychological plight of battered women. Such acknowledgement would surely serve to promote efforts currently underway to eradicate or at least reduce the incidence and severity of woman battering.

Legal recognition of the proposed doctrine of psychological self-defense would, of course, require a major change in substantive criminal law and would likely come about, if at all, only after significant public and political debate. Moreover, this doctrine seems bound to generate substantial opposition from at least some segments of the population. Even if the doctrine is never legally recognized, however, it represents an idea well worth considering. If nothing else, the public and political debate it might generate would serve to call significant attention to the serious problem of battering.

Appendix
100 Battered Women Who Killed

Adams, Ada Violet [Illinois][1]

Ada Violet Adams was convicted of murder in the death of Glenn Marshall and sentenced to 25 years imprisonment. At the time of killing, Adams had been living with Marshall for over a year, during which time he had beaten her on numerous occasions, often when he had been drinking. Adams testified that she stabbed Marshall to death when he swore at her and grabbed her by the throat. As she put it, "I had to do it in self-defense . . . He grabbed me, he was at my throat."

Autopsy revealed that when he died, Marshall had a blood alcohol content of .23 percent, more than twice the percentage required to be considered legally intoxicated. Evidence regarding Marshall's intoxication was excluded by the trial court as irrelevant, even though Adams presented evidence that Marshall had often beaten her when he was drunk.

Adams also presented the testimony of a psychiatrist who had examined her and concluded that she was sane. However, when her attorney attempted to have the psychiatrist testify regarding the battered woman syndrome, such testimony was excluded as irrelevant.

On appeal, Adams's conviction was reversed and the case was remanded for a new trial because the appellate court found that evidence of Marshall's intoxication was erroneously excluded and that the prosecutor, in his closing argument, had improperly referred to Adams's silence after her arrest.

Allery, Sherry Lynn [Washington][2]

Sherry Lynn Allery was convicted of second degree murder in the death of her husband, Wayne Allery. Throughout their five-year marriage, Ms. Allery had "suffered periodic pistol whippings, assaults with knives, and numerous beatings from her husband's fists." On one occasion, about two years before the killing, he had beaten her with a tire iron, causing injuries which required hospitalization.

In the year leading up to the killing, "the beatings had increased in severity and intensity." A week before the killing, Ms. Allery had filed for divorce and had served Mr. Allery with restraining orders.

On the night of the killing, Ms. Allery returned to her home. In view of the restraining orders, she did not expect to find Mr. Allery there. She entered the house and bolted the door behind her, only to find Mr. Allery lying on the couch. Mr. Allery threatened to kill her and she tried to flee through a bedroom window. While in the bedroom, she thought she heard a metallic sound from the kitchen. Believing that Mr. Allery had gone for a knife, she loaded a shotgun, returned to the living room area and shot her husband to death as he remained lying on the couch.

On appeal, Allery's conviction was reversed and the case remanded for a new trial because the trial court had excluded expert testimony regarding the battered woman syndrome.

Almond, Leslie [Pseudonym][3]

Leslie Almond had known Ronald Baxter for three years at the time she killed him. They had become romantically and sexually involved shortly after they met.

During the three-year relationship, Baxter had beaten Almond every few weeks. Some of the beatings were relatively minor, but others were more serious. In one incident, Baxter beat Almond for two and a half hours. In another battering incident, he beat her for "an hour or so" and struck her with the telephone when she tried to call the police. Baxter also raped and sexually assaulted Almond a number of times. In some of these attacks, he forced various objects, such as deodorant containers and cucumbers, into her vagina and choked or smothered her into unconsciousness.

Shortly before Almond killed Baxter, the couple began sharing an apartment, where the beatings and sexual attacks escalated. On the night of the killing, Almond awoke to find Baxter attempting to force a roll-on deodorant container between her legs. Baxter pushed her out of bed and grabbed her. She shook him off and ran to the kitchen, where she grabbed a knife. Baxter caught up with her and swung her around, at which point Almond stabbed him to death.

Almond was charged with first degree murder. After 14 hours of deliberation, a jury acquitted her on grounds of self-defense.

Anaya, Linda M. [Maine][4]

Linda Anaya was twice convicted of manslaughter in the death of her "lover," Frank Williams. At the time of the killing, she had been living with Williams for about five months. During those five months, Williams had beaten or threatened Anaya on a number of occasions. Williams had pushed and kicked her, threatened to kill her, chased her with a hammer, and cut her arms with a chisel. As a result of these batterings, Anaya had suffered bruises, a concussion, and a deep stab wound.

On at least two occasions, the police had been called to intervene as Williams was assaulting Anaya. Williams threatened to kill Anaya if she ever left him. Twice during this five-month period, Anaya attempted to kill herself.

Ultimately, Anaya stabbed Williams to death after an argument in which Williams, who was "quite intoxicated," had "pushed [Anaya] around." Anaya initially entered a plea of not guilty by reason of insanity, but withdrew that plea and went to trial claiming self-defense. Her first conviction was reversed and the case remanded for a new trial after the Maine Supreme Court concluded that the trial court had erred in excluding expert testimony regarding the battered woman syndrome.

Tried a second time on the same charges, Anaya presented both psychiatric and psychological expert testimony that she suffered from the battered woman syndrome throughout her relationship with Williams. She was again convicted and her conviction was affirmed on appeal.

Barham, Dorothy [Tennessee][5]

Dorothy Barham pleaded guilty to voluntary manslaughter in the shooting death of her ex-husband. In sentencing her to a six-year suspended prison term and 10 years probation, the Judge told her: "I do not send a message to battered wives in this community to take their husband's lives, when it is so easy to get divorced and walk away."

After 20 years of "drunken violence, abusive language and mental torture," Mrs. Barham divorced Mr. Barham. Seven months later Mr. Barham moved back into the family home and was shot to death as he lay sleeping on a couch. Attorneys said that Mr. Barham had beaten Mrs. Barham the night before the shooting, but Mrs. Barham had no recollection of the battering incident. As she later explained, "I don't know what happened to me that morning . . . All I know is that I was scared he was going to leave me again."

Barson, Diana Cervantes [Texas][6]

A jury found Diana Barson not guilty of murder in the death of her common-law husband. At trial, Barson testified that prior to the killing, her husband had beaten her for two years and that in the three days immediately prior to the killing, he had threatened and abused her with loaded revolvers and an ice pick.

Ultimately, Barson responded by shooting her husband, cutting his body into pieces, loading it into the trunk of her automobile, and driving to California to seek the help of relatives in disposing of it.

Bechtel, Donna [Oklahoma][7]

Donna Bechtel was convicted of first degree murder for killing her husband. Evidence at trial indicated that she was a battered woman who had been severely beaten by her husband the night of the killing.

Mrs. Bechtel testified that she shot her husband in the chest with a .357 Magnum during one of a series of battering incidents that night. Friends who saw Mrs. Bechtel the day after the killing testified that she had bruises on her face, neck, and arms. According to the prosecution, however, the physical evidence showed that Mr. Bechtel had been asleep when he was shot and killed. As the District Attorney put it, "This was not a battered woman's case . . . She shot him while he was sleeping."

Borders, Geraldine [Florida][8]

Geraldine Borders was convicted of second degree murder in the death of her husband, L.C. Borders. At the time of the killing, the couple apparently had been married for at least a decade. Throughout their marriage, Mr. Borders had beaten Mrs. Borders with his fists and other implements such as a frying pan. Some of these beatings were so severe that friends and relatives intervened for fear that Mrs. Borders would be killed. Both Mr. and Mrs. Borders had alcohol problems, but while Mrs. Borders had sought help for her alcoholism, Mr. Borders had refused to cooperate in any kind of treatment.

On the day of the killing, which occurred in the afternoon, Mr. Borders had been drinking heavily since 7:30 A.M. An autopsy revealed that his blood alcohol content at death was .42 percent.

Just prior to the killing, the couple had quarreled over money and Mrs. Borders had ordered Mr. Borders out of the house. He complied but then tried to force his way back into the home and Mrs. Borders armed herself with a kitchen knife. After Mr. Borders forced the door open and knocked her to the floor, she rose and stabbed him once in the neck, killing him.

On appeal, Mrs. Borders' conviction was reversed and remanded because, in the judgment of the appellate court, the trial court had erred in not reducing the charge against her to manslaughter before sending the case to the jury.

Branchal, Loretta [New Mexico][9]

Loretta Branchal was convicted of voluntary manslaughter in the death of Benjie Romero, the man with whom she had lived for over six years. Romero had frequently beaten Branchal during this period. Evidence at trial indicated, for example, that Romero had beaten Branchal with a board, broken out all the windows in her mother's house, threatened to kill her, thrown her daughter into a pigpen with a grown pig, forced her to eat at gunpoint, shot at her with a high-powered rifle, and forced her at gunpoint to touch a dead rattlesnake.

On at least one occasion, Branchal had called the police to intervene but had been told that the police could do nothing and that the family members should try to resolve problems on their own.

At the time of the killing Romero was intoxicated. Having returned home "drunk," Romero was verbally abusive to Branchal and threatened to kill her, her child, her mother, and her two brothers. When Romero subsequently left the house, Branchal locked him out. Romero then banged on the door and threatened to break it down. Finally, Branchal let him in and when he came at her with an "angry" expression on his face, she pulled a gun from her housecoat and shot him. As she explained at trial:

> I was scared. I was scared of my life. I thought to myself that if I would run away from him, he was going to find me . . . At the same time I thought to myself that if I would go away, my kids were gonna stay there and he could have killed one of them or hurt 'em.

On appeal, Branchal's conviction was reversed and the case remanded for a new trial because the trial court had failed to properly instruct the jury on the law of self-defense.

Brinker, Ruth [Minnesota][10]

Ruth Brinker was beaten by her husband every few weeks during their three-year marriage. On one occasion, Mr. Brinker held a loaded gun to her head. In another incident, he knocked her down and backed a car onto her, leaving tire marks on her shirt. Finally Mr. Brinker beat Mrs. Brinker and she responded by stabbing him in the chest with a knife, killing him.

Brinker was charged with second degree murder. After a psychological expert testified at her trial regarding the battered woman syndrome, Brinker was acquitted on grounds of self-defense.

Buhrle, Edith [Wyoming][11]

During 18 years of marriage, Edith Buhrle had been subjected to "numerous instances of physical and mental abuse" by her husband, Kenneth. The day before the killing, Mr. and Mrs. Buhrle had argued. She threatened him with a shovel and he beat her about the head, neck, and shoulders with a pair of work boots.

The following day, Mr. Buhrle moved into a motel room, to which he later asked Mrs. Buhrle to come for a talk. When Mrs. Buhrle arrived, she had with her a hunting rifle and a pair of rubber gloves. Mr. Buhrle kept the night chain on the motel room door and the couple argued for nearly two hours. Mrs. Buhrle then shot and killed Mr. Buhrle, fled the scene, and was later arrested with her husband's wallet in her possession.

Mrs. Buhrle was charged with second degree murder. She claimed self-defense, alleging that she believed that her husband had been reaching for a gun when she shot him, although no gun had been found in the motel room.

At trial, Mrs. Buhrle offered the testimony of Dr. Lenore Walker, a psychologist well known for her research and writing regarding battered women. The trial court excluded Dr. Walker's testimony and Mrs. Buhrle was convicted. On appeal, her conviction was affirmed by the Wyoming Supreme Court, which held that exclusion of Dr. Walker's testimony had been proper because the "state of the art" with regard to the battered woman syndrome was not such as to permit a reasonable expert opinion.

Burton, Leigh Guy [Louisiana][12]

Leigh Burton shot and killed her husband in a bar after he taunted her regarding his sexual relationship with another woman and then laughed at her. Burton was charged with second degree murder and entered a plea of not guilty by reason of insanity.

At trial, a psychiatrist testified that Burton had known right from wrong at the time of the killing. The psychiatric expert also testified, however, that Burton was a battered woman and that when she killed her husband she had been "in the highest degree of psychological pain with tremendous doubt over her self worth." The expert further testified that when Burton's husband laughed at her, "the shooting was like a reflex away from pain rather than a calculated act."

The jury rejected Burton's insanity claim and found her guilty of manslaughter. The court imposed a sentence of 13 years at hard labor. Subsequently, Burton's conviction was affirmed by a Louisiana appeals court which concluded that Burton had, by her own admission, shot her husband "to stop the pain" and thus not out of a reasonable belief that the killing was necessary to protect herself from death or serious bodily injury.

Bush, Una Alice [California][13]

Una Alice Bush was charged with murder and convicted of involuntary manslaughter in the death of her husband, Gary Bush.

At the time of the killing, the couple had been married for just over a year. Their brief marriage included numerous incidents in which Mr. Bush had beaten Mrs. Bush and threatened to kill her. In one battering incident, which occurred while Mrs. Bush was five months pregnant, Mr. Bush beat her so badly that she began to vomit blood and had to be hospitalized.

On the night of the killing, Mr. Bush arrived home at 2:45 A.M. An argument ensued and when Mrs. Bush tried to flee, Mr. Bush grabbed her arm and twisted it, taking her keys from her. Mrs. Bush ran to the telephone, intending to call the police, but was stopped by Mr. Bush, who grabbed her around the throat and began to choke her. Mr. Bush then beat her about the head and face and she responded by threatening to "hurt" him. Mr. Bush then threatened to kill her and continued beating her. Finally, Mrs. Bush noticed a knife on a nearby kitchen counter, grabbed it, and stabbed Mr. Bush to death.

On appeal, Bush's conviction was reversed because the trial court had (1) refused to instruct the jury, as requested by Bush's attorney, that a person whose life has been verbally threatened is justified in acting more quickly and in taking harsher measures to protect herself from assault; and (2) admitted evidence that Bush was the sole beneficiary of an insurance policy on her husband's life.

Caccavale, Frances [California][14]

Frances Caccavale, a 70-year-old grandmother, was convicted of second degree murder in the killing of her husband of 48 years. Despite Mrs. Caccavale's age and evidence that she was a battered woman, the judge imposed the maximum sentence: 15 years to life in prison. As he explained at sentencing: "Whether or not she is a battered wife was a matter for the jury to decide, and the jury heard the evidence and decided she wasn't."

At trial Mrs. Caccavale testified that her husband had begun abusing her three months after they were married in 1936: "He told me he was the man of the house. He punched me and threw me on the bed and started flipping cigarette ashes across my chest. He didn't stop until the cigarette was finished." Relatives and a former neighbor of the Caccavales testified that Mr. Caccavale had knocked Mrs. Caccavale unconscious, fractured her ribs, and broken her dentures. Expert testimony regarding the battered woman syndrome was presented to the jury, but the court refused to allow the expert to testify that Mrs. Caccavale suffered from the battered woman syndrome.

According to Mrs. Caccavale's taped confession, the killing took place while Mr. Caccavale was packing his bags to leave her. Mrs. Caccavale said she told her husband, "You're not leaving me stranded after 50 years," and that he responded, "If you don't leave me alone, I'll kill you." Mr. Caccavale then appeared to reach under the bed for a gun and Mrs. Caccavale stabbed him five times.

Caldwell, Marie [Oregon][15]

Charged with first degree manslaughter in the shooting death of her husband, Marie Caldwell pleaded guilty to criminally negligent homicide. In sentencing her to a year in jail, the judge explained that although Caldwell was a battered woman with no previous criminal record who had killed her batterer, "incarceration is to be expected when a life is taken."

Caldwell, who was described by a psychiatrist as a battered woman, shot her husband (who had a blood alcohol content of .25 percent) four times after he grabbed her by the neck and threatened to kill her.

Explaining the plea bargain, Caldwell's attorney said that the killing was "remarkably close" to being a matter of self-defense.

Carr, Wanda [California][16]

Wanda Carr was charged with murder in the death of her husband of 22 years. Mrs. Carr had pointed a loaded gun at her sleeping husband, awakened him, and asked him to talk to her. When he moved toward her, she shot and killed him.

The prosecutor reduced the charge to manslaughter before trial. Mrs. Carr pleaded not guilty by reason of insanity and waived a jury trial. A judge acquitted her, stating: "I don't think she had a viable alternative. This was a classic case in the sense of a long period of abuse and harassment . . . It was serious protracted mental and physical abuse."

Chandler, June [Idaho][17]

June Chandler, the mother of six children, was acquitted of murder in the death of her husband. Throughout their marriage, Mr. Chandler had beaten and sexually abused her when he became intoxicated.

On the night of the killing, Mr. Chandler had been drinking. After Mr. Chandler beat her and threatened to kill her, Mrs. Chandler shot him dead with one of his own weapons, an automatic rifle. Explaining why she chose this particular weapon, Mrs. Chandler said, "I knew all you had to do was keep pulling the trigger. You didn't have to stop and reload."

Crigler, Sharon [Washington][18]

Sharon Crigler was convicted of first degree manslaughter in the death of Keith Rolland, the man with whom she had formerly lived. Crigler was sentenced to five years in prison.

Crigler had lived with Rolland for several months, during which time "he brutally beat her on several occasions." Four days before the killing, Rolland moved out after an incident in which he repeatedly punched Crigler in the mouth.

On the evening before the killing, Crigler went to Rolland's new apartment, found another woman in his bed, and ransacked the apartment. At 2:00 the following morning, Rolland obtained the keys to Crigler's apartment. When he tried to unlock the door, Crigler told him to "back off." When she heard no response, Crigler fired a .22 caliber weapon through the door. The bullet struck Rolland and he bled to death within minutes.

On appeal, Crigler's conviction was reversed and the case was remanded for a new trial because of improper jury instructions on self-defense.

Davis, Patricia [Illinois][19]

Patricia Davis shot and killed her boyfriend as he slept alongside their 2-year-old son. Davis testified that her boyfriend had physically abused her in the past (including one incident in which he stabbed her). Just prior to the killing, while intoxicated, he had threatened her with a knife and then fallen asleep. Once he was asleep, Davis picked up a gun and shot him at point-blank range.

Davis's lawyer argued that she was a battered woman and she was acquitted of voluntary manslaughter.

Davis, Patricia [Kansas][20]

Patricia Davis was acquitted of murder in the shooting death of her husband. The killing took place on Christmas Day while Mr. Davis was asleep. Admitting the killing but claiming self-defense, Mrs. Davis testified that she shot Mr. Davis to keep him from carrying out his threat to wrap her up in tape like a "mummy" and keep her confined beneath their bed in a homemade coffin. Mrs. Davis further testified that prior to the killing, Mr. Davis had sexually abused and tortured her for many years.

Dozier, Deborah [West Virginia][21]

Deborah Dozier shot and killed the man with whom she had been living intermittently for about 10 years. Dozier claimed that she had been beaten by this man on a number of occasions prior to the killing. She was convicted of first degree murder, but her conviction was reversed and the case remanded for a new trial because the trial court's jury instructions impermissibly shifted the burden of proof to Dozier.

Edwards, Nancy [Louisiana][22]

Nancy Edwards was convicted of manslaughter in the death of her husband. Mrs. Edwards, who had previously been battered and threatened with death by her husband, shot him dead after she found him in bed nude with another woman, Audlee Outz. The killing occurred shortly after 6:00 A.M.

Around midnight on the morning of the killing, Mrs. Edwards had been beaten by her husband, who also threatened to beat their eight-year-old daughter to death. When Mr. Edwards moved toward the child, Mrs. Edwards grabbed a crowbar, struck her husband over the head, and fled with her child to a neighbor's home where she called the police. Mrs. Edwards then went to the home of her paramour, had sexual relations with him, and left for work at about 5:30 A.M.

Seeing her husband's car parked at Mrs. Outz's home, Mrs. Edwards picked up the gun she always carried in her car, broke into the Outz residence, and confronted her husband in bed with Mrs. Outz. Mr. Edwards sprang from the bed, telling Mrs. Edwards, "You God damn son of a bitch, I told you I'd kill you if you come here again." As her husband came at her with his hands raised, Mrs. Edwards shot him five times at a distance of less than two feet.

On appeal, Mrs. Edwards' conviction was reversed and the case remanded for a new trial because the trial court improperly excluded evidence regarding Mr. Edwards' dangerous character.

Emick, Leslie Ann [New York][23]

See Chapter 1 for a detailed description of this case.

Evans, Patricia [Illinois][24]

Patricia Evans pleaded guilty to killing her husband and was sentenced to two to six years in prison.

Mrs. Evans, the mother of four children, had complained to the police about being assaulted by her husband a number of times during the five years preceding the killing. At the time of the killing, she had filed for divorce.

Mrs. Evans shot and killed her husband after he pistol-whipped her. Explaining why she pleaded guilty rather than press her claim of self-defense, Mrs. Evans' attorney said, "I thought at the time it would have been very difficult to prove self-defense. She had to load the pistol, follow him down three flights of stairs, and shoot him."

Mrs. Evans' sentence was eventually commuted by the governor due to "extenuating circumstances and because of her children."

Felton, Rita [Wisconsin][25]

Rita Felton was convicted of second degree murder in the shooting death of her husband. Mrs. Felton had been beaten and sexually abused by her husband throughout their 23-year marriage, even during six pregnancies. On one occasion, Mr. Felton beat her, held her down, and threatened her with a blowtorch. Another time, he punched her so hard that he broke one of her dentures. On a number of other occasions, he threatened to kill her and forced her to commit degrading sexual acts. Additionally, Mr. Felton frequently beat the couple's children.

The police had been called to the Felton home numerous times and Mrs. Felton had once separated from her husband for 10 months. She resumed living with him, however, for several reasons. First, she was having serious financial problems during the separation. Second, Mr. Felton persuaded her that the children would have fewer problems at home and school if he were around to care for them. Finally, Mrs. Felton felt guilty because a minister from whom she sought counseling told her that she should try to be a better wife.

After the couple got back together, the batterings continued and, two or three weeks prior to the killing, Mrs. Felton attempted to commit suicide. On the day of the killing, the couple argued and Mr. Felton assaulted both Mrs. Felton and her 15-year-old daughter. After Mr. Felton went to bed and fell asleep, Mrs. Felton shot him dead with his own .22 caliber single shot rifle.

At trial, a psychologist testified that Mrs. Felton's experience was typical of that of a battered woman.

On appeal, Mrs. Felton's conviction was reversed and the case remanded for a new trial when the court found that she had been denied effective assistance of counsel because her attorney had not given adequate consideration to other defenses, including "heat of passion" and insanity.

Fennell, Karen [Pennsylvania][26]

Karen Fennell was convicted of voluntary manslaughter and sentenced to three and one-half to ten years imprisonment for killing her husband. Her conviction and sentence were affirmed on appeal and in federal court habeas corpus proceedings.

Mrs. Fennell, who was separated from her husband at the time of the killing, drove her car into the left side of his car while he was in the driver's seat. She then backed up, drove forward, and struck his vehicle again. When Mr. Fennell escaped from his car and tried to run away, Mrs. Fennell struck him with her car several times, killing him.

Evidence at trial indicated that Mr. Fennell had been an alcoholic and that while drunk he had often abused Mrs. Fennell. Mrs. Fennell testified that he had threatened, pushed, kicked, punched, and raped her on numerous occasions. The couple's son testified that he had seen his father knock Mrs. Fennell down and threaten her with a knife. Their daughter testified that she had seen Mr. Fennell sexually abuse Mrs. Fennell.

Both Mrs. Fennell and her children testified that even after Mr. Fennell was evicted from the family home by court order, he continued to harass and threaten Mrs. Fennell, often telephoning several hundred times a day and sometimes coming back to the house to threaten Mrs. Fennell in person.

Fielder, Pamela [Texas][27]

Pamela Fielder was convicted of voluntary manslaughter and sentenced to two years in prison for killing her husband. On appeal, her conviction was affirmed.

Throughout their marriage, Dr. Darwin Fielder (a gynecologist) had beaten, threatened, and sexually abused Mrs. Fielder. Explaining why she never left her husband, Mrs. Fielder testified that:

> Darwin told me that he would severely punish me. He told me, on occasions, he would kill me. He told me that there wasn't anything or any place on this earth that I could ever get away so that he wouldn't be able to find me. And I believed him.

At the time of the killing, Mrs. Fielder had just spoken with a lawyer about getting a divorce. When she told her husband she had talked to the attorney, he became furious and headed for what he called "the cave" (a utility closet in which he kept numerous sexual devices). At the suggestion of her attorney, Mrs. Fielder had earlier removed the contents of "the cave" and placed them in plastic bags.

Dr. Fielder started to enter "the cave" but then turned, grabbed a gun, and told Mrs. Fielder, "I've told you, I've told you." Mrs. Fielder testified that she understood this statement as a reference to Dr. Fielder's earlier threats to kill her if she ever revealed their unusual sexual activities to anyone. Mrs. Fielder responded by grabbing the gun from her husband and telling him to leave her alone. When he came at her, she fired the gun several times, killing him.

Fultz, Eleanor [Indiana][28]

Eleanor Fultz was convicted of manslaughter and sentenced to six years in prison for killing her alleged batterer. Ms. Fultz shot the man from a distance as he sat on the couch in her living room while a locksmith was in the house changing the locks on her doors. She testified that she shot him because he pointed his finger at her and muttered something inaudible, which she interpreted as a threat.

At trial, testimony (both expert and lay) which might have substantiated Ms. Fultz's claim to be a battered woman was excluded. Her conviction was affirmed on appeal.

Griffiths, Thelma [Idaho][29]

Thelma Griffiths was convicted of involuntary manslaughter and sentenced to three years in prison for killing her husband. Both the conviction and sentence were affirmed on appeal.

Mrs. Griffiths claimed that on many occasions prior to the killing she had been physically abused by her husband. On the evening of the killing, the couple argued and Mr. Griffiths pushed Mrs. Griffiths. She responded by reaching into an armoire and removing a gun. Mr. Griffiths then lunged at her "with the same expression on his face that she had noted on a previous occasion when he had choked her to near insensibility." Mrs. Griffiths fired the gun five times. Four shots hit Mr. Griffiths, killing him.

At the close of Mrs. Griffiths' trial, the prosecutor told the jury:

[Y]ou heard several of the stories by the defendant about Joe and her relationship together and how at times she stated in her story that Joe got violent.

I wish Joe were here to tell us his side of the story. I don't portray Joe as being a perfect individual, but I question if he was as bad as the picture that has been painted of him . . .

Ask yourselves this question: If Joe was that bad, if he did all those things, why didn't the defendant divorce him? Why didn't she leave him? If she was truly afraid for her life, why didn't she go to Idaho Falls, and visit with her family there? And her father said, "I love my daughter. The home is always open to her."

Hale, Cathryn [Florida][30]

Cathryn Hale pleaded no contest to a charge of second degree murder in the shooting death of her husband and was sentenced to 25 years probation.

Mrs. Hale had been married to her husband five months at the time of the killing. Throughout their short marriage, her husband had often beaten her when he was drinking. Two days before the killing, Mrs. Hale had been released from a hospital following surgery for uterine cancer.

On the day of the killing, her husband pulled her from her car, kicked her in the back, stomped on her foot and dragged her into the house. Once in the house, he knocked her across a couch and coffee table, then dragged her down the hallway to the bedroom, threatening to kill her. In the bedroom, he threw her onto the bed. She got up, took a revolver from a dresser drawer, pointed the gun at him, and told him to leave. When he blocked the doorway and lunged at her, she shot him in the chest, killing him.

In sentencing Mrs. Hale to probation, the Judge explained that "the battered woman syndrome as a defense is not recognized in Florida, nor is it a license for women to shoot their husbands in the back. However, these facts indicate classic self-defense."

Harrison, Betty Ann [Georgia][31]

Betty Ann Harrison was convicted of murder for killing Jack Calhoun, the man with whom she had lived, on and off, for a year and a half. She was sentenced to life in prison. Her conviction was affirmed on appeal.

Prior to the killing, Calhoun had physically abused Harrison on several occasions and had engaged in sexual intercourse with Harrison's 13-year-old daughter. When Harrison learned of Calhoun's sexual involvement with her daughter, she threatened to kill Calhoun.

On the evening of the killing, Harrison was visiting Calhoun's trailer home. When she tried to leave, Calhoun pulled her from the car, took her keys, struck her about the face and head, and insisted upon having sexual intercourse with her. As Calhoun was dragging her back toward his trailer, Harrison grabbed a kitchen knife and stabbed Calhoun. Harrison then drove Calhoun to her own trailer and called an ambulance. Calhoun was dead by the time the ambulance arrived.

Hawthorne, Joyce [Florida][32]

Joyce Hawthorne was convicted three times for killing her husband.

Mr. and Mrs. Hawthorne had been married for 17 years at the time of the killing. Throughout their marriage, Mr. Hawthorne had often beaten Mrs. Hawthorne and the couple's five children. Mr. Hawthorne also had threatened to kill both Mrs. Hawthorne and the children and had tried to molest their 15-year-old daughter.

On the morning of the killing, the couple argued and Mr. Hawthorne grabbed Mrs. Hawthorne around the neck, choking her. She broke loose and shot him six times with two shotguns.

In her first trial, Mrs. Hawthorne was convicted of murder and sentenced to life in prison. That conviction was reversed on appeal and the case remanded for a new trial because, in part, the trial court had improperly excluded expert testimony on the battered woman syndrome.

On remand, the trial court again excluded this expert testimony and Mrs.

Hawthorne was convicted of manslaughter. Again, an appellate court reversed her conviction and remanded the case for yet another trial.

In Mrs. Hawthorne's third trial, the court again refused to admit expert testimony on the battered woman syndrome and once more Hawthorne was convicted of manslaughter. This time an appellate court affirmed the trial court's refusal to admit the expert testimony but reversed the conviction and remanded the case for still another trial on the grounds that the State had used an illegally obtained statement to impeach Mrs. Hawthorne's testimony.

Heidmous, Pamela [North Carolina][33]

Pamela Heidmous pleaded guilty to voluntary manslaughter in the shooting death of her husband. She was sentenced to the statutory maximum of twenty years in prison despite evidence that she had been physically abused repeatedly by her husband and suffered from the battered woman syndrome.

Mrs. Heidmous claimed that on the night of the killing Mr. Heidmous slapped her face, punched her repeatedly, knocked her to the floor, and told her he was going to kill her. As a result, she suffered abrasions and bruises to the head, neck, back, knee, and shins, all of which were observed by the police after the killing.

According to Mrs. Heidmous, when her husband knocked her to the floor, she got up and grabbed a nearby shotgun and loaded it. As she backed away from her husband, she tripped, fell backwards, and the gun went off, killing him.

The prosecution challenged this version of the incident, noting that Mr. Heidmous had been found lying in bed—dressed only in his underwear and with the bedcovers pulled up to his waist—in "a position he was known to have slept in during his life."

Hodges, Joan [Kansas][34]

Joan Hodges was convicted of voluntary manslaughter in the shotgun slaying of her husband and sentenced to serve from four to 12 years in prison. Since the killing was committed with a firearm, Hodges was required by state law to serve a minimum of four years before becoming eligible for parole.

Hodges admitted shooting her husband twice with a 12-gauge shotgun while he was lying in bed. She claimed, however, that she intended not to kill him but to prevent him from continuing to abuse her. A psychologist's expert testimony that Hodges suffered from the battered woman syndrome was excluded at trial.

On appeal, Hodges' conviction was reversed and the case remanded for a new trial when the Kansas Supreme Court concluded that the expert's testimony had been improperly excluded by the trial court.

Holbron, Judith [Hawaii][35]

Judith Holbron was acquitted of manslaughter in the killing of her husband.

At trial, Holbron testified that in the years prior to the killing, her husband had beaten her and their two children with ax handles and clotheslines and had threatened to kill her if she ever left him.

Mrs. Holbron also testified that she shot Mr. Holbron while he was lying on the floor after he had verbally abused her, handed her a gun, and told her to kill herself. According to her testimony, "I didn't want to shoot myself, [so] I shot him."

Hornbuckle, Janice [Washington][36]

Janice Hornbuckle was acquitted of first degree murder in the shooting death of her husband. Prior to the killing, Hornbuckle had been physically abused by her husband and, on a number of occasions, had sought assistance from the police. The killing took place during a battering incident. Hornbuckle's husband beat her and threatened her at knifepoint. She grabbed a nearby shotgun and shot him.

Hoy, Barbara [New York][37]

Barbara Hoy was charged with manslaughter but convicted of the lesser offense of criminally negligent homicide in the shooting death of her husband.

Mrs. Hoy testified at trial that she shot her husband because he beat her repeatedly during their marriage. The jury also heard testimony that Mrs. Hoy suffered from the battered woman syndrome. The prosecutor argued, however, that Mr. and Mrs. Hoy "had a sadomasochistic relationship in which they enjoyed beating each other."

Hughes, Francine [Michigan][38]

Francine Hughes was charged with first degree murder in the death of her husband. She pleaded not guilty by reason of insanity and was acquitted on that basis.

Hughes had been severely beaten and psychologically abused by her husband throughout their marriage. She had sought assistance from the police and other legal authorities many times, all to no avail. Hughes had separated from her husband numerous times and had even divorced him, but he always found a way to force her to return to him.

On the night of the killing, he beat her, smeared her with garbage and food, forced her to burn the books and papers she used in her business school classes, and demanded that she have sex with him. After the couple had sex, Mr. Hughes fell asleep. Mrs. Hughes then removed her children from the house, poured gasoline on the bed in which her husband slept, and set a match to it. Mr. Hughes was killed in the ensuing blaze.

Hundley, Betty [Kansas][39]

Betty Hundley was convicted of involuntary manslaughter for killing her husband and sentenced to serve from two to five years in prison. On appeal, her conviction was reversed and the case remanded for a new trial because the trial court had used the term "immediate" instead of "imminent" in instructing the jury as to the nature of the threat required for a justification of self-defense. Hundley avoided a retrial by pleading no contest to the original charge and was sentenced to five years supervised probation.

At the time of the killing, Mr. and Mrs. Hundley had been married for about 10 years. During that time, Mr. Hundley had frequently beaten and kicked Mrs. Hundley. He had knocked out several of her teeth, broken her nose at least five times, repeatedly broken her ribs, and threatened to cut her eyeballs out and her head off. Mrs. Hundley was a diabetic. On numerous occasions, Mr. Hundley had hidden her insulin or diluted it with water, causing her to lapse into diabetic comas.

Six weeks prior to the killing, Mrs. Hundley had been hospitalized. When she returned home from the hospital, Mr. Hundley knocked her down, kicked her, and choked her into unconsciousness. Subsequently, Mrs. Hundley moved out and went to live in a nearby motel. Mr. Hundley then started calling her day and night, threatening to kill her and members of her family.

On the day of the killing, Mr. Hundley called Mrs. Hundley and told her that he was coming to her motel room to kill her. A short while later, Mr. Hundley broke into the motel room, hit Mrs. Hundley, choked her, and threatened to kill her. Mr. Hundley then forced her to shower with him and to submit to having him shave her pubic hair "in a rough and violent fashion." Mr. Hundley then forced Mrs. Hundley to have sexual intercourse with him.

After the intercourse, Mr. Hundley continued to threaten Mrs. Hundley. He pounded a beer bottle on a table, threw a dollar bill at her, and told her to go out and buy him some cigarettes. At that point, Mrs. Hundley, who was closer to the door than her husband, pulled a gun from her purse and told Mr. Hundley to leave. Mr. Hundley laughed and told her, "You are dead, bitch, now!" As he reached for the beer bottle, Mrs. Hundley closed her eyes and fired the gun five times, shooting Mr. Hundley in the back.

Hutto, Cynthia [South Carolina][40]

Cynthia Hutto was acquitted of homicide charges in the shooting death of her husband. Hutto had been beaten repeatedly by her husband throughout their marriage. Just prior to the killing, her husband had beaten her for about 45 minutes. After the beating, he handed her a gun, told her that if she didn't kill him he would kill her, and retired to their bedroom. Shortly thereafter, Hutto entered the bedroom and shot her husband twice in the back, killing him.

Ibn-Tamas, Beverly [District of Columbia][41]

Beverly Ibn-Tamas was convicted of second degree murder and sentenced to serve from one to five years in prison for killing her husband. At trial, expert testimony regarding the battered woman syndrome was excluded. On appeal, the case was remanded to the trial court for clarification of its ruling that such testimony was inadmissible. On remand, the trial court again concluded that such testimony was inadmissible. Once more, Ibn-Tamas appealed and her conviction was affirmed.

The Ibn-Tamas's marriage was marked by recurring episodes of violence. Dr. Ibn-Tamas, a physician, had often beaten Mrs. Ibn-Tamas. For instance, he had struck her with fists, shoes, and other objects, knocked her to the floor, rendered her unconscious by pushing his knee into her neck, and forced her out of a moving car on an interstate highway. While Mrs. Ibn-Tamas was pregnant, Dr. Ibn-Tamas punched her in the face and neck and threatened her with a fractured skull if she ever left him.

Dr. Ibn-Tamas's former wife testified that Dr. Ibn-Tamas had treated her in a similar fashion while they were married. He had beaten her with his fists, fired a gun at her, broken down a door, and thrown her belongings out the window.

The killing occurred after an altercation in which Mrs. Ibn-Tamas, then pregnant, was beaten by Dr. Ibn-Tamas. The dispute began at the breakfast table. Dr. Ibn-Tamas hit Mrs. Ibn-Tamas over the head with a magazine and then with his fists. He then dragged her upstairs and told her to pack a suitcase and leave the house. When she resisted, he beat her with his fists and a wooden hairbrush, grabbed a revolver, pointed it at Mrs. Ibn-Tamas and said, "You are going out of here this morning one way or another."

Dr. Ibn-Tamas then left, leaving the gun behind, but returned a short while later and resumed the attack. When Dr. Ibn-Tamas pushed her against a bureau, Mrs. Ibn-Tamas grabbed the gun, warned her husband to leave, and fired the gun at the bottom of the door. Dr. Ibn-Tamas then left the room and headed downstairs. Mrs. Ibn-Tamas followed shortly and shot Dr. Ibn-Tamas when he jumped at her from behind a wall on the stairway landing.

Wounded, Dr. Ibn-Tamas retreated. Mrs. Ibn-Tamas then followed him down the rest of the stairs, saw him crouching, and shot and killed him.

Jen, Cheng Chin [Missouri][42]

Cheng Chin Jen was acquitted of second degree murder charges in the shooting death of her husband. Prior to the killing, Mrs. Jen had been battered by her husband for 17 years. Mr. Jen had also abused the couple's children, once holding a shotgun to his daughter's head to force her to practice playing the piano.

Mrs. Jen admitted that she shot her husband to death while her eight-year-old watched, but claimed she did so because she feared for the safety of herself and her two daughters. Her claim to self-defense was supported at trial by an expert who testified that Mrs. Jen was a battered woman.

Jones, Helen [Pseudonym][43]

Helen Jones was convicted of reckless homicide and sentenced to serve one year in prison for killing her husband.

For years prior to the killing, Mrs. Jones had been physically and psychologically abused by her husband. After one beating early in their marriage, Mrs. Jones threatened to leave. Mr. Jones responded by stripping her, locking all of her clothes in the car, and leaving her alone and naked, without a telephone, miles from the nearest neighbor.

The beatings continued. When Mrs. Jones called the police, she was told that nothing could be done unless the police actually saw the assault. The cycle repeated itself over and over: Mr. Jones beat her, she left, and he either talked her into returning or forced her to do so. On one occasion, Mrs. Jones left, but Mr. Jones found her, beat her, and held her captive for several days. On another occasion, he forced her back home at the gunpoint, shooting at her and grazing her scalp.

On the day of the killing, Mrs. Jones, who was then separated from her husband, had been drinking with a friend. Mr. Jones found her, forced her into his car, and drove to the apartment complex where they had lived together. Mr. Jones took Mrs. Jones's wallet, which contained nearly $1,000 in cash. He also grabbed a small handgun from between the car seats.

An argument ensued. Mr. Jones dropped the gun and it went off. Mrs. Jones grabbed the gun and Mr. Jones fled. She followed him up two flights of stairs, demanding her wallet, but when she reached the second landing, Mr. Jones knocked her down the stairs. Mrs. Jones got up and shot Mr. Jones, who died a short while later from the wound. Autopsy revealed that Mr. Jones's blood alcohol content had been .17 percent at the time of his death.

Joslyn, Shirley May [Iowa][44]

Shirley May Joslyn was convicted of first degree murder and conspiracy to commit first degree murder in the shooting death of her husband. She was sentenced to life imprisonment.

Prior to the killing, Mrs. Joslyn had been beaten repeatedly by her husband. Following the killing, her brother, Edward Waterbury, confessed that he and Mrs. Joslyn had decided that Mr. Joslyn should be killed because of the repeated beatings he had inflicted upon Mrs. Joslyn.

Waterbury bought a six-shot revolver with $200 Mrs. Joslyn had given him for that purpose. Later, Waterbury went to the Joslyn home, waited until Mr. Joslyn fell asleep, and then shot him, reloaded the gun, and shot him again to be certain that he was dead.

On appeal, Waterbury's convictions for murder and conspiracy to commit murder were affirmed. The appellate court, however, reversed Mrs. Joslyn's convictions and remanded the case for a new trial because the trial court had improperly admitted Waterbury's confession into evidence against her.

Kaplan, Kathy [New Hampshire][45]

Kathy Kaplan pleaded guilty to second degree murder and was sentenced to 30 years to life in prison after she admitted that she paid a "hit man" $5,000 to kill her husband. The "hit man," who allegedly shot and killed Mrs. Kaplan's husband, was acquitted.

Mrs. Kaplan married her husband, who was 32 years older than she, when she was 14 years old, using another woman's birth certificate. Throughout their marriage, Mr. Kaplan had abused her physically, psychologically, and sexually. He beat her so badly that at times she needed medical attention. He cut her with a knife, hired her out as a prostitute, and forced her to act in pornographic movies. Mrs. Kaplan says she reached the "breaking point" and decided to have Mr. Kaplan killed when he threatened to kill the couple's two-year-old son.

Kelly, Gladys [New Jersey][46]

Gladys Kelly was convicted of reckless manslaughter in the stabbing death of her husband. On appeal, her conviction was reversed and the case remanded for a new trial because the New Jersey Supreme Court found that the trial court had erred in excluding expert testimony regarding the battered woman syndrome.

Prior to the killing, Mr. Kelly had beaten Mrs. Kelly almost weekly throughout their marriage, usually while he was intoxicated. In addition to beating Mrs. Kelly, Mr. Kelly had often threatened to kill her and cut off parts of her body if she ever left him.

On the day of the killing, the Kellys met at a friend's house. When the couple left the house, Mr. Kelly, who was intoxicated, asked Mrs. Kelly, "What the hell did you come around here for?" He then grabbed her collar and the two of them fell to the ground. Mr. Kelly then choked Mrs. Kelly, struck her in the face, and bit her leg.

A crowd gathered and two men separated Mr. and Mrs. Kelly. Mrs. Kelly then left the crowd to look for her daughter, from whom she had become separated in the scuffle. Her daughter, who had picked up Mrs. Kelly's pocketbook, was standing nearby. Mrs. Kelly retrieved her pocketbook. When she then observed Mr. Kelly running toward her with raised hands, she reached into the pocketbook and removed a pair of scissors. When Mr. Kelly reached her, she used the scissors to stab him to death.

Kelly, Ivy Gail [Washington][47]

Ivy Gail Kelly was found guilty of second degree murder and sentenced to a maximum term of 20 years in prison for killing her husband. Her conviction was affirmed by an appeals court but eventually reversed by the Washington Supreme Court, which remanded the case for a new trial because the trial court had erred in admitting evidence that Mrs. Kelly was verbally and physically abusive to her neighbors.

Evidence adduced at trial, including expert testimony that Mrs. Kelly was a battered woman, supported her claim that she had been beaten and threatened with death repeatedly by her husband.

Mrs. Kelly admitted killing her husband with a single gunshot, but claimed that she had been trying to scare him, not shoot him. According to Mrs. Kelly, her husband had been drinking, was angry with her, and had blocked her only exit from the house. She claimed that she believed he was going to kill her, so she pointed the gun at him and it discharged.

Kontos, Hazel [Alabama][48]

Hazel Kontos was convicted of first degree murder and sentenced to life imprisonment in the shooting death of her ex-husband. Her conviction was affirmed on appeal.

Mrs. Kontos, whose first husband died after they had been married for 25 years, married Mr. Kontos in January, separated from him in April, and divorced him in July of that same year. Despite their divorce, Mr. Kontos continued to harass Mrs. Kontos. On one occasion, he called her and threatened to kill her. Another time, he broke windows at her home and chopped at her door with an ax.

On the day of the killing, about four months after their divorce, Mr. Kontos came to the beauty salon where Mrs. Kontos was employed and stated that he intended "to perform kidney surgery" that night, flee to Hawaii, and never work again. At 11:00 that evening, Mrs. Kontos was awakened by loud knocking at her door. Mrs. Kontos went to the door, opened it and admitted Mr. Kontos.

Once inside the house, Mr. Kontos began to call Mrs. Kontos obscene names. Mr. Kontos then went to another room and returned with a pistol. After holding the pistol to Mrs. Kontos's throat for about 10 minutes, Mr. Kontos slapped her face, forbade her to read the Bible, smashed some of her religious pictures, and made derogatory remarks about various religious figures. Mr. Kontos then ripped a religious medal from Mrs. Kontos's neck and flushed it down the toilet.

Roughly two hours after arriving, Mr. Kontos undressed and went to bed, taking with him the pistol with which he had threatened Mrs. Kontos. Once Mr. Kontos fell asleep, Mrs. Kontos took another pistol from a drawer and shot Mr. Kontos, killing him.

Landfried, Cindy [Minnesota][49]

Cindy Landfried shot and killed her battering husband. At the time of the shooting, Mr. Landfried was lying down, resting. He had just finished beating Mrs. Landfried and had told her that after he rested he would continue the beating.

The case was presented to a grand jury which refused to indict Mrs. Landfried, concluding that she had killed her husband in self-defense.

Leaphart, Rose [Tennessee][50]

Rose Leaphart, M.D., was convicted of second degree murder in the slaying of her husband, a fourth year dental student. She was sentenced to serve a minimum of 15 years in prison. Her conviction was affirmed on appeal.

Prior to the killing, Dr. Leaphart had been married to Mr. Leaphart for two years. Throughout these two years, Mr. Leaphart had beaten and abused Dr. Leaphart. On one occasion he broke her arm. Another time, he blackened both of her eyes. Additionally, Mr. Leaphart, who was a drug abuser, once forcibly injected Dr. Leaphart with a drug. An expert witness testified at the trial that Dr. Leaphart was a battered woman.

In response to Mr. Leaphart's abuse, Dr. Leaphart moved several times, installed an expensive alarm system in her apartment, hired a body guard, and took out a number of criminal warrants against Mr. Leaphart.

The prosecution's theory, apparently accepted by the jury, was that, in desperation, Dr. Leaphart paid two men $10,000 to kill her husband. The two men beat Mr. Leaphart to death with a baseball bat. In his closing argument to the jury, Dr. Leaphart's attorney conceded that Dr. Leaphart had been present at the killing, but argued that she was a battered wife who never actually intended that her husband be killed.

Ledford, Barbara [Georgia][51]

Barbara Ledford was convicted of murder in the death of Jose Leon and sentenced to life in prison.

At trial, Ledford testified that Leon, her common-law husband, had beaten her severely on a number of occasions. She also testified that Leon had beaten her on both the morning and the afternoon of the day she killed him.

According to Ledford, the killing took place during a fight precipitated by an argument over Leon's threat to take the couple's daughter out-of-state. During the fight, Leon "bashed [Ledford's] head against the kitchen floor and punched her in the stomach. Ledford responded by taking a rifle from a kitchen closet and fleeing into the yard.

While Ledford was standing in the yard, she heard Leon "rampaging through their trailer." When Leon emerged from the trailer and approached Ledford, he was carrying a belt with a large metal buckle. After warning Leon that unless he backed off she would kill him, Ledford shot Leon twice in the chest and six times in the back and then watched as he bled to death. Once Leon was dead, Ledford "wrapped his body in a blanket, soaked it with gasoline, and burned it."

In a subsequent statement to the police, Ledford admitted that within the preceding month she had told a number of people that she wanted to shoot Leon and burn his body. She also admitted that after the killing she staged a burglary to avoid suspicion.

Leidholm, Janice [North Dakota][52]

Janice Leidholm was convicted of manslaughter and sentenced to five years imprisonment (with three years of the sentence suspended) for killing her husband. Expert testimony presented at trial established that Mrs. Leidholm was a battered woman. Mrs. Leidholm argued that the killing was done in self-defense and was in response to years of abuse by her husband.

On the evening of the killing, Mr. and Mrs. Leidholm had both consumed large quantities of alcohol at a gun club party. On the drive home from the party, the couple began to argue. Upon arriving home, Mrs. Leidholm tried several times to telephone the police, but each time Mr. Leidholm knocked her to the floor.

A short while later, Mr. Leidholm went to bed. When he fell asleep, Mrs.

Leidholm went to the kitchen, got a butcher knife, and used it to stab him. In a matter of minutes, Mr. Leidholm bled to death.

On appeal, Mrs. Leidholm's conviction was reversed and the case remanded for a new trial because the trial court had improperly instructed the jury as to the standard to be applied in assessing a claim of self-defense. Significantly, however, the appeals court concluded that the trial court had not erred in refusing to give the jury the "battered woman" instruction requested by Mrs. Leidholm's attorney. That instruction would have charged the jury that "evidence that the accused acted or failed to act while suffering the condition known as the 'battered wife syndrome' may be considered . . . in determining whether or not the accused act in self-defense."

Rather than face another trial, Mrs. Leidholm agreed to a plea bargain: she would plea guilty to manslaughter and be sentenced to serve no more than a year in prison, with three months suspended and credit given for the 76 days she had already spent in jail. After pleading guilty, however, Leidholm successfully argued that she should be given a suspended sentence.

Lynch, Sheral [Louisiana][53]

Sheral Lynch was convicted of manslaughter and sentenced to 21 years at hard labor for killing Jimmy Dyess, the man with whom she was living. Although she waited more than three years to appeal her conviction, the Louisiana Supreme Court granted her leave to file an "out of time" appeal and reversed her conviction. That court concluded that the prosecution had not proven beyond a reasonable doubt that the killing was not in self-defense.

At the time of the killing, Lynch was 19 years old and had lived with Dyess since she was 16. During those three years, Dyess had beaten Lynch 20 or 30 times. On one occasion, he beat her with a bat until she was unable to walk for several weeks. Another time, he knocked out one of her teeth.

Just prior to the killing, Dyess struck Lynch and threw her on the bed, telling her, "I'm going to beat your goddam [sic] ass . . ." Lynch grabbed a gun from a dresser drawer and ran out the back door. Dyess followed her and kept advancing toward her despite several warnings. Finally, Lynch shot Dyess, killing him.

Maldonado, Gloria [Illinois][54]

Gloria Maldonado shot and killed her battering husband, Juan, after he beat the couple's eight-year-old son with a shoe. After reviewing the evidence, the state's attorney ruled that there was insufficient evidence to warrant prosecution.

Marshall, Lorretta [District of Columbia][55]

Lorretta Marshall was arrested and taken into custody on murder charges after stabbing to death Adolphus Thompson, the man with whom she had lived, on and off, for about two years.

Throughout their relationship, Marshall had been beaten by Thompson. Indeed, during the nine months prior to the killing, the police had been called to Marshall's home 13 times. Only once, however, was Thompson arrested. Even then, Marshall subsequently dropped the charges.

Sixteen months after the killing, Marshall was tried on a charge of second degree murder. Marshall claimed to have killed Thompson in self-defense. Four of the 40 police officers who had responded to her calls for help testified on her behalf. Ultimately Marshall was acquitted.

Martin, Helen [Missouri][56]

Helen Martin was convicted of capital murder in the death of her husband. She was sentenced to life imprisonment without parole for 50 years. Martin appealed her conviction, claiming that the trial court erred in excluding expert testimony that she was a battered woman. The appellate court, however, affirmed her conviction, holding that absent a prima facie showing of self defense, expert testimony on the battered woman syndrome was inadmissible.

During the course of their marriage, Mr. Martin had repeatedly abused Mrs. Martin, both physically and psychologically. Eventually, several months before the killing, the couple separated. Mrs. Martin remained in the marital home with her daughter while Mr. Martin moved into an apartment with his girlfriend.

Shortly after the separation, Mrs. Martin learned that Mr. Martin had threatened to blow up the house, which he had insured for $380,000. A month or so later, Mrs. Martin offered Robert Brasher $10,000 to kill Mr. Martin. Shortly thereafter, Brasher ambushed Mr. Martin in the Martin home and shot him in the back, killing him.

Mrs. Martin was present at the killing and helped Brasher dispose of the gun and Mr. Martin's body. Subsequently, Mrs. Martin reported her husband missing, but three days later confessed to her role in his death.

McKendrick, Carolyn [Pennsylvania][57]

Carolyn McKendrick was convicted of third degree murder in the shooting death of her boyfriend, Tyrone Everett, a professional boxer. McKendrick claimed that Everett had often beaten her and that she killed him during an argument because she feared that he would beat her again.

On appeal, McKendrick's conviction was affirmed without opinion.

McNearney, Sharon [Michigan][58]

Sharon McNearney was acquitted of homicide charges in the shooting death of her husband.

The couple had been married 24 years. Throughout that time, Mr. McNearney had beaten Mrs. McNearney on the average of once a month. At one point during the marriage, Mr. McNearney had been jailed for 18 months for shooting at Mrs. McNearney with a gun.

Mrs. McNearney testified that her husband had threatened to kill her and that she shot him as he walked through the front door, unarmed, because she feared that he would make good on his threat.

Meeks, Lorraine [Michigan][59]

Lorraine Meeks was convicted of second degree murder for killing her common law husband, James Satchel. She was sentenced to serve a term of from 10 to 20 years in prison. Her conviction was affirmed on appeal and she was denied habeas corpus relief in the federal courts. In upholding her conviction, the courts concluded that she was not denied effective assistance of counsel by her attorney's failure to present expert testimony regarding the battered woman syndrome.

Meeks claimed that Satchel had beaten and threatened her throughout their 10 years together. The day before the killing, Satchel had beaten Meeks into unconsciousness and threatened to kill her. On the day of the killing, Satchel telephoned Meeks and told her that he planned "to finish the job that I didn't do yesterday." Meeks prepared for Satchel's arrival by removing some gasoline from the garage, intending to douse Satchel with it if he tried to assault her.

Later that day, Satchel returned home and threatened Meeks with a knife. Meeks fled to a bedroom and tried to lock the door. When Satchel entered the bedroom, Meeks doused him with gasoline, lit a piece of paper, and ignited him. Satchel died four days later from the injuries he suffered.

Minnis, Jeannette [Illinois][60]

Jeannette Minnis was convicted of murder and sentenced to 25 years imprisonment for killing her husband and dismembering his body.

At trial, Minnis testified that her husband had beaten her at least once a week throughout their marriage and had sexually abused her for years. The killing, she testified, was immediately preceded by an incident in which her husband and another man pinned her down with a set of weights, had sexual relations with each other in front of her, and then raped her. The details of Mrs. Minnis's testimony are set forth in Chapter 3 of this volume.

According to Mrs. Minnis's testimony, her husband left following this incident, but later returned and choked her while forcing her to have sexual intercourse with him. She described her response as follows:

> So, as he tried to choke me, I almost wanted to die. So, I don't know where— where I got the strength—but . . . all of a sudden . . . I just gave it all I had. I kicked him off of me . . . And when he fell back he just laid there.

The precise cause of Mr. Minnis' death was never determined because, after the above-described incident, Mrs. Minnis cut Mr. Minnis' body into pieces, wrapped the pieces in trash bags, and disposed of the bags in various places, including dumpsters and a nearby river.

On appeal, Mrs. Minnis' conviction was reversed and the case remanded for a new trial. The appeals court concluded that the trial erred in excluding expert testimony regarding the battered woman syndrome. Such testimony, the appeals court found, was relevant to the issue of why Mrs. Minnis dismembered her husband's body:

> It is true that in nearly all the reported cases, the syndrome evidence has been utilized, if permitted, as a form of self-defense in a confrontational situation . . . We agree that defendant's testimony, if believed by the jury, clearly establishes [self-defense] and thus expert testimony was unnecessary to explain it. However, her reasons for dismembering [the] body were very much at issue. The prosecutor used the dismemberment as substantive evidence to prove defendant's consciousness of guilt. A defendant clearly has the right to introduce evidence to rebut the State's evidence of consciousness of guilt.

Rather than risk a second murder conviction, Minnis pleaded guilty to a reduced charge of voluntary manslaughter and was sentenced to 11 years imprisonment.

Moran, Betty [Ohio][61]

Over a claim of self-defense supported by evidence that she suffered from the battered woman syndrome, Betty Moran was convicted of murder for killing her husband, Willie Moran. Her conviction was affirmed on appeal in state courts and in subsequent federal habeas corpus proceedings.

Prior to the killing, Mrs. Moran had been severely beaten and abused by her husband on numerous occasions. As two justices of the U.S. Supreme Court put it, Mr. Moran "had repeatedly beaten and brutalized her."

On the day of the killing, Mr. Moran demanded that Mrs. Moran give him some money he believed she had saved. He told her that if she didn't produce the money by the time he awoke from his nap, he would "blow [her] damn brains out."

Since Mr. Moran "virtually always carried firearms and owned a collection of pistols, rifles and shotguns," Mrs. Moran took his threat seriously. Realizing that she had no money to give him, she picked up one of his guns and shot him to death as he lay sleeping.

Mullis, Elaine [Georgia][62]

Elaine Mullis was convicted of murder and sentenced to life imprisonment for killing her husband. Her conviction was affirmed on appeal when the Georgia Supreme Court found that the trial court had not erred in excluding expert testimony regarding the battered woman syndrome.

Mrs. Mullis testified that her husband had beaten her on a number of occasions prior to the killing. According to her testimony, she accidentally stabbed her husband with a kitchen knife she was using to slice tomatoes. According to Mrs. Mullis's version of the killing, her husband slapped her face, hit her on the head with a can or bottle, threatened to kill her, knocked her head into a wall, grabbed her by the throat, and was stabbed to death sometime during the struggle.

Necaise, Cecelia [Louisiana][63]

Cecelia Necaise was convicted of manslaughter and sentenced to 12 years at hard labor for killing her husband. Her conviction and sentence were affirmed on appeal.

At trial, Mrs. Necaise testified that she had been beaten by her husband many times prior to the killing. Her testimony was corroborated by hospital records and by the testimony of the couple's three daughters. There was also evidence that Mrs. Necaise had made numerous attempts to separate her husband and had instituted divorce proceedings against him. Expert psychiatric testimony indicating that Mrs. Necaise was a battered woman was excluded by the court.

Mrs. Necaise also testified that immediately prior to the killing, Mr. Necaise held a knife to her throat, threatened to cut her head off, kicked her in the back, and forced her to have sexual relations with him. Mr. Necaise then forced her to lie in bed with him and told her to "count every second . . . [and] wonder what minute I'm going to cut your throat."

In response she removed a gun from beneath the mattress and tried to escape. When she saw Mr. Necaise coming after her with a clenched fist, "I panicked. And before I knew it, the gun just went off."

Newhouse, Tammie [Kansas][64]

Tammie Newhouse was charged with murder and convicted of involuntary manslaughter in the shooting death of her husband. Under Kansas law, she must serve a minimum of three years in prison because the homicide was committed with a firearm.

At trial, Mrs. Newhouse testified that she had often been beaten by her husband, but the court refused to admit expert testimony on the battered woman syndrome. According to Mrs. Newhouse, she feared for her life when she fired at least five shots at her husband's car as he drove away from the parking lot after threatening her with a knife.

Norris, Marie [Georgia][65]

Marie Norris was charged with murder in the shooting death of her husband. She pleaded not guilty by reason of insanity and expert testimony regarding the battered woman syndrome was admitted into evidence at her trial. Mrs. Norris was found guilty as charged and was sentenced to life imprisonment. Her conviction was affirmed on appeal.

Mrs. Norris had been physically abused by her husband throughout their marriage and was diagnosed by two psychiatrists as suffering from the battered woman syndrome. Just prior to the killing, she had been hospitalized for "acute severe depression."

Mrs. Norris was unable to recall the full details surrounding the killing. According to her testimony, her husband struck her on the head. He then gave her a codeine tablet and sent her to bed. She recalled awakening once and taking another tablet. Her next recollection was finding herself in the yard the next morning, playing with her dog. Her husband's body was found in the house. A gun, "the murder weapon," was in his hand. He had been shot several times and there was evidence that the killing had taken place during a struggle.

Nunn, Barbara Ann [Iowa][66]

Barbara Ann Nunn was convicted of second degree murder in connection with the death of Bernard Boyce, the man with whom she had lived for about two years. Her conviction was affirmed on appeal.

Nunn and Boyce had engaged in physical fights about once a week throughout their relationship. Evidence at trial indicated that Boyce "had treated [Nunn] violently in the past and had threatened to kill her on the day he died." A social worker testified that Nunn suffered from the battered woman syndrome.

Just before the killing, Nunn and Boyce had a heated argument, during which both had been armed with knives. When the argument ceased, Boyce retreated to another room. A few minutes later, Nunn followed Boyce and stabbed him to death.

In affirming Nunn's conviction, the appellate court found that Nunn's motion for acquittal on grounds of self-defense had been properly denied. As the court explained, "We cannot ignore the fact that there was a cooling-off period before the actual stabbing."

Olsen, Rachel [Pseudonym][67]

Rachel Olsen had been beaten by her husband throughout their three year marriage. During several battering incidents, Mrs. Olsen had called the police. Each time, the police responded, but never arrested Mr. Olsen. Instead they advised Mrs. Olsen to consider divorce.

On the day before his death, Mr. Olsen had beaten and choked Mrs. Olsen so severely that she was unable to eat. The following day, after a bout of heavy drinking, Mr. Olsen again beat Mrs. Olsen and began to taunt her about his sexual relationship with another woman.

An argument ensued and Mr. Olsen threatened to kill Mrs. Olsen. He then grabbed her by the wrists, shoved her into a corner, and started to bang her head against the wall. During the struggle, Mrs. Olsen stabbed Mr. Olsen once with a kitchen knife, killing him.

Mrs. Olsen was charged with murder, but claimed self-defense and was acquitted.

Ortiz, Donna [New York][68]

Donna Ortiz was acquitted of murder and other charges stemming from the shooting death of her married "boyfriend," Mark McMiller.

According to testimony at trial, McMiller had often beaten Ortiz during the 12 years they lived together. In one incident, he stabbed her, puncturing one of her lungs. In another incident, he injured her ear when he beat her with a shotgun. On other occasions, McMiller's abuse left Ortiz with a broken pelvis, two fractured ankles, and knife wounds to both arms. Testimony regarding these batterings was corroborated by medical evidence as well as the testimony of the director of a local shelter for battered women.

The killing took place about an hour after McMiller beat the couple's eight-year-old son with a broom handle. According to Ortiz, McMiller attacked her and threatened to kill her, telling her at one point in the encounter:

"Only one of us is leaving alive." While choking Ortiz and pulling her hair, McMiller tossed his automatic pistol on the kitchen table. Ortiz grabbed the gun and shot McMiller once in the chest.

Patri, Jennifer [Wisconsin][69]

Jennifer Patri was convicted of manslaughter and sentenced to 10 years in prison in the shooting death of her estranged husband. Her conviction was affirmed on appeal and she was denied habeas corpus relief in the federal courts. Mrs. Patri served three years and three months of her sentence and was then paroled.

Prior to the killing, throughout their 14 year marriage, Mr. Patri had repeatedly beaten and threatened to kill Mrs. Patri. One of these beatings resulted in a miscarriage. Allegedly, Mr. Patri also had sexually abused the couple's 12-year-old daughter.

Several months before the killing, the Patris separated, Mr. Patri moved in with another woman, and Mrs. Patri filed for divorce. Mr. Patri sought custody of the couple's two children and a month before the killing threatened to kidnap the children. At that time, Mrs. Patri purchased a shotgun.

On the day of the killing, Mr. Patri came to Mrs. Patri's home. Mrs. Patri gave two conflicting accounts of what then happened.

According to one account, the couple argued and Mrs. Patri confronted Mr. Patri with allegations of child molestation. When Mr. Patri responded by saying, "I'm going to shut your fucking mouth once and for all," Mrs. Patri ran to the basement. When Mr. Patri followed her, carrying a knife, she grabbed the shotgun and warned him to leave. When he continued toward her, she shot and killed him.

According to Mrs. Patri's other account of the killing, the couple argued and when Mr. Patri got ready to leave, she shot him once in the back, then reloaded the gun and shot him again in the head.

In both accounts, Mrs. Patri admitted that she dragged her husband's body from the house, covered it with dirt and debris, and then tried to set her house on fire.

Player, Mary Louise [California][70]

Mary Louise Player was convicted of second degree murder and sentenced to three years in prison for killing her husband.

Mrs. Player, who had been beaten by her husband numerous times in the past, shot and killed him as he lay on the couch. A few minutes earlier, he had beaten and raped her in front of her children, threatened to kill her when he got up, and warned her not to leave. Mrs. Player claimed she killed her husband in self-defense.

At sentencing, Mrs. Player's attorney depicted her as a battered woman who had "suffered enough through seven years of brutal beatings" and urged the judge to impose probation. The judge, however, sentenced Mrs. Player to prison, explaining that, "The jury has spoken, and women in Mrs. Player's situation have to know that they cannot commit second degree murder and expect to walk out the door free."

Powell, Bernadette [New York][71]

Bernadette Powell was charged with second degree murder in the shooting death of her ex-husband, Herman Smith. Subsequently, Powell refused a plea bargain in which the prosecutor offered to allow her to plead guilty to criminally negligent homicide, an offense carrying sanctions ranging from probation to a maximum of four years imprisonment.

Insisting that she killed Smith in self-defense, Powell chose to go to trial. A jury found Powell guilty of second degree murder and the judge imposed the minimum sentence allowed by law: 15 years to life imprisonment. Convicted in 1979, Powell will not even be eligible for parole until 1994.

Powell had been abused by Smith throughout their seven-year marriage. Smith beat Powell on the average of twice a week. A number of times, injuries he inflicted upon her required hospitalization. The police were called on several of these occasions and Powell obtained court orders of protection, which Smith repeatedly violated.

A year before the killing, Powell had divorced Smith. Between the time of the divorce and the killing, Powell and Smith had gotten along fairly well and there had been no further instances of abuse until the day of the killing.

On the day of the killing, Powell drove to the nearby city in which Smith was living. The purpose of Powell's trip was to pick up the couple's son, who had been visiting Smith. Smith asked Powell to drive him to another nearby city and the three of them left together in Powell's truck.

While on the road, Smith pulled a gun and forced Powell to drive him to a number of locations before eventually stopping at a motel for the night. Once in the motel room, Smith told Powell, "Don't try anything—you can't run from a bullet." After their son fell asleep, Smith ordered Powell to join him on the bed. Powell complied and Smith fell asleep. A short while later, Powell grabbed the gun, which was under Smith. According to Powell, Smith jumped up and the gun went off, killing him.

Ratcliffe, ———[72]

Mrs. Ratcliffe pleaded guilty to manslaughter in the death of her husband. She was sentenced to two years probation.

Throughout their marriage, Mr. Ratcliffe had physically abused Mrs.

Ratcliffe. While she was pregnant, he forced her to have sexual intercourse with him by burning her with a lighted cigarette. Mrs. Ratcliffe then borrowed a knife, intending to kill Mr. Ratcliffe. Six days later, she stabbed him to death.

Reese, Beverly [*Georgia*][73]

Beverly Reese was acquitted of homicide charges in the shooting death of her husband.

According to Mrs. Reese, the shooting took place after years of abuse by her husband and one "long night of violence." A psychologist gave expert testimony that Mrs. Reese "exhibited many classic characteristics of the 'battered woman syndrome.'" Pictures of Mrs. Reese taken shortly after the killing showed her with a bruised and swollen face.

While Mrs. Reese recalled grabbing a gun from a dresser, pointing it at her husband (who was "lying on the bed with his eyes closed"), and hearing the gun fire, she claimed she did not remember pulling the trigger.

According to one juror, the jury's judgment "pretty much came down to not guilty or not guilty by reason of insanity" but "[i]t didn't take long to reach the conclusion she wasn't guilty." In the view of the prosecutor, the jury concluded that Mr. Reese "deserved what he got."

Reeves, Barbara [*Illinois*][74]

Barbara Reeves was convicted of murder and sentenced to 14 years in prison for killing her husband.

Prior to the killing, Mr. Reeves had beaten Mrs. Reeves on many occasions. Several of these beatings were so severe that hospitalization was required. Mr. Reeves had also threatened Mrs. Reeves with a gun a number of times.

On the night of the killing, the couple argued in a bar. Mr. Reeves left and Mrs. Reeves said several times that she was "going to kill that son-of-a-bitch Charlie Reeves." Subsequently, Mrs. Reeves was joined by two friends who took her home. Mrs. Reeves went into the house and removed a gun and some ammunition.

A short while later, Mrs. Reeves and her friends went to a local cafe and ordered breakfast. When they started to leave the cafe, they were confronted by Mr. Reeves, who grabbed Mrs. Reeves around the neck in a chokehold and dragged her out of the cafe and down the street. As Mr. Reeves dragged Mrs. Reeves, he continuously hit her with his free hand. After Mr. Reeves had dragged her some distance (estimated to be from 20 to 75 feet), the gun Mrs. Reeves was carrying went off once, killing Mr. Reeves.

On appeal, Mrs. Reeves' conviction was reversed when the appellate court concluded that the prosecution failed to prove beyond a reasonable doubt that Mrs. Reeves had not killed in self-defense.

Roan Eagle, Marlene [South Dakota][75]

Marlene Roan Eagle was acquitted of murder in the killing of her husband.

Prior to the killing, Mrs. Roan Eagle had been beaten by her husband on a number of occasions, the most recent beating having occurred about six months prior to the killing. As a result of these beatings, Mrs. Roan Eagle had been hospitalized twice, once for a full month.

Immediately prior to the killing, her husband had come at her with a broken broomstick. Mrs. Roan Eagle responded by stabbing him through the heart, killing him.

Robertson, ————[76]

Mrs. Robertson pleaded guilty to manslaughter in the death of her husband and was sentenced to a conditional discharge.

Mrs. Robertson had often been beaten by her husband. Three times she suffered miscarriages as a result of these beatings. On a number of occasions, Mr. Robertson threatened Mrs. Robertson and her children with a knife. Finally, unable to withstand any more abuse, Mrs. Robertson stabbed Mr. Robertson in the chest, killing him while he slept.

Sanchez, Sylvia [Texas][77]

Sylvia Sanchez was charged with murder but allowed to plead guilty to voluntary manslaughter in the shooting death of her husband. Accepting this plea bargain, a judge sentenced her to eight years probation and payment of $1,250 in costs (half the expense of her husband's funeral).

Mrs. Sanchez admitted that she confronted her husband in the parking lot of a saloon and shot him eight times, but told authorities that the killing was a last resort to end months of physical and emotional abuse. Sanchez said her husband was in the habit of getting drunk, coming home, and beating her. On the day of the killing, she said, she went looking for him with a gun because she feared he would come home and batter her again.

Mrs. Sanchez purchased the gun a month earlier after her husband threatened her with a knife. She wrestled the knife away from him and took it to the police, who told her there was nothing they could do: "They told me to go back home and 'be careful with the knife.'"

On earlier occasions, when her husband had beaten her, Mrs. Sanchez received essentially the same kind of response from the police: "I called the police so many times they wouldn't pay attention anymore. Sometimes they would get him outside and talk to him and then turn him loose, or they would say, 'this is his house and there's nothing we can do.'"

Shropshire, Billie [Illinois][78]

Billie Shropshire was convicted of murder for killing her ex-boyfriend.

Shropshire had moved three times to escape from the abuse inflicted upon her by the man she killed. Each time, he followed her. He beat her, slashed the tires on her car, followed her children after school, stood outside her window and aimed a shotgun at her head, and threatened her face-to-face with a knife and a gun. Shropshire reported this abuse to the police and took the man to court, but the abuse continued. Finally, Shropshire shot and killed her abuser.

In the words of the public defender: "It was a classic case of self-defense—except for the last minute and a half."

Smith, Jeannette [Michigan][79]

Jeannette Smith was acquitted of murder charges in the death of her 66-year-old husband.

During her five-week trial, Mrs. Smith testified at length regarding the severe abuse she had suffered at the hands of Mr. Smith during their marriage. According to Mrs. Smith's testimony, Mr. Smith often pistol-whipped her, beat her and poured salt into her wounds, threatened her with guns and knives, and awakened her at night, pulling her out of bed by her hair.

Several times, Mrs. Smith left Mr. Smith, but each time she returned, persuaded to do so by Mr. Smith's promises to reform or his threats to kill her or have her killed. During one separation, Mr. Smith threw a can of gasoline through Mrs. Smith's window and told her that he had "put a contract out" on her life.

Shortly before the killing, the couple separated again. On the day of the killing, Mrs. Smith went to her husband's home seeking financial help. There she was beaten by her husband and his 17-year-old pregnant "housekeeper-secretary."

Mrs. Smith called the police, who removed the 17-year-old from the house. While the police remained outside the house with the girl, Mr. Smith came at Mrs. Smith, threatening to kill her. Moments later, Mr. Smith stumbled out of the house with a five-inch kitchen knife in his back. Mrs. Smith testified that she could not recall what had happened.

Smith, Josephine [Georgia][80]

Josephine Smith was convicted of voluntary manslaughter and sentenced to 15 years in prison for killing her "live-in boyfriend." Her conviction was affirmed by the state court of appeals but eventually reversed by the Georgia Supreme Court, which concluded that the trial court erred in refusing to admit expert testimony that Smith was a battered woman.

Smith met the man she eventually killed when she was 17 years old. During their six-year relationship, he had beaten her periodically. On the evening of the killing, Smith returned to her apartment and found her boyfriend waiting for her. Shortly thereafter she went to bed. Her boyfriend followed her and started touching her. When she told him to stop, he said: "You don't tell me when to touch you."

Smith then got out of bed, dressed, and started to leave but remained in the bedroom when her boyfriend threatened her with his fist. He then kicked her, hit her in the head, grabbed her by the throat, choked her, and threw her against the door. Smith broke loose, grabbed a gun, and ran out of the room. Her boyfriend followed her and grabbed her. Once again, she broke loose. As she tried to leave the apartment, he slammed the door on her foot and she shot the gun three times, killing him.

Snyder, Deborah [Pennsylvania][81]

Deborah Snyder was acquitted of murder charges after she shot and killed her "boyfriend" of 10 years, Timothy Tilmon. A psychologist testified that she was a battered woman who was in a "state of terror" at the time of the killing. The evidence indicated that Snyder had been beaten by Tilmon for years.

On the night of the killing, Snyder and Tilmon returned home after visiting three bars. Tilmon, who was intoxicated, threatened to kill Snyder and "pushed around" their six-year-old son. When Tilmon left the house to buy some beer, Snyder locked him out and got a gun from an upstairs bedroom. When Tilmon returned, he went to the back door and tried to force his way into the house. Snyder responded by shooting him through the heart, killing him.

Strong, Laverne [Georgia][82]

Laverne Strong was convicted of felony murder and sentenced to life imprisonment in the death of her common-law husband, Johnny Lamar. Her conviction was affirmed on appeal.

Evidence at Strong's trial indicated that she had been beaten by Lamar during their relationship and that Lamar had once broken Strong's jaw. Expert testimony on the battered woman syndrome was offered and admitted into evidence.

According to Strong's testimony, she arrived home, walked into the house, and was attacked by Lamar, who cut her with a knife. She seized the knife and stabbed him in the arm, severing an artery. In an earlier statement given to police, Strong said that after Lamar cut her, she grabbed a knife from a nearby table and slashed him with it.

Taylor, Bernestine [Illinois][83]

Bernestine Taylor withstood nine years of severe physical abuse from her husband before stabbing him to death. An eight-man, four-woman jury acquitted her of homicide charges.

Terry, Shirley [Florida][84]

Shirley Terry was convicted of manslaughter with a firearm and sentenced to 20 years in prison for killing her boyfriend, Oscar Mercer.

At trial, Terry testified that she had an intimate relationship with Mercer for four years and that during that time Mercer had often beaten her. Some of these beatings had been administered with bottles and boards and resulted in injuries requiring hospital care.

Eventually, Terry moved in with her mother. When Mercer followed her and threatened to shoot her, she moved to an apartment of her own. Mercer again followed her, broke in several times, and continued to beat her. About three weeks before the killing, Mercer tied Terry up and threatened to dump her in an alligator swamp.

On the day of the killing, Terry telephoned Mercer from a bar and told him where she was, fearful that he would beat her if he found out from someone else. Mercer then picked her up, drove her to her apartment, and demanded sexual relations. Afterwards, Mercer forced Terry into his car. As they were driving away, he again threatened to feed her to the alligators. Terry then pulled a gun from her purse and shot Mercer, killing him.

On appeal, Terry's conviction was reversed and the case remanded for a new trial, in part because the trial court had excluded expert testimony on the battered woman syndrome.

Thomas, Gladys [Ohio][85]

Gladys Thomas was indicted for murder and convicted of voluntary manslaughter for killing her common-law husband, Dennis Brown. On appeal, her conviction was reversed and the case remanded for a new trial because the trial court had improperly excluded expert psychiatric testimony regarding Thomas's "paranoid personality."

Thomas and Brown had lived together, on and off, for several years prior to the killing. Brown was a drug abuser who forced Thomas into life as a prostitute to support his drug habit. Brown had also beaten Thomas throughout the course of their relationship. A number of these beatings left Thomas with injuries requiring hospital treatment.

At the time of the killing, Thomas and Brown had been separated for about a month. Brown called Thomas and arranged to visit her. Thomas prepared for Brown's visit by getting out a gun. When Brown arrived, an argument ensued and Thomas shot and killed him as he approached her.

Thomas, Juanita [Michigan][86]

Juanita Thomas was convicted of first degree murder and sentenced to life imprisonment in the stabbing death of her "live-in boyfriend," Willie Hammond. Her conviction was affirmed on appeal.

Over a six-year period prior to the killing, Thomas had been repeatedly beaten and abused by Hammond. At one point, Thomas changed the lock on her door to keep Hammond out, but he broke in and told her she might as well give him a key.

In the days immediately prior to the killing, Thomas complained to others that Hammond was seeing another woman and that she (Thomas) was going to kill Hammond. Thomas also displayed a knife to several witnesses and told them it was the weapon she intended to use on Hammond.

Thomas claimed that she killed Hammond in self-defense, but there was both physical and testimonial evidence suggesting that Hammond was asleep at the time Thomas stabbed him.

Thomas, Kathy [Ohio][87]

Kathy Thomas was convicted of murder for killing her common-law husband, Reuben Daniels, and was sentenced to 15 years to life in prison. Her conviction was affirmed on appeal when the Ohio Supreme Court concluded that the trial court had not erred in refusing to admit expert testimony on the battered woman syndrome at Thomas's trial. Subsequently, Thomas was denied habeas corpus relief in the federal courts.

Thomas and Daniels had lived together for about three years before the killing. During those years, Thomas was repeatedly beaten by Daniels.

Thomas admitted shooting Daniels once in the forehead and once in the left arm. She claimed self-defense, but gave the police three different versions of what happened.

In Thomas's first version of the events surrounding the killing, she stated that the couple had argued over Thomas's cooking. Daniels slapped Thomas, pushed her down onto a couch, and she picked up the gun. Thomas then walked to a chair where Daniels was seated and shot him.

In Thomas's second account of the killing, she told the police that she and Daniels had argued over a pawn ticket for her watch. Daniels pushed her down and as he was arising from a chair, about to attack her, she reached for the gun and shot him.

In Thomas' final version, the couple had argued about burned fish. Daniels pushed Thomas down, Thomas picked up the gun, stood up and told Daniels, "I've had enough." Thomas then aimed the gun at Daniels and shot him.

Thompson, Toni [Texas][88]

Toni Thompson was convicted of murder for killing her husband. Her conviction was affirmed on appeal.

The Thompsons had been married three months at the time of the killing. During those three months, Mr. Thompson, while intoxicated, had abused Mrs. Thompson on a number of occasions. In one incident, he held a sawed-off shotgun to her head and threatened to kill her. On another occasion, he punched her in the jaw with his fist, knocked her off a bar stool, and dragged her away by her hair. Mr. Thompson also allegedly had a reputation for violent acting-out and had been convicted five times for carrying weapons.

On the evening of the killing, Mr. and Mrs. Thompson had been drinking in a bar. Mr. Thompson left to run an errand but returned about an hour and a half later, asking Mrs. Thompson why she was still there. An argument ensued and Mrs. Thompson told Mr. Thompson, "Get off my fucking case, Bobby, or I'll shoot you." Mr. Thompson then approached Mrs. Thompson with his arms outstretched "like he was going to grab and choke" her. Mrs. Thompson backed away, pulled a pistol from her purse, and shot and killed Mr. Thompson.

Three Stars, Paula [Washington][89]

Paula Three Stars pleaded guilty to first degree manslaughter after being charged with murder in the killing of Sonny Evening, Jr., the man with whom she lived. As part of the plea bargain, the prosecutor agreed to recommend that Three Stars be sentenced to serve only one year in jail. A county judge, rejecting this agreement, sentenced Three Stars to 10 years in prison and then refused to allow her to withdraw her guilty plea. Subsequently, however, following major media coverage and demonstrations by Three Stars' supporters, the judge concluded that Three Stars had killed in self-defense. Thus, he reduced her sentence to three years probation.

The evidence indicated that Evening had often beaten Three Stars. As a result of these beatings, Three Stars had suffered a dislocated shoulder, broken fingers, black eyes, and bruises. Ultimately, Evening was killed by shotgun blasts to his head and neck. Three Stars claimed that she fired the fatal shots in self-defense.

Tisland, Lucile [Minnesota][90]

Lucile Tisland was acquitted of first degree murder. Tisland, who claimed to be a battered woman, killed her sleeping husband after he threatened to kill her and their children. According to Tisland, her husband had earlier demanded that she keep a miscarried fetus in the family freezer.

Torres, Lydia [New York][91]

Lydia Torres was acquitted of second degree murder in the killing of her common-law husband, Ruperto Rosado.

During their ten-year relationship, Rosado had often beaten and threatened Torres, generally while he was intoxicated. At times he menaced her with a knife and a gun. A psychologist testified that Torres suffered from the battered woman syndrome.

The killing occurred after an argument in which Rosado, who had been drinking, accused Torres of having sexual relations with his son. When Torres denied the accusation, Rosado grabbed her by the hair and repeatedly beat her about the face and back. Then, screaming that "This will be your last night," Rosado put a gun against Torres' mouth, threw her down, placed the gun on a table, and sat down in a chair.

After he was seated, Rosado continued to threaten to kill Torres. In response, Torres grabbed the gun from the table and shot Rosado three times, fatally wounding him as he sat in the chair.

Ware, Evelyn [California][92]

Evelyn Ware was acquitted of murder charges in the killing of her husband. Mr. Ware had beaten and tormented Mrs. Ware repeatedly throughout their marriage. He continued to beat and harass her even after she divorced him. Finally, after one battering incident, Mrs. Ware shot Mr. Ware five times, killing him.

Watson, Barbara [Pennsylvania][93]

Barbara Watson was convicted of manslaughter for killing her common-law husband, Matt Lee Black. On appeal, her conviction was reversed when the Pennsylvania Supreme Court held that the evidence had not been sufficient to establish that the killing was not in self-defense.

Watson and Black had lived together for 10 years, during which time they had three children. Watson had been beaten by Black throughout their relationship.

On the night of the killing, Watson and Black argued. Black knocked

Watson down in the street and threatened her with a baseball bat. Later that night, as the couple walked down the street about 40 feet ahead of some friends, the arguing continued. At trial, Watson testified as follows:

> So we was walking, you know, up the street. And he just hauled off and grabbed me around the neck and shoulders and started choking me. And he had me down on the ground. And I was scared. And he said, "You black bitch, I should have killed you a while ago when we was at the house."
>
> And I was scared. It was me or him. I didn't know what to do. I was so scared. I was scared that he was going to kill me, because he told me he was going to kill me.
>
> That's why I shot him. I don't know how I managed to get the gun. I was just scuffling down on the ground. It was me and him.

White, Dorothy [Missouri][94]

Dorothy White was convicted of manslaughter for killing her husband. The jury recommended a sentence of one year in prison.

A psychiatrist testified at the trial that Mrs. White was suffering from the battered woman syndrome when she shot and killed Mr. White. The evidence showed that Mr. White was an alcoholic who had terrorized Mrs. White for years and had threatened to kill her for months prior to the shooting.

The evidence further showed that, just prior to the killing, the couple had argued over some furniture Mrs. White had placed in storage and planned to sell to pay for a divorce. Mr. White told Mrs. White not to sell the furniture, but return it to their home. According to Mrs. White, he told her, "You've got two days and don't forget what I've been telling you—I'm going to kill you."

A short while later, Mrs. White shot and killed Mr. White as he stood unarmed in the bathroom of the couple's home.

In response to Mrs. White's claim of self-defense, the prosecutor told the jury, "This makes a mockery of people who do act in self-defense. This woman could have left at any time."

White, Odessa [Illinois][95]

Odessa White was charged with murder and convicted of voluntary manslaughter for killing George Butler, the man with whom she had lived for about five years. White was sentenced to four years probation, with the first year to include periodic imprisonment. Her conviction was affirmed on appeal.

White was beaten by Butler throughout their life together. Butler broke

White's ankle and ribs, dislocated her elbow, twisted her arm (causing an injury which required surgery), beat her on the face with a bottle, blackened her eyes, struck her on the breast (resulting in yet another injury that required surgery), and hit her over the head with a car jack.

On the day of the killing, White and Butler were drinking and arguing. Butler told White he was going out to buy more liquor. When White objected, Butler told her that he was going to whip her. He grabbed her by the arm, but she broke loose and fled to a bedroom, where she remained for four or five minutes before removing a pistol from a dresser. According to White, Butler then came toward her, "walking fast," and she shot him once. When he continued toward her, "running," she shot him again. In White's own words:

> I wasn't intending to kill him, but I didn't want him to hurt me no more . . .
> I thought maybe if I shoot the first time he would go back. but instead of
> him going back, he started coming faster upon me.

Wilds, Carol Ann [Indiana][96]

Carol Ann Wilds was convicted of murder and sentenced to a term of 15 to 25 years in prison for killing her husband. Her conviction was affirmed on appeal.

The couple had a long history of marital problems, including arguments and violence toward one another.

The day before the killing, Mrs. Wilds purchased a gun and some ammunition and test-fired the gun in the presence of two witnesses. The next day, the couple argued in front of friends and Mrs. Wilds told Mr. Wilds that if he ever beat her again, "I will blow you away while you are asleep."

That night, the couple argued and Mr. Wilds beat Mrs. Wilds and then walked off. The next thing Mrs. Wilds remembered was the gun going off.

Mr. Wilds body was found on his bed. An autopsy revealed fingernail scratches on his face as well as seven bullet wounds to his neck. It was determined that the bullets that killed him were fired from a distance of about 15 inches. This evidence, the prosecution suggested, indicated that Mr. Wilds was probably asleep when he was killed.

Williams, Viola [Louisiana][97]

Viola Williams was charged with first degree murder in the shooting death of her common-law husband, Harold Randolph. The charges against Williams were dropped after the prosecutor learned that Randolph had abused Williams for more than 10 years prior to the shooting. Among other forms of abuse, Randolph had beaten Williams with a baseball bat, slashed her with a knife, and pushed her face into a mound of red ants. There was evidence that Williams had sought help many times and that Randolph had once been convicted of simple battery for beating Williams with a baseball bat.

Ultimately, Williams shot Randolph 13 times. She shot him twice in the head, reloaded the gun, and then fired 11 shots into his back. Describing the killing, the prosecutor, who agreed to drop the charges, said: "The first two [shots] were in self-defense and the rest for what he'd done to her for years."

Winstead, Mary [Illinois][98]

Mary Winstead was acquitted of murder charges in the shooting death of her husband.

Mrs. Winstead admitted shooting her husband seven times with a single-shell shotgun while he was resting on a bed at home. Evidence at trial indicated that Mr. Winstead had abused Mrs. Winstead throughout their 11-year marriage. A sociologist testified that many of Mrs. Winstead's responses to this abuse were characteristic of the battered woman syndrome. The prosecutor, however, claimed that the killing was committed in a "cold calculated manner" and that Mrs. Winstead had not been abused during the six months immediately preceding the homicide.

Wisecup, Jo Nell [Georgia][99]

Jo Nell Wisecup killed her husband, was charged with murder, convicted of voluntary manslaughter, and sentenced to eight years in prison to be followed by four years on probation. Her conviction was affirmed on appeal.

Prior to the killing, Mrs. Wisecup had often been abused by her husband. According to Ms. Wisecup, the killing took place when Mr. Wisecup assaulted her with a .38 caliber pistol. She struggled with him to keep the gun pointed away from her body, the gun went off accidentally, and Mr. Wisecup was shot. The bullet severed an artery and Mr. Wisecup bled to death before Mrs. Wisecup could summon help.

Zenyuh, Mary [Pennsylvania][100]

Mary Zenyuh was convicted of involuntary manslaughter and sentenced to serve between two and four years in prison for killing her husband. On appeal, the conviction was reversed because the court found that the prosecution had failed to prove beyond a reasonable doubt that the killing was not in self-defense.

Prior to their one-year marriage, which ended with Mr. Zenyuh's death, the Zenyuhs had dated for six years. Throughout their relationship, Mr. Zenyuh had beaten Mrs. Zenyuh. A number of these beatings resulted in injuries requiring emergency medical treatment. Mr. Zenyuh had also threatened to kill Mrs. Zenyuh if she ever left him.

On the evening of the killing, both Mr. and Mrs. Zenyuh had been drinking at a family gathering (tests established that his blood alcohol content was .17 percent and that hers was .13 percent). The couple argued and when Mrs. Zenyuh tried to leave, Mr. Zenyuh beat and kicked her, leaving bruises on her legs, arms, and neck.

Later, when the Zenyuh's arrived home, the argument continued and Mrs. Zenyuh picked up a kitchen knife, fearing that Mr. Zenyuh was going to beat her again. Mr. Zenyuh came at Mrs. Zenyuh, grabbed her by the arm, and struggled with her. During the struggle, he was stabbed several times. He later died from the stab wounds he suffered.

Notes

Chapter 1

1. *Sentence in Emick Case Is Fair, Compassionate,* Editorial, BUFFALO NEWS, Apr. 15, 1985, at B2, cols. 1–2.
2. People v. Emick, 481 N.Y.S. 2d 552, 553 (1984).
3. *Id.* at 557–559.
4. *Id.* at 555–557.
5. *Id.* at 558.
6. *Id.* at 557.
7. *Id.* at 559.
8. *Id.*
9. *Id.* at 555.
10. *Id.*
11. *Id.* at 560.
12. *Id.*
13. *Id.* at 562.
14. *Id.* at 560.
15. *Id.*
16. *Id.* at 562.
17. *Emick Gets Probation in Manslaughter Case,* BUFFALO NEWS, Apr. 11, 1985, at C5, cols. 5–6.
18. *Id.*
19. *Id.*
20. Estimates of the number of battered women in the United States vary widely:

> It is estimated that one-third to one-half of all women who live with male companions experience such forms of brutality as threats of severe harm, degradation, beatings, or torture.

Schneider, *Equal Rights to Trial for Women: Sex Bias in the Law of Self-Defense,* 15 HARVARD C. R.–C. L. L. Rev. 623, 624–625 (1980).

> Nearly six million wives will be abused by their husbands in any one year.

Wife Beating: The Silent Crime, TIME, Sept. 5, 1983 at 23.

> Throughout the hearings it became clear to the Task Force that current knowledge about the incidence of family violence is based mostly on estimates. Effective re-

sponses to the problem require much more accurate data. There is no shortage of figures, yet estimates . . . vary greatly. In addition, legal experts regard family violence to be among the most underreported of any crime.

United States Attorney General's Task Force on Family Violence, FINAL REPORT 82 (1984).

21. *See, e.g.,* MacPherson, *Battered Wives and Self-Defense Pleas,* WASHINGTON POST, Dec. 4, 1977, at A1, cols. 2–4 and A16, cols. 1–6; *A Killing Excuse,* TIME, Nov. 28, 1977 at 108; Quindlen, *Women Who Kill Their Spouses: The Causes, the Legal Defenses,* N.Y. TIMES, March 10, 1978, at B4, cols. 1–6; Lewin, *When Victims Kill,* NAT'L. LAW J., Oct. 29, 1979 at 1, cols. 2–3; King, *Right of Self-Defense Gaining in "Battered Wife" Cases,* N.Y. TIMES, May 7, 1979, at A1, cols. 1–2; *Driven to Kill: Battered Women Strike Back,* A.B.A.J., Dec. 1984 at 25.

22. *See, e.g.,* the 100 cases summarized in the appendix to this volume, nearly all of which involved claims of self-defense. *See also* chapter 4, *infra.*

23. *Id.*

24. *Id.*

25. *See generally,* L. Walker, THE BATTERED WOMAN SYNDROME (1984).

Chapter 2

1. For an historical analysis of the 1860s through the mid-1970s, *see* Davidson, *Wifebeating: A Recurring Phenomenon Throughout History,* in BATTERED WOMEN 2 (M. Roy, ed., 1977).

2. Gayford, *Battered Wives,* 15 MEDICINE, SCIENCE AND THE LAW 237 (1975).

3. *Id.* at 237–238.

4. *Id.* at 238.

5. Hilberman and Munson, *Sixty Battered Women,* 3–4 VICTIMOLOGY 460, 462 (1977-78).

6. *Id.*

7. Rounsaville and Weissmann, *Battered Women: A Medical Problem Requiring Detection,* 8 INT'L J. PSYCH. 191 (1977).

8. L. Walker, THE BATTERED WOMAN SYNDROME 26 (1984).

9. Kuhl, *Community Responses to Battered Women,* 7 VICTIMOLOGY 49, 52 (1982).

10. M. Pagelow, WOMAN BATTERING: VICTIMS AND THEIR EXPERIENCE (1981).

11. K. Hofeller, SOCIAL, PSYCHOLOGICAL AND SITUATIONAL FACTORS IN WIFE ABUSE (1982).

12. Gayford, *supra* note 2 at 237. In Walker's study of 435 battered women, the subjects reported that "psychological abuse . . . caused them the most pain." L. Walker, THE BATTERED WOMAN SYNDROME 27 (1984).

13. L. Walker, THE BATTERED WOMAN at xv (1979).

14. *Id.*

15. *Id.*

16. L. Walker, *supra* note 12 at 27–28.

17. Hilberman and Munson, *supra* note 5 at 461–462.

18. Hofeller, *supra* note 11 at 118.

19. Kuhl, *supra* note 9 at 52.

20. L. Walker, *supra* note 12 at 28.

21. Waits, *The Criminal Justice System's Response to Battering,* 60 WASH. L. REV. 267, 280–281n.60 (1985).

22. L. Walker, *supra* note 12 at 48.

23. *Id.*

24. Kuhl, *supra* note 9 at 52.

25. Hilberman and Munson, *supra* note 5 at 462.

26. *See, e.g.,* L. Walker, *supra* note 12 at 27; L. Walker, *supra* note 13 at 49–50.

27. *Id. See also* Walker, *What Counselors Should Know about the Battered Woman,* in THE MALE BATTERER 151, 158–160 (D. Sonkin, D. Martin & L. Walker, eds., 1985).

28. *See, generally,* M. Seligman, HELPLESSNESS: ON DEPRESSION, DEVELOPMENT AND DEATH (1975).

29. L. Walker, *supra* note 13 at 49–50.

30. *Id.*

31. For example, Hilberman and Munson, *supra* note 5 at 464, report that more than half of the battered women in their study presented with evidence of psychological dysfunction. Gayford, *supra* note 2 at 242, reports that 71 of the 100 battered women he studied had been treated by their general medical practitioners for psychological symptoms and that 46 of these women were referred for psychiatric evaluation.

32. Hilberman and Munson, *supra* note 5 at 465.

33. *See* Rounsaville and Weissmann, *supra* note 7.

34. Gayford, *supra* note 2 at 242.

35. Hoffeler, *supra* note 11 at 118.

36. M. Pagelow, *supra* note 10 at 240.

37. Rounsaville and Weissman, *supra* note 7 at 195.

38. Hilberman and Munson, *supra* note 5 at 464.

39. *Id.* at 464–465.

40. *Wife Beating: The Silent Crime,* TIME, September 5, 1983 at 23, 24.

41. L. Walker, *supra* note 12 at 188.

42. *Id.*

43. Gayford, *Battered Wives,* in VIOLENCE AND THE FAMILY 19, 25 (J.P. Martin ed. 1978).

44. Hilberman and Munson, *supra* note 5 at 463.

45. *See, e.g.,* L. Walker, *supra* note 12 at 42:

Women commonly reported phrases such as, "If I can't have you, no one will." "If you leave, I'll find you wherever you go." "Just do that and you'll see how mean I can really be." Threats of bodily mutilation such as cutting up her face, sewing up her vagina, breaking her kneecaps, and knocking her unconscious also served to terrify women . . .

State v. Kelly, 478 A. 2d 364, 369 (N.J. 1984):

During the attacks, which generally occurred when Mr. Kelly was drunk, he threatened to kill Mrs. Kelly and to cut off parts of her body if she ever tried to leave him.

A. Jones, WOMEN WHO KILL 299 (1980):

> There are cases on record of men still harassing and beating their wives twenty-five years after the wives left them and tried to go into hiding. If researchers were not quite so intent upon assigning the pathological behavior to the women, they might see that the more telling question is not "Why do the women stay?" but "Why don't the men let them go?"

46. *See* L. Walker, *supra* note 12 at 42–43.

47. *See* L. Walker, *supra* note 13 at 180.

48. *See* D. Martin, BATTERED WIVES 84 (1976); Roy, *A Current Survey of 150 Cases*, in BATTERED WOMEN 25, 31 (M. Roy ed. 1977); L. Walker, *supra* note 12 at 28, 172.

49. Rounsaville, Lifton, and Bieber, *The Natural History of a Psychotherapy Group for Battered Women*, 42 PSYCHIATRY 63 (1979).

50. Goodstein and Page, *Battered Wife Syndrome: Overview of Dynamics and Treatment*, 138 AM. J. PSYCH. 1036, 1041 (1981).

51. *Id.* at 1040. *See also* Kuhl, *supra* note 9 at 55. Many family members, friends, and neighbors who learn of the battered woman's situation refuse to get involved.

52. *Id.* Where the battered women Kuhl studied told others of their abuse, they were believed by only 20 percent of family members, 15 percent of friends, and 20 percent of neighbors. Of those who believed the woman, 5 percent of family members, 4 percent of friends, and 4 percent of neighbors blamed her. Few family members, friends, or neighbors offered help, and a number of those who tried to help the woman "made things worse."

53. *See generally* B. Warrior, BATTERED WOMEN'S DIRECTORY (1985). *See also* L. Okun, WOMAN ABUSE: FACTS REPLACING MYTHS 141–144 (1986).

54. B. Warrior, *supra* note 53.

55. *Id.*

56. *Id. See also* L. Okun, *supra* note 53 at 141–144; *Wife Beating: The Silent Crime*, *supra* note 40 at 24 (YWCA shelters are unable to accomodate 80 percent of those who seek refuge).

57. A look at a recent nationwide list of shelters indicates that there are many areas of the United States in which no shelters exist. B. Warrior, *supra* note 53.

58. In September of 1984, Congress enacted and the President signed into law Pub. L. No. 98–457, which appropriated $62 million over a three-year period to help fund shelters for victims of domestic violence.

59. *See* Walker, *Psychological Causes of Family Violence*, in M. Lystad (ed.), VIOLENCE IN THE HOME 71, 90, who explains that while "shelter women" may be able to provide researchers with "important insights," they are not representative of battered women because "only a small percentage of battered women use the shelter[s]."

60. *See, e.g.*, Walker, Thyfault & Browne, *Beyond the Juror's Ken: Battered Women*, 7 VERMONT L. REV. 1, 12 (1982):

> Many of these women had tried to leave and were badly beaten for it. Some actually had gotten away but their husbands traced them and followed them, even to another state . . . Some of the women . . . had been separated or divorced for up to two years . . . and yet still experienced life-threatening harassment and abuse.

61. *See* Walker, *supra* note 12 at 141.

62. *See* Buzawa & Buzawa, *Legislative Trends in the Criminal Justice Response to Domestic Violence,* in A. Lincoln & M. Straus (eds.), CRIME AND THE FAMILY 134, 135 (1985):

> The police and local law enforcement agencies have traditionally been the primary societal institution intervening in domestic violence. Such agencies have the initial contact with violence-prone families as they provide free services, are highly visible authoritative figures, maintain central dispatch and are usually the only public agency in a position to provide rapid 24-hour-a-day assistance.

63. *Id.* at 136–138. *See also* J. Hendricks, CRISIS INTERVENTION: CONTEMPORARY ISSUES FOR ON-SITE INTERVENERS 49–51 (1985).

64. *Id.* at 64–76.

65. *Id.*

66. Sherman & Berk, *The Specific Deterrent Effects of Arrest for Domestic Assault,* 49 AMER. SOC. REV. 261 (1984).

67. J. Hendricks, *supra* note 63 at 51: "Arrest of the abuser is seen by many police and citizens as a last resort disposition in domestic violence calls. The International Association of Chiefs of Police recommends that arrest be used as a last resort."

68. In many jurisdictions, police officers are unable, as a matter of law, to make an arrest for a misdemeanor unless the criminal act was committed in their presence or an arrest warrant was previously obtained. *See* Buzawa & Buzawa, *supra* note 62 at 138.

69. Waits, *supra* note 21 at 311–312:

> Police questioning of the couple typically reflects inaccurate suppositions about the abusive relationship. Officers may consider the victim's hysteria as evidence of her untrustworthiness, and they may rebuff her attempts to tell her story or may not believe it once told.

70. Buzawa & Buzawa, *supra* note 62 at 140.

71. *See* Waits, *supra* note 21 at 309–310.

72. *See* Gombossy, *Battered Wife Who Sued Police Wins $2.3 Million,* NATIONAL LAW JOURNAL, July 15, 1985 at 6.

73. *See* Buzawa & Bazawa, *supra* note 62 at 137; Waits, *supra* note 21 at 321; Fromson, *The Prosecutor's Responsibilities in Spouse Abuse Cases,* in U.S. Department of Justice, PROSECUTOR'S RESPONSIBILITY IN SPOUSE ABUSE CASES 1–2 (1978).

74. Hendricks, *supra* note 63 at 51.

75. Threats and acts of retaliation are common in battering relationships and the likelihood of serious or lethal violence is greatest when the battered woman asserts control or acts to terminate the relationship. *See* Walker, Thyfault & Browne, *supra* note 60 at 12; L. Walker, *supra* note 12 at 42–43.

76. *Id.* at 141.

77. *See* Waits, *supra* note 21 at 328; Buzawa & Bazawa, *supra* note 62 at 137.

78. *Id.* at 143–144. *See also* Waits, *supra* note 21 at 328 (referring to "knee-jerk referrals to counseling").

79. *Id.* at 321–329 (suggested changes in prosecutorial and judicial response). *See also* Buzawa & Buzawa, *supra* note 62 at 143–146 (legislative changes which may alter prosecutorial and judicial response).

80. Stark, Flitcraft and Frazier, *Medicine and Patriarchal Violence: The Social Construction of a "Private" Event,* 9 INT'L J. OF HEALTH SERVICES 461 (1979).

81. *See* Klingbeil & Boyd, *Emergency Room Intervention: Detection, Assessment and Treatment,* in A. Roberts (ed.), Battered Women and Their Families 7 (1984).

82. *See, e.g.,* Gayford, *supra* note 2 at 242 (71 of 100 battered women studied had been treated with antidepressants and/or tranquilizers by their general physicians).

83. *See, e.g.,* Hilberman, *Overview: The "Wife-Beater's Wife" Reconsidered,* 137 Am. J. Psych. 1336 (1980) that describes traditional psychological and psychiatric assumptions about battered women:

> Wife abuse, when it was identified, was generally thought to represent some intrapsychic liability on the part of the victim. This psychiatric labeling or attribution of blame reflected and reinforced the societal belief that spouse abuse was an isolated problem in unusually disturbed couples in which the violence was viewed as "fulfilling masochistic needs of the wife and necessary for the wife's (and the couple's) equilibrium."

84. *See generally* A. Roberts (ed.), Battered Women and Their Families: Intervention Strategies and Treatment Programs (1984).

85. "Client resistance" is a major problem in counseling batterers, even where their participation is made a condition of probation. For a discussion of problems in gaining cooperation and maintaining a treatment relationship with batterers, *see* D. Sonkin, D. Martin & L. Walker, The Male Batterer: A Treatment Approach 90–149 (1985).

86. L. Walker, *supra* note 12 at 117.

87. *See* Hilberman, *supra* note 83; N. Shainess, *Psychological Aspects of Wife-battering,* in M. Roy (ed.), Battered Women 111, 155-116 (1977); Snell, Rosenwald & Robey, *The Wifebeater's Wife: A Study of Family Interaction,* 11 Archives of General Psych. 107 (1964).

88. *See* D. Martin, Battered Wives 67–71 (1976) describing "Freudian notions of the submissive, masochistic female and the dominant, sadistic male."

89. *See generally* L. Walker, *supra* notes 12 and 13; Gelles, *Abused Wives: Why Do They Stay?,* 38 J. of Marriage and the Family 659 (1976); Hilberman, *supra* note 83.

90. *See, e.g.,* L. Walker, *supra* note 13 at 33–35.

91. Wetzel & Ross, *Psychological and Social Ramifications of Battering: Observations Leading to a Counseling Methodology for Victims of Domestic Violence,* 1983 Personnel and Guidance 423 (1983).

92. *See* L. Walker, *supra* note 13 at 33–35; Ferraro and Johnson, *How Women Experience Battering: The Process of Victimization,* 30 Soc. Prob. 325, 330 (1983).

93. *See* L. Okun, *supra* note 53 at 94–95; D. Martin, *supra* note 88 at 79–83.

94. *Id.*

95. *Id. See also* M. Schulman, A Survey of Spousal Violence Against Women in Kentucky 3 (1981), reporting that 43 percent of battered women studied had not told anyone about the abuse they suffered.

96. *See, e.g.,* Roy, *supra* note 48 at 31–32; Ferraro & Johnson, *supra* note 92 at 330: D. Martin, *supra* note 88 at 80.

97. L. Walker, *supra* note 13 at 55–70.

98. *Id.* at xv.

99. *Id.* at 56–59.

100. *Id.* at 59–65.

101. *Id.* at 65–70.

102. *Id.* at 69.

103. *Id.* at 70.

104. Dutton & Painter, *Traumatic Bonding: The Development of Emotional Attachments in Battered Women and Other Relationships of Intermittent Abuse,* 6 VICTIMOLOGY 139 (1981).

105. *Id.* at 146–147.

106. *Id.*

107. *Id.* at 147.

108. *Id.*

109. *Id.*

110. *Id.*

111. *Id.* at 148.

112. *Id.*

113. *Id.* at 152.

114. *See* L. Walker, *supra* notes 27 and 29.

115. *Id.*

116. M. Seligman, *supra* note 28.

117. *Id.* at 74.

118. *Id.* at 82.

119. *Id.* at 36.

120. *Id.* at 23–25.

121. *See* Hiroto, *Locus of Control and Learned Helplessness,* 102 J. OF EXPERIMENTAL PSYCH. 187 (1974). Other human studies have reached similar results. *See, e.g.,* Fosco & Geer, *Effects of Gaining Control over Aversive Stimuli after Differing Amounts of No Control,* 29 PSYCH. REP. 1153 (1971); Thornton & Jacobs, *Learned Helplessness in Human Subjects,* 87 J. OF EXPERIMENTAL PSYCH. 369 (1971).

122. L. Walker, *supra* note 13 at 49–50.

123. *See* Gayford, *supra* note 2 at 242; Hilberman & Munson, *supra* note 5 at 463–466; Goodstein & Page, *supra* note 50 at 72.

124. M. Seligman, *supra* note 28 at 82.

125. *Id.*

126. A. Beck, DEPRESSION: CLINICAL, EXPERIMENTAL, AND THEORETICAL ASPECTS 28 (1967).

127. Hilberman & Munson, *supra* note 5 at 465.

Chapter 3

1. U.S. Department of Justice, Federal Bureau of Investigation, UNIFORM CRIME REPORTS: CRIME IN THE UNITED STATES 169–177 (1985).

2. *Id.* at 8.

3. In 1984, men were the victims in 82 percent of the reported homicides known to be perpetrated by females. *Id.* While the relationship of these men to the

women who killed them cannot be ascertained from the data provided in the UNI-
FORM CRIME REPORTS, other data consistently show that most male homicide victims
of female offenders are husbands, common-law husbands, or "lovers." *See* Benedek,
Women and Homicide in THE HUMAN SIDE OF HOMICIDE 151–152 (1982); Daniel
& Harris, *Female Homicide Offenders,* 10 Bull. AM. ACAD. PSYCH. AND L. 261
(1982); A. Jones, WOMEN WHO KILL 320-321 (1980); Rasko, *The Victim of the
Female Killer* 1 VICTIMOLOGY 396 (1976); Rosenblatt & Greenland, *Female Crimes
of Violence,* 16 CANADIAN J. CRIMINOLOGY AND CORRECTIONS 173 (1974); Ward,
Jackson, & Ward, *Crimes of Violence by Women,* in CRIMES OF VIOLENCE 868–869
(D. Mulvihill et al., eds. 1969); M. Wolfgang, PATTERNS OF CRIMINAL VIOLENCE 55
(1958).

4. C. McCormick, BATTERED WOMEN (Cook County Department of Corrections 1977), cited in Schneider & Jordan, *Representation of Women Who Defend
Themselves in Response to Physical or Sexual Assault,* 4 WOMEN'S RIGHTS L. REP.
149, 151 (1978). This widely quoted but apparently never published study was conducted by the Superintendant of the Cook County Women's Correctional Institution
in Chicago in the mid-1970s. Of the 132 female homicide defendants studied, 53 were
charged with killing husbands, common-law husbands, or boyfriends who these
women claimed had beaten them over extended periods of time.

5. J. Totman, THE MURDERESS: A PSYCHOSOCIAL STUDY OF CRIMINAL
HOMICIDE 33–36 (1978).

6. *Id.* at 48.

7. *See, e.g., The Right to Kill,* NEWSWEEK, Sept. 1, 1973 at 69; *A Killing
Excuse,* TIME, November 28, 1977 at 108; MacPherson, *Battered Wives and Self-
Defense Pleas,* WASHINGTON POST, Dec. 4, 1977 at 1, 14; Meyers, *Battered Wives,
Dead Husbands,* STUDENT LAW., Mar. 1978 at 46; Eisenberg & Seymour, *The Self-
Defense Plea and Battered Women,* TRIAL, July, 1978 at 34; Quindlen, *Women Who
Kill Their Spouses: The Causes, the Legal Defenses,* N.Y. TIMES, May 7, 1979 at Al,
A18; Lewin, *Self-Defense for Battered Women: When Victims Kill,* NAT'L. L. J., Oct.
29, 1979 at 1, 11–12; *Driven to Kill: "Battered Women Strike Back,* A.B.A. J., Dec.
1984 at 25–26.

8. Walker, *Battered Women, Psychology and Public Policy,* 39 Am. Psych.
1178,1179 (1984).

9. L. Walker, *The Battered Woman Syndrome* 40–44 (1984). *See also* Walker,
Thyfault & Browne, *Beyond the Juror's Ken: Battered Women,* 7 VERMONT L. REV.
1 (1982), in which Walker and her colleagues describe aspects of this research.

10. L. Walker, *supra* note 9 at 40.

11. *Id.* at 40–44.

12. Walker, Thyfault & Browne, *supra* note 9 at 11.

13. L. Walker, *supra* note 9 at 40-44.

14. *Id.* at 42.

15. *Id.*

16. *Id.*

17. Walker, Thyfault & Browne, *supra* note 9 at 11–12.

18. *Id.* at 12.

19. L. Walker, *supra* note 9 at 41–43.

20. Walker, Thyfault & Borwne, *supra* note 9 at 11.

21. *Id.* at 12; L. Walker, *supra* note 9 at 40.
22. *Id.* at 41.
23. *Id.* at 42.
24. *Id.* at 40.
25. *Id.*
26. Walker, Thyfault & Browne, *supra* note 9 at 11; L. Walker, *supra* note 9 at 43.
27. *Id.* at 41.
28. *Id.*
29. A Browne, *Assault and Homicide at Home: When Battered Women Kill,* paper presented at the Second National Conference for Family Violence Researchers, Durham, N.H., August 1984.
30. *Id.* at 9.
31. *Id.*
32. *Id.*
33. *Id.* at 16.
34. *Id.*
35. *Id.*
36. *Id.* at 10.
37. *Id.* at 16.
38. *Id.* at 17.
39. *Id.*
40. *Id.*
41. *Id.*
42. "The study focused on the women's actions (i.e., the killing of a mate) in the context of their perceptions based on prior physical assaults by that partner, and the impact that the abuse and situational or societal variables had on their assessment of the danger and of the alternatives available to them." *Id.* at 9.
43. A. Jones, WOMEN WHO KILL 281–321 (1980).
44. *Id.* at 298.
45. *Id.* at 312.
46. *Id.* at 313–314.
47. *Id.* at 315.
48. *Id.* at 298.
49. *Id.* at 294, 313.
50. *Id.* at 294.
51. *Id.* at 290, 318.
52. *Id.* at 298–299.
53. *Id.* at 298.
54. *Id.*
55. *Id.*
56. *Id.*
57. *Id.* at 298–299.
58. *Id.*
59. *Id.* at 298.
60. *Id.* at 299.
61. *Id.* at 292, 311–313.

62. *Id.* at 313–314.
63. *Id.* at 315.
64. *Id.* at 281, 287, 290, 317.
65. J. Totman, *supra* note 5 at 33–36, 48.
66. See Chapter 2 for various research and clinical definitions of "battered woman."
67. J. Totman, *supra* note 5 at 42–47.
68. *Id.* at 42.
69. *Id.* at 44–45.
70. *Id.* at 43.
71. *Id.* at 44.
72. *Id.* at 45.
73. *Id.* at 43.
74. *Id.* at 45.
75. *Id.* 46.
76. *Id.*
77. *Id.* at 47.
78. *Id.*
79. *Id.*
80. *Id.* at 46.
81. *Id.*
82. *Id.* at 37.
83. Barnard, Vera, Vera & Newman, *Till Death Do Us Part: A Study of Spouse Murder,* 10 Bull. Am. Acad. of L. and Psych. 271 (1980).
84. *Id.* at 274.
85. *Id.* at 273.
86. *Id.* at 275.
87. *Id.* at 274.
88. The year 1978 was selected as the cutoff because it was not until that year that such cases were reported on a consistent basis. Wire service reports were obtained through a commercial computerized data base known as NEXIS. Several of the cases located were ones also described by A. Jones, *supra* note 3. The degree of overlap between this sample and the samples examined by Walker, *supra* note 9, and Browne, *supra* note 19, is unclear, since neither of these researchers referred to their subjects by name. The present sample, however, is more than twice the size of either of these researchers' samples.
89. People v. White, 414 N.E. 2d 196, 198 (Ill. 1980).
90. People v. Minnis, 455 N.E. 2d 209 (Ill. App. 1983)
91. *Id.* at 214–215.
92. *Courts Recognizing "Battered Wife Syndrome",* APA Monitor, Apr. 1983 at 27 (describing Joyce Hawthorne).
93. People v. Emick, 481 N.Y.S. 2d 552, 556 (1984).
94. *Woman in Michigan Is Freed in Slaying,* N.Y. Times, Apr. 15, 1979 at A-28, col. 1 (describing Jeannette Smith).
95. People v. Felton, 329 N.W. 2d 161, 163 (Wis. 1983).
96. Meyers, *supra* note 7 at 47–48 (describing Billie Shropshire).

97. Fennell v. Goolsby, U.S. Dist. Ct. E.D. Pa. (Slip Opinion, Aug. 28, 1985).
98. *See* W. LaFave & A. Scott, CRIMINAL LAW 454, 457 (1986); P. Robinson, CRIMINAL LAW DEFENSES (v.2) 56 (1984).
99. A. Browne, *supra* note 19 at 10.
100. *Id.*
101. *Id.* at 16.
102. *Id.*
103. L. Walker, *supra* note 9 at 44.
104. *Id.* at 43–44.
105. A. Browne, *supra* note 19 at 16.
106. *Id.* at 16–17.
107. L. Walker, *supra* note 9 at 42.
108. *Id.*
109. *Id.* at 188.
110. Gayford, *Battered Wives,* in VIOLENCE AND THE FAMILY 19, 25 (J.P. Martin, ed., 1978).
111. A. Browne, *supra* note 19 at 15.
112. *Id.*
113. *Id.* at 17.
114. *Id.*
115. L. Walker, *supra* note 9 at 183.
116. A. Browne, *supra* note 19 at 17.
117. *Id.*
118. *Id.*
119. L. Walker, *supra* note 9 at 183.
120. *Id.* at 42.
121. *Id.* at 43.
122. *Id.* at 157; A. Browne, *supra* note 19 at 13.
123. *Id.*; J. Totman, *supra* note 5 at 39.
124. A. Browne, *supra* note 19 at 13.
125. A. Jones, *supra* note 3 at 316 (calculated from racial descriptions provided by the author).
126. A. Browne, *supra* note 19 at 13.
127. J. Totman, *supra* note 5 at 39.
128. Barnard et al., *supra* note 83 at 273.
129. L. Walker, *supra* note 9 at 156.
130. A. Browne, *supra* note 19 at 13.
131. A. Jones, *supra* note 3 at 316.
132. L. Walker, *supra* note 9.
133. *Id.* at 156; A. Browne, *supra* note 19 at 13.
134. L. Walker, *supra* note 9 at 156.
135. A. Browne, *supra* note 19 at 13.
136. J. Totman, *supra* note 5 at 39.
137. Barnard et al., *supra* note 83 at 273.
138. *See* D. Sonkin, D. Martin, & L. Walker, THE MALE BATTERER 41–42 (1985).

139. For example, among the 100 cases summarized in the appendix to this volume are women from virtually all socioeconomic levels, ranging from welfare recipients to highly educated professionals and wives of such professionals.

140. A. Browne, *supra* note 19 at 13.

141. *Id.* at 14.

142. L. Walker, *supra* note 9 at 43.

143. A. Browne, *supra* note 19 at 15.

144. L. Walker, *supra* note 9 at 43.

145. A. Browne, *supra* note 19 at 15.

146. Barnard et al., *supra* note 80 at 274–275.

147. A. Browne, *supra* note 19 at 15.

148. L. Walker, *supra* note 9 at 42.

149. Barnard et al., *supra* note 80 at 274.

150. *See, e.g.*, M. Wolfgang, Patterns in Criminal Homicide 55 (1958).

Chapter 4

1. *A Killing Excuse*, Time, Nov. 28, 1977 at 108; *See also* MacPherson, *Battered Wives and Self Defense Pleas*, Washington Post, Dec. 4, 1977 at A1, A16; Note, *Does Wife Abuse Justify Homicide*, 24 Wayne L. Rev. 705 (1978); *Wives Who Batter Back*, Newsweek, January 30, 1978 at 54; Quindlen, *Women Who Kill Their Spouses: The Causes, the Legal Defenses*, N.Y. Times, Mar. 10, 1978 at B4; Eisenberg & Seymour, *The Self-Defense Plea and Battered Women*, 14 Trial 34 (1978); King, *Right of Women to Self-Defense Gaining in "Battered Wife" Cases*, N.Y. Times, May 7, 1979 at A1, A18; Lewin, *When Victims Kill*, Nat'l. L. J., Oct. 29, 1979 at 1, 10–11; *Driven to Kill*, A.B.A.J., Dec. 1984 at 25.

2. Schneider & Jordan, *Representation of Women Who Defend Themselves in Response to Physical or Sexual Assault*, 4 Women's Rights L. Rep. 149, 149–150 (1978).

3. Walker, Thyfault & Browne, *Beyond the Juror's Ken: Battered Women*, 7 Vermont L. Rev. 1, 14 (1982).

4. A. Browne, *Assault and Homicide at Home: When Battered Women Kill*, paper presented at the Second National Conference for Family Violence Researchers, Durham, N.H., August 1984.

5. A. Jones, Women Who Kill 281-321 (1980).

6. Barnard, Vera, Vera & Newman, *Til Death Do Us Part: A Study of Spouse Murder*, 4 Bull. Am. Academy of Psych. and L. 271, 276 (1982).

7. J. Totman, The Murderess: A Psychosocial Study of Criminal Homicide 36 (1978).

8. *See generally* R. Perkins & R. Boyce, Criminal Law 46–119 (1982); W. LaFave & A. Scott, Criminal Law 605–683 (1986).

9. *Id.* at 612.

10. *Id.* at 616–617.

11. *Id.* at 617–618.

12. *See, e.g.,* State v. Kelly, 655 P. 2d 1202 (Wash. App. 1982).

13. W. LaFave & A. Scott, *supra* note 8 at 642.

14. R. Perkins & R. Boyce, *supra* note 8 at 131.

15. W. LaFave & A. Scott, *supra* note 8 at 648.

16. *Id.* at 668–672.

17. *Id.* at 653–660.

18. *See, e.g.,* N.Y. Penal Law § 125.25 (1)(a).

19. R. Perkins & R. Boyce, *supra* note 8 at 99.

20. W. LaFave & A. Scott, *supra* note 8 at 661–662.

21. *Id.*

22. *Id.* at 661–662.

23. *See* P. Robinson, CRIMINAL LAW DEFENSES (v.1) 509 (1984) for a fairly complete catalog of such defenses.

24. For example, in none of the 100 cases described in the appendix did the battered woman defendant deny having killed her batterer.

25. Among the 100 cases described in the appendix, 85 of the defendants pleaded self-defense while three entered pleas of not guilty by reason of insanity and were acquitted on that basis.

26. *Id.* See also text accompanying notes 2 and 5 *supra*.

27. M'Naughten's Case, 8 ENG. REP. 718 (1843).

28. MODEL PENAL CODE § 4.01 (Proposed Official Draft 1982).

29. *See* Dvoskin, *Legal Alternatives For Battered Women Who Kill Their Abusers*, 6 BULL. AM. ACAD. OF PSYCH. AND L. 335, 343–345.

30. *See* L. Walker, THE BATTERED WOMAN SYNDROME 40–44 (1984).

31. *See* Steadman, Keitner, Braff & Arvanites, *Factors Associated with a Successful Insanity Plea*, 140 AM. J. PSYCH. 401 (1983).

32. Schneider & Jordan, *supra* note 2 at 160.

33. *Id.*

34. *See* R. Reiser, LAW AND THE MENTAL HEALTH SYSTEM 647 (1985).

35. In Jones v. United States, 103 S. Ct. 3043 (1983), the U.S. Supreme Court held that the maximum sentence a defendant could have received if convicted places no constitutional limit on the amount of time the defendant may be held in a mental institution following acquittal by reason of insanity. The defendant so acquitted may be retained under commitment laws until he or she is no longer regarded as mentally ill and dangerous.

36. Schneider & Jordan, *supra* note 2 at 159–160.

37. L. Walker, *supra* note 30 at 40.

38. Schneider & Jordan, *supra* note 2 at 150.

39. W. LaFave & A. Scott, *supra* note 8 at 454.

40. *Id.* at 456.

41. *See* P. Robinson, CRIMINAL LAW DEFENSES (v.2) 96–100, 280–313 (1984).

42. G. Fletcher, RETHINKING CRIMINAL LAW 759 (1978).

43. *See* Greenawalt, *The Perplexing Borders of Justification and Excuse*, 84 COLUM. L. REV. 1897 (1984).

44. "The distinction is arguably superfluous because whether a person's . . . conduct [is] justified, or whether it is merely . . . excused, the end result is the same,

namely the person avoids punishment for his conduct." State v. Leidholm, 334 N.W. 2d 811, 815 (1983).

45. *See* Annotation, 43 A.L.R. 3d 221 (1972).

46. *Id.*

47. *See, e.g.,* State v. Felton, 329 N.W. 2d 161, 163 (Wis. 1983); People v. Emick, 481 N.Y.S. 2d 552, 558 (1984).

48. R. Perkins & R. Boyce, *supra* note 8 at 116.

49. *See, e.g.,* State v. Felton, *supra* note 47; People v. Emick, *supra* note 47; Kontos v. State, 363 So. 2d 1025 (Alabama 1978); State v. Leidholm, 334 N.W. 2d 811 (N.D. 1983); J. Kaplan & R. Weissberg, CRIMINAL LAW: CASES AND MATERIALS 818 (1986); People v. Thomas, 126 Mich. App. 611 (1983); State v. Heidmous, 331 S.E. 2d 200 (1985); Bond, *Women's Groups Support Alleged Battered Wife Convicted of Murder,* United Press International P.M. Cycle, May 5, 1985; *Wife Gets Suspended Sentence,* United Press International P.M. Cycle, Feb. 16, 1985.

50. *See, e.g.,* among the most recent such cases: State v. Branchal, 684 P.2d 1163 (N.M. App. 1984); Harris, *Battered Wife,* United Press International A.M. Cycle, Sept. 16, 1985 (describing case of Frances Caccavale); Fielder v. State, 683 S.W. 2d 565 (1985); *"Newhouse",* United Press International B.C. Cycle, November 8, 1985 (describing case of Tammie Newhouse).

51. Patri v. Percy, 530 F. Supp. 591 (1982); *See also* Quindlen, *supra* note 1 at 12.

52. Hawthorne v. State, 377 So. 2d 780 (Fla. 1979), 408 So. 2d 801 (1982). *See also Cunningham, Courts Recognizing "Battered Wife Syndrome",* APA MONITOR, Apr. 1983 at 24.

53. Harrison v. State, 310 S.E. 2d 506 (Ga. 1984).

54. Most homicides by battered woman seem to occur outside the presence of witnesses. Thus in most cases, since the victim is dead, the only "eyewitness" testimony regarding the killings comes from the women defendants themselves.

55. A common scenario: *See, e.g.,* State v. Griffiths, 610 P. 2d 522, 524 (Idaho 1980); State v. Kelly, 655 P. 2d 1202, 1203 (Wash. App. 1982); State v. Edwards, 420 So. 2d 663, 668 (La. 1982); Thompson v. State, 659 S.W. 2d 649, 651 (Tex Crim. App. 1983); State v. Branchal, 684 P. 2d 1163, 1166 (N.M. App. 1984).

56. *See, e.g.,* State v. Edwards, State v. Thompson, State v. Branchal, *supra* note 55.

57. *See* Schneider, *Equal Rights to Trial for Women: Sex Bias in the Law of Self-Defense,* 15 HARV. C.R.–C.L. L. REV. 623, 631–632 (1980).

Chapter 5

1. *See* Annotation, 43 A.L.R. 3d 221 (1972).

2. E. Schneider, *Describing and Changing: Women's Self-Defense Work and the Problems of Expert Testimony on Battering,* Unpublished Paper (1986) at 8–9 (to be published in *Women's Rights Law Reporter*).

3. *See, e.g.,* State V. Kelly, 478 A.2d 364, 371–373 (1984) (citing L. Walker, THE BATTERED WOMAN 56–70 (1979).

4. *Id.* at 371–372.

5. *Id.* at 372.

6. *Id.* at 373.

7. Brief for American Psychological Association, *Amicus Curiae,* at 4–5, Hawthorne v. State, District Court of Appeal for Florida (1st District), No. An–435 (1983).

8. *See* W. LaFave and A. Scott, CRIMINAL LAW 454–455 (1986).

9. *See, e.g.,* State v. Borders, 433 So. 2d 1325 (Fla. Dist. Ct. App. 1983); Smith v. State, 277 S.E. 2d 678 (1981); Strong v. State, 307 S.E. 2d 912 (1983) 912 (Ga. 1983).

10. Crocker, *The Meaning of Equality for Battered Women Who Kill Men in Self-Defense,* 8 HARV. WOMEN'S L. J. 121, 143 (1985).

11. State v. Kelly *supra* note 3 at 375.

12. *Id.* at 377.

13. *Id.* at 378.

14. *See, e.g.,* State v. Thomas, 423 N.E. 2d 137, 139 (Ohio 1981); Fultz v. State, 439 N.E. 2d 659, 662 (Ind. App. 1982); State v. Martin, 666 S.W. 2d 895, 899 (Mo. App. 1984); Fielder v. State, 683 S.W. 2d 565, 594 (Tex. App. 1985).

15. People v. White, 414 N.E. 2d 196, 200 (Ill. App. 1980).

16. *Id.*

17. State v. Thomas, 423 N.E. 2d 137, 139 (Ohio 1981).

18. *See, e.g.,* State v. Griffiths, 610 P. 2d 522, 524 (Idaho 1980); Mullis v. State, 282 S.E. 2d 334, 337 (Ga. 1981); Fielder v. State, 683 S.W. 2d 565, 594 (Tex. App. 1984).

19. State v. Griffiths, *supra* note 18 at 524.

20. *See, e.g.,* State v. Thomas, *supra* note 17 at 139; Buhrle v. State, 627 P. 2d 1374, 1378 (Wyo. 1981).

21. *Id. See Also* State v. Griffiths, *supra* note 17 at 524.

22. *See, e.g.,* State v. Thomas, *supra* note 17 at 140; Fielder v. State, *supra* note 18 at 594.

23. Brief for American Psychological Association, *supra* note 7 at 13–14.

24. *See, e.g.,* Walker, Thyfault & Browne, *Beyond the Juror's Ken: Battered Women,* 7 VERMONT L. REV. 1 (1982); Thyfault, *Self-Defense: Battered Woman Syndrome on Trial,* 20 CALIF. WESTERN L. REV. 485 (1984); Buda & Butler, *The Battered Wife Syndrome: A Backdoor Assault on Domestic Violence,* 23 J. OF FAMILY L. 359 (1984–1985).

25. *See* W. LaFave & A. Scott, *supra* note 8 at 454–457.

26. *See, e.g.,* State v. Kelly, *supra* note 3 at 378.

27. As noted in the preceding chapter, among the cases examined in the appendix in which information regarding the homicidal act was available, only one-third (29 of 87) of the killings took place during the course of a battering incident.

28. In 34 of the 87 cases in the appendix, the killing occurred after either a battering incident or a threat to kill or injure the woman. Two killings occurred after the batterer had beaten the woman's child, 10 after an argument, and 18 while the batterer was asleep.

29. *See* Dix, *Self-Defense,* in Encyclopedia of Crime and Justice 948, 948–950 (1983):

> Threatened harm can usefully be regarded as nonimminent if the period before the harm will occur permits utilization of alternatives to self-defense. Battered women may assault and even kill their husbands at a time when anticipated injuries may be hours or even days in the future. [U]se of force in some of these situations, objectively considered, appears to be quite inappropriate . . .

30. Schneider, *supra* note 2 at 44.

31. *Id.* at 36.

32. *Id.* at 24.

33. *Id.* at 16.

34. *See, e.g.,* N.Y. Penal Law Sect. 125.25 (1)(a). *See also* People v. Emick, 481 N.Y.S. 2d 552 (1984), in which a battered woman defendant was convicted of first degree (i.e., voluntary) manslaughter.

35. Walker (Participant in panel discussion at the Annual Meeting of the American Psychological Association, Los Angeles, Cal., August 1985), *Diagnosing Battered Spouse and Rape Trauma Syndromes: Are Psychologists Experts?*

36. *Cf.* Bochnak, Women's Self-Defense Cases: Theory and Practice 36, 89–90 (1981).

37. *See, e.g.,* State v. Kelly, *supra* note 3 at 372, 377.

38. Crocker, *supra* note 10 at 144.

39. *Id.*

40. Schneider, *supra* note 2 at 5.

41. *Id.*

42. E. Cleary (Ed.), McCormick's Handbook of the Law of Evidence 29 (1972).

43. *See, e.g.,* Ibn-Tamas v. United States, 407 A.2d 626 (D.C. 1979); State v. Dozier, 255 S.E. 2d 552 (W.Va. 1979); State v. Baker, 424 A.2d 171 (N.H. 1980); Buhrle v. State, 627 P. 2d 1374 (Wyo. 1981); State v. Anaya, 438 A. 2d 892 (Me. 1981); Smith v. State, 277 S.E. 2d 678 (Ga. 1981); Hawthorne v. State, 408 So. 2d 801 (Fla. Dist. Ct. App. 1982).

Chapter 6

1. *See* W. LaFave & A. Scott, Criminal Law 454–457 (1986); P. Robinson, Criminal Law Defenses (v. 2) 96–100 (1984).

2. In the often quoted words of Justice Holmes: "Detached reflection cannot be demanded in the presence of an uplifted knife." Brown v. United States, 256 U.S. 335, 343 (1921).

3. H. Kalven & H. Zeisel, The American Jury 231–236 (1966).

4. Acker & Toch, *Battered Women, Straw Men, and Expert Testimony: A Comment on State v. Kelly,* 21 Crim. L. Bull. 125, 147–148 (1985).

5. *See generally* R. Harre, Personal Being: A Theory for Individual Psychology (1983); F. Mikhailov, The Riddle of the Self (1980); T. Mischel (ed.), The Self: Psychological and Philosophical Issues (1977).

6. *See* L. Zurcher, THE MUTABLE SELF 24–28 (1977); Lester, *Self: Psychological Portraits,* in THE EXISTENTIAL SELF IN SOCIETY 25–27 (J. Kotarba & A. Fontana, eds., 1984); L. Myers, SELF: AN INTRODUCTION TO PHILOSOPHICAL PSYCHOLOGY 14–17 (1969).

7. *Id.*

8. W. James, THE PRINCIPLES OF PSYCHOLOGY (v.1) 279 (1890) (Harvard ed. 1981).

9. *See generally* J. Kotarba & A. Fontana (eds.), THE EXISTENTIAL SELF IN SOCIETY (1984).

10. *See* C. Rogers, CLIENT-CENTERED THERAPY: ITS CURRENT PRACTICE, IMPLICATIONS AND THEORY 510–517 (1951); Douglas, *The Emergence, Security, and Growth of the Sense of Self,* in J. Kotarba & A. Fontana, *supra* note 6 at 69–99; R. Laing, THE DIVIDED SELF 39–43 (1970);

11. *Id. See also* I. Yalom, EXISTENTIAL PSYCHOTHERAPY (1980); Douglas, *supra* note 10 at 77–80.

12. H. Kohut, THE RESTORATION OF THE SELF 103–105 (1977).

13. R. Laing, *supra* note 10 at 39.

14. *Id.* at 41–42.

15. *Id.* at 42.

16. *Id.*

17. *Id.*

18. *Id.* at 42–43.

19. *Id.* at 43.

20. H. Kohut, *supra* note 12 at 63.

21. *Id.* at 103.

22. *Id.* at 104.

23. *Id.* at 103.

24. *Id.* at 77.

25. Johnson & Ferraro, *The Victimized Self: The Case of the Battered Woman,* in THE EXISTENTIAL SELF IN SOCIETY 118 (J. Kotarba & A. Fontana, eds., 1984).

26. *Id.* at 119–120.

27. *Id.* at 120.

28. *Id.* at 121–124.

29. *Id.* at 120.

30. *Id.* at 127.

31. *Id.* at 126.

32. *Id.* at 128–129.

33. *See* L. Walker, THE BATTERED WOMAN SYNDROME 42 (1984); A. Jones, WOMEN WHO KILL 298–299 (1980).

34. R. Laing, *supra* note 10 at 40.

35. L. Walker, *supra* note 33; L. Walker, THE BATTERED WOMAN (1979). *See also* D. Martin, BATTERED WIVES (1976); M. Roy (ed.), BATTERED WOMEN (1977); L. Okun, WOMAN ABUSE: FACTS REPLACING MYTHS (1986).

36. M. Seligman, HELPLESSNESS: ON DEPRESSION, DEVELOPMENT AND DEATH 9–20 (1975).

37. L. Walker, THE BATTERED WOMAN 75 (1979); Walker, *Victimology and the Psychological Perspectives of Battered Women,* 8 VICTIMOLOGY 82, 93–98

(1983); Walker, Thyfault & Browne, *Beyond the Juror's Ken: Battered Women*, 7 VERMONT L. REV. 1, 8 (1982).

38. *Id.*

39. M. Seligman, *supra* note 36 at 95.

40. *Id.* at 82-92.

41. *Id.* at 93.

42. Bibring, *The Mechanism of Depression*, in P. Greenacre (ed.), AFFECTIVE DISORDERS 13 (1948).

43. Melges & Bowlby *Types of Hopelessness in Psychopathological Process*, 20 ARCHIVES OF GENERAL PSYCH. 690 (1969).

44. Lichtenberg, *A Definition and Analysis of Depression*, 77 ARCHIVES OF NEUROLOGY AND PSYCH. 519 (1957).

45. *See* Hilberman & Munson, *Sixty Battered Women*, 2 VICTIMOLOGY 791 (1979).

46. *See e.g.*, E. Schneiderman, N. Farberow & R. Litman, THE PSYCHOLOGY OF SUICIDE 434-435 (1983).

47. Silverman, *The Epidemiology of Depression: A Review*, 124 AM. J. PSYCH. 883, 887 (1968).

48. L. Hankoff & B. Einsidler, SUICIDE: THEORY AND CLINICAL ASPECTS xiii (1979); M. Seligman, *supra* note 36 at 77.

49. Suicidal ideation is one of the most common symptoms of depression. It has been estimated that 30 percent of all clinically depressed patients and 75 to 80 percent of the most severely depressed express such ideation. F. Ayd, CLINICAL DEPRESSION 43 (1980); J. Page, PSYCHOPATHOLOGY (1975). Additionally, it is estimated that the number of suicide attempts is at least six to 10 times greater than the number of suicides. D. DeCatanzaro, SUICIDE AND SELF-DAMAGING BEHAVIOR 17 (1981).

50. *See* Jeger, *Behavior Theories and Their Applications*, in L. Hankoff and B. Einsidler (eds.), SUICIDE: THEORY AND CLINICAL ASPECTS 179, 186–192; R. Maris, PATHWAYS TO SUICIDE 212–216 (1981).

51. Beck, Steer, Kovacs & Garrison, *Hopelessness and Eventual Suicide: A Ten Year Perspective Study of Patients Hospitalized with Suicidal Ideation*, 142 AM. J. PSYCH. 559 (1985).

52. *Id.*

53. Minkoff, Bergman, Beck et al., *Hopelessness, Depression and Attempted Suicide*, 130 AM. J. PSYCH. 455 (1973).

54. Beck, Kovacs & Weissman, *Hopelessness and Suicidal Behavior*, 234 J.A.M.A. 1146 (1975).

55. *See, e.g.*, Wetzel, *Hopelessness, Depression and Suicidal Intent*, 33 ARCHIVES OF GENERAL PSYCH. 1069 (1976); Beck, Weissman & Kovacs, *Alcoholism, Hopelessness and Suicidal Behavior*, 33 J. OF STUDIES OF ALCOHOL 66 (1976); Wetzel, Margulies & Davis, *Hopelessness, Depression and Suicidal Intent*, 412 J. OF CLINICAL PSYCH. 159 (1980); Petrie & Chamberlain, *Hopelessness and Social Desirability as Moderator Variables in Predicting Suicidal Behavior*, 51 J. OF CONSULTING AND CLINICAL PSYCH. 485 (1983); Dyer & Keitman, *Hopelessness, Depression and Suicidal Intent in Parasuicide*, 144 BRIT. J. PSYCH. 127 (1984).

56. Gayford, *Battered Wives,* 15 MEDICINE, SCIENCE AND L. 237, 242 (1975).

57. L. Walker, THE BATTERED WOMAN SYNDROME 42 (1984).

58. A. Browne, *Assault and Homicide at Home: When Battered Women Kill,* paper presented at the Second Annual Conference for Family Violence Researchers, Durham, N.H. (August 1984) at 17.

59. Johnson & Ferraro, *supra* note 25 at 124.

60. L. Walker, *supra* note 57 at 34-35.

61. *Id.* at 40.

62. *See generally* Schneider, *The Present Situation of Victimology in the World,* in THE VICTIM IN INTERNATIONAL PERSPECTIVE 11 (H. Schneider, ed., 1982).

63. *See* Frieze, Hymer & Greenberg, *Describing the Victims of Crime and Violence,* in A. Kahn, FINAL REPORT: AMERICAN PSYCHOLOGICAL ASSOCIATION TASK FORCE ON THE VICTIMS OF CRIME AND VIOLENCE 19, 19–29 (1984).

64. *Id.*

65. *See, e.g.,* Friedman, Bischoff, Davis & Person, VICTIMS AND HELPERS: REACTIONS TO CRIME (National Institute of Justice 1982); Symonds, *Victim Responses to Terror,* in F. Wright, C. Bahn & R. Reiber, FORENSIC PSYCHOLOGY AND PSYCHIATRY 129, 130 (1980).

66. *Id.* at 129.

67. *Id.*

68. Symonds, *Victims of Violence: Psychological Effects and Aftereffects,* 35 AM. J. PSYCHOANALYSIS 19, 22 (1975).

69. Symonds, *supra* note 65 at 129.

70. *Id.*

71. *Id.*

72. *Id.*

73. *Id.* at 129–130.

74. *Id.* at 132.

75. *See* Frieze et al., *supra* note 63.

76. Martin, *Foreword* to S. Morgan, CONJUGAL TERRORISM iii (1982).

77. *See* A. Schmid, Political Terrorism: A Research Guide to Concepts, Theories, Data Bases and Literature (1983).

78. L. Walker, THE BATTERED WOMAN SYNDROME 27–28 (1984).

79. Dutton & Painter, *Traumatic Bonding: The Development of Emotional Attachments in Battered Women and Other Relationships of Intermittent Abuse,* 6 VICTIMOLOGY 139 (1981).

80. Martin, *supra* note 76 at iii.

81. *See* Eitenger, *The Effects of Captivity,* in VICTIMS OF TERRORISM 73 (F. Ochberg & D. Soskis, eds., 1982).

82. *Id.*

83. S. Morgan, *supra* note 76 at 30–31.

84. Fields, *Research on the Victims of Terrorism,* in VICTIMS OF TERRORISM 137 (F. Ochberg & D. Soskis, eds., 1982).

85. Strentz, *The Stockholm Syndrome: Law Enforcement Policy and Ego Defenses of the Hostage,* in FORENSIC PSYCHOLOGY AND PSYCHIATRY 137 (F. Wright, C. Bahn & R. Reiber, eds., 1980).

86. Dutton & Painter, *supra* note 79.
87. *See, e.g.,* Carmen, Rieker & Mills, *Victims of Violence and Psychiatric Illness,* 141 Am. J. Psychiatry 378 (1984).
88. *See* Symonds, *supra* note 65.
89. *Id.*
90. Ochberg, *A Case Study: Gerard Vaders,* in Victims of Terrorism 9, 31 (F. Ochberg & D. Soskis, eds., 1982).
91. Hilberman & Munson, *supra* note 45 at 464.

Chapter 7

1. *See, e.g.* Acker & Toch, *Battered Women, Straw Men, and Expert Testimony: A Comment on State v. Kelly,* 21 Crim. L. Bull. 125 (1985):
> The battered wife syndrome is yet another new defense competing for the attention of criminal law specialists. This defense seeks to explain the violence of wives directed at their husbands as the product of prior batterings.

2. *See* Buda & Butler, *The Battered Wife Syndrome: A Backdoor Assault on Domestic Violence,* 23 J. Family L. 359, 373–374 (1984–1985):
> Defense attorneys with battered woman clients must, in short, adopt the battered woman syndrome defense with a profound sense of its limitations. No American court has recognized this defense as existing outside the realm of established self-defense rules, and the likelihood of such recognition is remote.

3. *See* Rittenmeyer, *Battered Wives, Self-Defense and Double Standards of Justice,* 9 J. Crim. Just. 389, 394 (1981), who argues that allowing a "battered wife syndrome defense in homicide cases would amount to gender-based discrimination contrary to the Equal Protection Clause of the 14th Amendment.

4. L. Walker, The Battered Woman xv (1979).
5. *See, e.g.,* Jahnke v. State, 682 P.2d 991 (Wyo. 1984), affirming the manslaughter conviction of a 16-year-old boy who killed his father after being abused by the father for 14 years; G. Morris, The Kids Next Door: Sons and Daughters Who Kill Their Parents 143–184 (1985).
6. *See* Note, *Partially Determined Imperfect Self-Defense: The Battered Wife Kills and Tells Why,* 34 Stanford L. Rev. 615 (1982).
7. G. Fletcher, Rethinking Criminal Law 856 (1978).
8. *Id.*
9. J. Hall, Principles of Criminal Law 415 (1947).
10. G. Fletcher, *supra* note 7 at 856.
11. Kadish, *Respect for Life and Regard for Rights in the Criminal Law,* 64 Calif. L. Rev. 871, 871–872 (1976).
12. *Id.*
13. W. LaFave & A. Scott, Criminal Law 454 (1986).
14. N.Y. Penal Law, Section 3515 (2)(a). *See also* Connecticut General Statutes Sec. 53a–19(b); Delaware Code Annotated Title 11, Sec. 464(e); New Hampshire Revised Statutes Title 62, Sec. 627:4(III).
15. W. LaFave & A. Scott, *supra* note 13 at 460–461; R. Perkins & R. Boyce, Criminal Law 133 (1982).

16. *See, e.g.,* Beard v. United States, 158 U.S. 550 (1895): "A True Man, who is without fault, is not obliged to fly from an assailant who by violence or surprise maliciously seeks too take his life, or to do him enormous bodily harm."

17. W. LaFave & A. Scott, *supra* note 13 at 460.

18. Beale, *Retreat from a Murderous Assault,* 16 HARV. L. REV. 567, 581 (1903).

19. W. LaFave & A. Scott, *supra* note 13 at 461; R. Perkins & R. Boyce, *supra* note 13 at 1133.

20. *Id.* at 1133–1137.

21. *See* P. Robinson, CRIMINAL LAW DEFENSES (v. 2) 110 (1984).

22. W. LaFave & A. Scott, *supra* note 13 at 467.

23. *Id.* at 467–468.

24. Model Penal Code § 3.06, Comment (Tentative Draft no. 8, 1958).

25. *See* P. Robinson, *supra* note 21 at 33-84; R. Perkins & R. Boyce, *supra* note 13 at 1112; Note, *The Impact of the Model Penal Code on Statutory Reforms,* 75 COLUM. L. REV. 914, 933–934 (1975).

26. *See, e.g.* People v. Evans, 379 N.Y.S. 2d 912 (1975). *See also* Burgess & Holstrom, *Adaptive Strategies and Recovery from Rape,* in R. Moos (ed.), COPING WITH LIFE CRISES 353-414 (1986).

27. *See* note 25 *supra.*

28. *See generally* D. Finkelhor & K. Yllo, LICENSE TO RAPE (1985).

29. *See* note 25 *supra.*

30. Kadish, *supra* note 11 at 888 (emphasis added).

31. G. Fletcher, *supra* note 7 at 860.

32. J. Locke, TWO TREATISES OF GOVERNMENT 320–321 (Rev. ed. 1960).

33. G. Fletcher, *supra* note 7 at 861–862.

34. *Id.* at 857–860.

35. Fletcher, *Proportionality and the Psychotic Aggressor,* in E. Wise & G. Mueller, STUDIES IN COMPARATIVE CRIMINAL LAW 123, 135 (1975).

36. *Id.* at 135-136.

37. *Id.* at 136. *See also* Fletcher, *supra* note 7 at 858.

38. U.S. Department of Justice, Federal Bureau of Investigation, UNIFORM CRIME REPORTS: CRIME IN THE UNITED STATES 11 (1985).

39. *See, e.g.,* UNIFORM CRIME REPORTS 11 (1984): "Nineteen percent of all killings involved family relationships, one-half of which involved spouse killing spouse."

40. The actual incidence of lethal domestic violence is unknown. UNIFORM CRIME REPORTS data are based primarily upon reports forwarded to the FBI by local law enforcement agencies. "[N]ot all law enforcement agencies provide data for complete reporting periods . . ." U.S. Dept. of Justice, *supra* note Department of Justice, *supra* note 38 at 3.

41. S. Kadish, S. Schulhofer & M. Paulsen, CRIMINAL LAW AND ITS PROCESSES 195–196 (1983).

42. *Id.* at 196–203.

43. *See* M. Dan-Cohen, *Decision Rules and Conduct Rules: On Acoustic Separation in Criminal Law,* 97 HARV. L. REV. 625, 637–641 (1984).

44. *Id.*

45. "Incapacitation as a goal of punishment is in many ways the cleanest form of individual prevention. Its objective is to deny, or at least greatly reduce, the opportunity to commit future offenses . . . We know that incapacitation prevents crime." P. Low, J. Jeffries & R. Bonnie, CRIMINAL LAW: CASES AND MATERIALS 24 (1982).

46. "The concept of special deterrence is difficult to separate from rehabilitation" and contains elements of both intimidation and reform. *Id.* at 23.

47. *See,* Ewing & Jamieson, *The Battered Woman Syndrome: Expert Testimony and Public Attitudes,* paper presented at the Annual Meeting of the American Psychological Association, Washington, D.C., August 1986 (reports findings of community survey showing that substantial proportions of the public hold such beliefs); Gentemann, *Wife-Beating: Attitudes of a Non-Clinical Population,* 9 VICTIMOLOGY 109 (1984) (20 percent of those questioned in a cross-section survey of adult women blamed the victim of wife-beating for her beatings).

48. *See, e.g.,* Kuhl, *Personality Traits of Abused Women: Masochism Myth Refuted,* 9 VICTIMOLOGY 450 (1984); Symonds, *Violence against women—The Myth of Masochism,* 33 AM. J. PSYCHOTHERAPY 161 (1979).

49. *See generally* D. Sonkin, D. Martin, L. Walker, THE MALE BATTERER: A TREATMENT APPROACH (1985).

50. *See* P. Robinson, *supra* note 21 at 99; P. Robinson, CRIMINAL LAW DEFENSES (v. 1) 19–40 (1984).

51. *Id.* at 35–36.

52. *Id.* at 41–54.

53. P. Robinson, *supra* note 21 at 99–100.

54. *Id.*

55. *Id.*

56. *See* P. Robinson, *supra* note 50 at 46–50.

57. 432 U.S. 197 (1977).

58. P. Robinson, *supra* note 50 at 48–50.

59. *Id.* at 51-52.

60. *See* R. Epstein, C. Gregory & H. Kalven, CASES AND MATERIALS ON TORTS 1049–1055 (1984).

61. *Id.* at 1055–1056.

62. *See* P. Robinson, *supra* note 21 at 275–313.

63. *See* P. Robinson, *supra* note 50 at 207–236.

64. W. Lafave & A. Scott, *supra* note 13 at 653–654.

65. *See, e.g.,* N.Y. Penal Law Sec. 125.5 (1)(a).

66. *Id.*

67. *See* R. Epstein et al., *supra* note 60 at 1035–1039.

68. *See* Weissman, *Psychological and Psychiatric Evaluation of Workers' Compensation Claimants,* in PSYCHOLOGY, PSYCHIATRY AND THE LAW 363 (C. Ewing, ed., 1985).

69. *See* R. Miller, *Clinical and Legal Aspects of Civil Commitment,* in PSYCHOLOGY, PSYCHIATRY AND THE LAW 181 (C. Ewing, ed., 1985).

70. *See* T. Gutheil & P. Appelbaum, CLINICAL HANDBOOK OF PSYCHIATRY AND THE LAW 268–269 (1982).

71. *See* Chapter 4, *supra.*

Chapter 8

1. *Wife Beating: The Silent Crime,* TIME, Sept. 5, 1983 at 23.
2. *See, e.g.,* A. Roberts (Ed.), BATTERED WOMEN AND THEIR FAMILIES: INTERVENTION STRATEGIES AND TREATMENT PROGRAMS (1984).
3. *Id. See also* D. Sonkin, D. Martin & L. Walker, THE MALE BATTERER: A TREATMENT APPROACH (1985).
4. *See* B. Warrior, BATTERED WOMEN'S DIRECTORY (9th ed. 1985).
5. *See* Waits, *The Criminal Justice System's Response to Battering: Understanding the Problem, Forging the Solutions,* 60 WASH. L. REV. 267, 305–329 (1985).
6. Sherman & Berk, *The Specific Deterrent Effect of Arrest for Domestic Assault,* 49 AM. SOC. REV. 261 (1984).
7. *See* A. Roberts, *supra* note 2.
8. *See* L. Walker, THE BATTERED WOMAN SYNDROME 117 (1984).
9. *Wife-Beating: The Silent Crime, supra* note 1 at 24.
10. *See* Waits, *supra* note 5 at 305–329.

Appendix

1. People v. Adams, 403 N.E. 2d 267 (1981).
2. *Washington Supreme Court Rules "Battered Woman" Testimony Vital,* Associated Press [hereinafter AP] A.M. Cycle, May 17, 1984; State v. Allery, 682 P. 2d 312 (1984).
3. E. Bochnak, WOMEN'S SELF-DEFENSE CASES 147–177 (1981).
4. 438 A. 2d 892 (Me. 1981), *appeal after remand,* 456 A. 2d 1255 (Me. 1983); Goldsmith, *"Battered",* United Press International [hereinafter UPI] A.M. Cycle, December 29, 1981.
5. *Wife Gets Suspended Sentence,* UPI P.M. Cycle, February 16, 1985.
6. King, *Right of Women to Self-Defense Gaining in "Battered Wife" Cases,* N.Y. TIMES, May 7, 1979 at A1, A18.
7. Bond, *Women's Groups Support Alleged Battered Wife Convicted of Murder,* UPI P.M. Cycle, May 5, 1985.
8. Borders v. State, 433 So. 2d 1325 (1983).
9. State v. Branchal, 684 P. 2d 1163 (1984).
10. Lewin, *Self-Defense for Battered Women: When Victims Kill,* NAT'L. L. J., Oct. 29. 1979 at 1, 11–12.
11. Buhrle v. State, 627 P. 2d 1374 (Wyo. 1981).
12. State v. Burton, Slip Opinion, Court of Appeals of Louisiana (No. 84 KA 0694, Feb. 26, 1985).
13. People v. Bush, 84 Cal. App. 3d 294, 148 Cal. Rptr. 430 (1978).
14. *Battered,* UPI A.M. Cycle, April 24, 1985; Crane, *Wifebeater,* UPI P.M. Cycle, August 21, 1985; Harris, *Battered Wife,* UPI A.M. Cycle, September 16, 1985.

15. *Wife Gets Year in Jail for Slaying Husband,* UPI B.C. Cycle, August 6, 1984.

16. Note, *Does Spouse Abuse Justify Homicide?,* 24 WAYNE LAW REV. 1705, 1717 (1978).

17. *Id.*

18. State v. Crigler, 598 P. 2d 739 (Wash. 1979).

19. *Judge Acquits "Battered Woman',* UPI A.M. Cycle, March 3, 1983; *"Battered Woman" Acquitted,* UPI P.M. Cycle, March 4, 1983.

20. SAN FRANCISCO CHRONICLE, June 3, 1980 at 5.

21. State v. Dozier, 255 S.E. 2d 552 (W. Va. 1979).

22. State v. Edwards, 420 So. 2d 663 (La. 1982).

23. Dickenson, *Emick Testifies of Beatings, Threats Leading up to Slaying in Trailer,* BUFFALO NEWS, Dec. 1, 1983 at 1, A2; Margolick, *A Battered Woman Goes on Trial,* N.Y. TIMES, Dec. 2, 1983 at B1, B6; People v. Emick, 481 N.Y.S. 2d 552 (1984); *Emick Sentenced to Probation for Killing Boyfriend,* UPI A.M. Cycle, April 10, 1985; *Emick Gets Probation in Manslaughter Case,* BUFFALO NEWS, April 11, 1985 at C5;

24. *Does Spouse Abuse Justify Homicide? supra* note 16 at 1718.

25. State v. Felton, 329 N.W. 2d 161 (Wis. 1983).

26. Fennell v. Goolsby, No. 84–1351 (E.D. Pa. August 28, 1985).

27. *Fielder,* UPI P.M. Cycle, January 24, 1985; Fielder v. State, 683 S.W. 2d 565 (Tex. 1985).

28. Fultz v. State, 439 N.E. 2d 659 (Ind. 1982).

29. State v. Griffiths, 610 P. 2d 522 (Idaho 1980).

30. *Judge Gives Woman Probation for Shooting Husband,* AP A.M. Cycle, May 24, 1982; *Battered,* UPI A.M. Cycle, May 24, 1982.

31. Harrison v. State, 310 S.E. 2d 506 (Ga. 1984).

32. Hawthorne v. State, 377 So. 2d 780 (Fla. Dist. Ct. App. 1979), *appeal after remand,* 408 So. 2d 801 (Fla. Dist. Ct. App. 1982), *cert. denied,* 415 So. 2d 1361 (Fla. 1982), *appeal after second remand,* 470 So. 2d 770 (Fla. Dist. Ct. App. 1985); Cunningham, *Courts Recognizing "Battered Wife Syndrome",* APA MONITOR, Apr. 1983 at 27.

33. State v. Heidmous, 331 S.E. 2d 200 (N.C. 1985).

34. *Hodges Denied New Trial,* UPI A.M. Cycle, January 5, 1985; *Kansas City Area News Briefs,* UPI B.C. Cycle, January 15, 1985; *Judge Denies New Trial Sought by "Battered Wife",* UPI A.M. Cycle, January 24, 1985; *"Battered Wife" Sentenced to Prison,* UPI A.M. Cycle, Jan. 25, 1985.

35. *Jury Acquits Woman, 26, Who Killed Ex-Husband,* N.Y. TIMES, April 23, 1978 at A23.

36. MacPherson, *"Battered Wives and Self-Defense Pleas,* WASHINGTON POST, Dec. 4, 1977 at 1, 14.

37. *Jury Deliberates in Battered Wife Case,* UPI A.M. Cycle, Oct. 7, 1985; *Woman Convicted in Death of Husband,* UPI A.M. Cycle, Oct. 8, 1985; *Woman Gets One Year for Killing Husband,* UPI A.M. Cycle, Nov. 12, 1985; *New York News Summary,* UPI P.M. Cycle, Nov. 13, 1985.

38. *A Killing Excuse,* TIME, Nov. 28, 1977 at 108; *Does Spouse Abuse Justify Homicide?, supra* note 16 at 1716; F. McNulty, THE BURNING BED (1980); *Driven to Kill: "Battered Women" Strike Back,* A.B.A.J., Dec. 1984 at 25–26.

39. State v. Hundley, 693 P. 2d 475 (Kan. 1985); *High Court to Hear 38 Cases,* UPI B.C. Cycle, Oct. 20, 1985.

40. King, *supra* note 6; Lewin, *supra* note 10.

41. Ibn-Tamas v. United States, 407 A. 2d 626 (D.C. 1979), *appeal after remand,* 455 A. 2d 893 (D.C. 1983).

42. *Jury Acquits Woman in Murder Trial,* UPI A.M. Cycle, Oct. 7, 1983; *Jury Acquits Battered Wife of Murder,* UPI A.M. Cycle, Oct. 8, 1983; *Battered Woman Not Guilty in Murder Trial,* UPI P.M. Cycle, Oct. 8, 1983; *Battered Woman Found Innocent in Murder of Husband,* UPI P.M. Cycle, Oct. 9, 1983.

43. Vaughan & Moore, *The Battered Spouse Defense in Kentucky,* 10 N. KENTUCKY L. REV. 399 (1983).

44. State v. Waterbury and Joslyn, 307 N.W. 2d 45 (Iowa 1981).

45. *Leave Before You Kill, Advises Battered Wife,* BUFFALO NEWS, Jan. 18, 1985 at C7–C8.

46. Brownstein, *Battered-N.J.,* UPI P.M. Cycle, May 10, 1983; State v. Kelly, 478 A. 2d 364 (N.J. 1984);

47. State v. Kelly, 655 P. 2d 1202 (Wash. App. 1982); *Battered,* UPI B.C. Cycle, July 31, 1984.

48. Kontos v. State, 363 So. 2d 1025 (Alabama 1978).

49. Lewin, *supra* note 10.

50. State v. Leaphart, 673 S.W. 2d 870 (Tenn. 1984).

51. Ledford v. State, 333 So. 2d 576 (Ga. 1985).

52. State v. Leidholm, 334 N.W. 2d 811 (N.D. 1983); J. Kaplan & R. Weissberg, CRIMINAL LAW: CASES AND MATERIALS 818 (1986).

53. State v. Lynch, 436 So. 2d 567 (La. 1983).

54. *A Killing Excuse, supra* note 38.

55. Mann, *Spouse Abuse: A Problem That Cries for Answers,* WASHINGTON POST, May 13, 1981.

56. *"Battered Woman" Testimony Barred in Murder Trial,* UPI A.M. Cycle, Feb. 27, 1982; *Battered,* UPI A.M. Cycle, Feb. 28, 1982; State v. Martin, 666 S.W. 2d 895 (Mo. 1984); Court *Upholds Contract Murder Conviction,* UPI B.C. Cycle, February 7, 1984.

57. Commonwealth v. McKendrick, 453 A.2d 328 (Pa. 1982).

58. *Does Spouse Abuse Justify Homicide?, supra* note 16 at 1717.

59. Meeks v. Bergen, 749 F. 2d 322 (1984); Sussman, *Torch Murder Conviction Reinstated,* UPI P.M. Cycle, Nov. 28, 1984.

60. People v. Minnis, 455 N.E. 2d 209 (Ill. 1983); *Woman Who Hacked Up Husband Goes Back to Prison,* UPI B.C. Cycle, April 12, 1985.

61. Moran v. Ohio, 105 S. Ct. 350 (1984).

62. Mullis v. State, 282 S.E. 2d 334 (Ga. 1981).

63. State v. Necaise, 466 So. 2d 660 (La. 1985).

64. *Newhouse,* UPI B.C. Cycle, Nov. 8, 1985.

65. Norris v. State, 295 S.E. 2d 321 (Ga. 1982).

66. State v. Nunn, 356 N.W. 2d 601 (Iowa App. 1984).

67. E. Bochnak, *supra* note 3 at 107-145.

68. Gryta, *Jury Acquits Woman in Murder Trial,* BUFFALO NEWS, Dec. 20, 1985 at C5.

69. Harper, *Patri Trial,* AP A.M. Cycle, December 5, 1977; *Does Spouse Abuse Justify Homicide?, supra* note 16 at 1718–1719; *A Killing Excuse, supra* note 38; Patri v. Percey, 530 F. Supp 591 (1982).

70. *Player,* UPI P.M. Cycle, Feb. 7, 1983; *National News Briefs,* UPI P.M. Cycle, Feb. 7, 1983.

71. People v. Powell, 424 N.Y.S. 2d 626 (1980); Case Histories Project, DO THEY BELONG IN PRISON: THE IMPACT OF NEW YORK'S MANDATORY SENTENCING LAWS 34–35 (1985); L. Shepherd, *Bernadette Powell: A Degree and a Book,* ITHACA JOURNAL, June 27, 1985 at 1; J. Mann, *A Woman Who Killed,* WASHINGTON POST, July 24, 1985 at C3.

72. Wasik, *Cumulative Provocation and Domestic Killing,* 29 CRIM. L. REV. 29, 33 (1982).

73. *Jury Acquits Woman Who Shot Husband, Feeling She Was Battered Wife,* AP P.M. Cycle, June 21, 1985; *Battered Wife Cleared on Murder Charges,* UPI B.C. Cycle, June 21, 1985.

74. People v. Reeves, 362 N.E. 2d 9 (Ill. 1977).

75. Eisenberg & Seymour, *The Self-Defense Plea and Battered Women,* TRIAL, July 1978 at 34.

76. Wasik, *supra* note 72 at 34.

77. *Battered,* UPI B.C. Cycle, September 16, 1985; Sisk, *Interest High in Trial of Woman for Slaying of Husband,* UPI B.C. Cycle, Sept. 21, 1985; Sisk, *Lawmaker Eyes Battering as Murder Defense,* UPI P.M. Cycle, Oct. 23, 1985; Sisk, *Battered Wife Pleads Guilty to Killing Her Husband,* UPI A.M. Cycle, Oct. 23, 1985.

78. Meyers, *Battered Wives, Dead Husbands,* STUDENT LAW., March 1978 at 46, 47–48.

79. *Woman in Michigan Is Freed in Slaying,* N.Y. TIMES, Apr. 15, 1979 at 28.

80. State v. Smith, 274 S.E. 2d 703 (Ga. 1981).

81. Ray, *Jury Acquits City Woman,* ALTOONA MIRROR, Nov. 7, 1985 at A–1.

82. Strong v. State, 307 S.E. 2d 912 (Ga. 1983).

83. Meyers, *supra* note 78 at 47.

84. Terry v. State, 467 So. 2d 761 (Fla. 1985); *Murder Conviction Overturned for Battered Woman,* UPI A.M. Cycle, Apr. 10, 1985.

85. State v. Thomas, 468 N.E. 2d 763 (Ohio App. 1983).

86. Thomas, *Letters from Prison,* in F. Delacoste & F. Newman (eds.), FIGHT BACK: FEMINIST RESISTANCE TO MALE VIOLENCE 156 (1981); People v. Thomas, 126 Mich. App. 611 (1983).

87. State v. Thomas, 423 N.E. 2d 137 (Ohio 1981); Thomas v. Arn, 728 F.2d 813 (1984); *Battered,* UPI A.M. Cycle, Mar. 4, 1985; Carelli, *Murder Conviction of Woman Who Claimed She Was Battered Wife Upheld,* AP P.M. Cycle, Dec. 4, 1985.

88. Thompson v. State, 659 S.W. 2d 649 (Tex. Crim. App. 1983).

89. *Threestars,* UPI A.M. Cycle, April 18, 1984; *Threestars,* UPI B.C. Cycle, Apr. 20, 1984; *Threestars,* UPI B.C. Cycle, Apr. 25, 1984; *Threestars,* UPI B.C. Cycle, June 14, 1984.

90. *Driven to Kill, supra* note 38 at 25.

91. Fox, *Battered Woman Claim Aids Acquittal in Murder Trial,* N.Y.L.J., Apr. 26, 1985 at 1, 3; People v. Torres, 488 N.Y.S. 2d 35 (1985).

92. *A Killing Excuse, supra* note 38 at 108.

93. Commonwealth v. Watson, 431 A.2d 949 (Pa. 1981).

94. *Year Sentence Recommended in Husband Shooting*, UPI A.M. Cycle, Mar. 1, 1983.

95. People v. White, 414 N.E. 2d 196 (Ill. 1980).

96. Wilds v. State, 383 N.E. 2d 326 (1978).

97. King, *supra* note 6.

98. *Battered*, UPI B.C. Cycle, Jan. 25, 1985.

99. Wisecup v. State, 278 S.E. 2d 682 (Ga. 1981).

100. Commonwealth v. Zenyuh, 453 A. 2d 338 (Pa. 1982).

Index

Abuse: child, 12, 20; physical, 8–9, 25–30, 31–32, 34–35; psychological, 9–12, 25–30, 32, 35–36; sexual, 9–12, 26–27, 32–33, 36
Acker, J., 62
Age. *See* Demographic factors
Alcohol abuse, 31, 39–40
Allison, Marshall, 1–5
American Psychological Association, 54–55
Anxiety. *See* Disintegration anxiety
Autonomy principle, 83–84

Barnard, G., 30–31, 37–39, 43
Barriers to leaving: battered women who killed, 33–34; battering cycle, 18–19; depression, 21; economic, 13; environmental, 13–17; learned helplessness, 20–21, 67; lethality risk, 37; psychological, 17–21; sex-role stereotypes and expectations, 17–18; traumatic bonding, 19–20, 75
Battered woman: defined, 7–12; number, 95. *See also* Demographic factors
Battered woman syndrome, 3. *See also* Expert testimony
Beck, A., 21
Bibring, G., 67
Bowlby, J., 68
Browne, A., 25–27, 34–39, 41–42
Burden of persuasion, 90–91
Burden of production, 89–91
Burden of proof. *See* Burden of persuasion.

"Castle" doctrine, 81
Child abuse, 12, 24–25, 36, 40
Convictions, criminal, 41–43
Crocker, P., 52, 58
Cycle theory of violence, 18–19, 51–52, 65

Defense of habitation, 81–82
Demographic factors: age, 37, 40; education, 38, 40; race, 37–38; social class, 38
Depression: incidence among battered women, 11; learned helplessness and, 66–70; reason for not leaving batterer, 21; suicide and, 68–69
Deterrence: general, 86–88; special, 88–89
Disintegration anxiety, 63–66
Drug abuse, 39–40
Dutton, D., 19–20, 73

Education. *See* Demographic factors
Eitenger, L., 73
Emick, Leslie Ann, 1–5
Excuse versus justification, 47
Expert testimony: battered woman syndrome, 51–60, 94

Ferraro, K., 64–66
Fields, R., 74
Firearms. *See* Weapons used to kill; Threats
Fletcher, G., 83–85

Gayford, J., 8–12, 36

Harrison, Betty Ann, 48
Hawthorne, Joyce, 48
Hilberman, E., 8–12
Hoeffler, M., 8–9
Homicidal incidents: details of, 28–30, 34, 39–40, 48, 55, 70; precipitating event(s), 25, 55; sleeping victim, 28, 34, 47–49, 55
Homicide: defenses to charge of, 41–50; perpetrators, 23, 86; victims, 23, 86

Injuries to battered women. *See* Abuse
Insanity, 45–46
Isolation: financial, 10, 13, 33, 36; social, 10, 27, 33, 37, 40

James, W., 63
Johnson, J., 64–66
Jones, A., 27–28, 37–38
Jury deliberations, 61–62, 94
Justification versus excuse, 47

Kadish, S., 83
Kalvin, H., 62
Kelly, State v., 52–53
Kidnapping, 82–83
Kohut, H., 63–66
Kuhl, A., 8, 10

Laing, R., 63–66
Learned helplessness, 21, 67–70
Legal response to batterers. *See* Police response to battered women; Prosecutors' response to battered women
Lesser evils principle, 84–85
Lichtenberg, G., 68
Locke, J., 83–84

Manslaughter, 41–45
Martin, D., 73–74
Medical professionals' response to battered women, 16, 95
Mental health professionals' response to battered women, 17–18, 95
Meyers, Richard, 2–4
Minnis, Jeannette, 32–33
Morgan, S., 74
Munson, K., 8–12
Murder, 41–44

Ontological insecurity, 63–66

Pagelow, M., 8–9
Painter, S., 19–20, 73
Patri, Jennifer, 48
Patterson v. New York, 90
Physical abuse. *See* Abuse
Police response to battered women, 15, 29, 95
Prison. *See* Sentences, criminal
Probation. *See* Sentences, criminal
Prosecutors' response to battered women, 15–16
Psychological abuse. *See* Abuse
Psychological effects of battering. *See* Abuse; Depression; Disintegration anxiety; Learned helplessness; Ontological insecurity; Psychophysiological disorders; Suicide; Victimology
Psychological self-defense: 62, 76, 77–94, 96–97. *See also* Burden of persuasion; Burden of production; Psychopathology; Self, psychology of; Terrorism, conjugal; Victimology
Psychopathology, 66–70
Psychophysiological disorders, 12
Psychotherapy: battered women, 17; batterer, 17

Race. *See* Demographic factors
Rape, 10, 26, 32, 40, 71, 82–83. *See also* Abuse
Retreat doctrine, 80–81
Rounsaville, B., 8, 11–12

Schneider, E., 41, 46, 51, 56, 58
Self: aspects of, 62–63; psychology of, 63–66; victimized, 63–66
Self-defense, 4, 42, 46–50, 77, 79. *See also* Burden of persuasion; Burden of production; Defense of habitation; Expert testimony; Psychological self-defense; Retreat doctrine
Seligman, M., 20–21, 67–68
Sentences, criminal, 4, 41–43, 48
Sex role stereotypes, 17–18, 56–57
Sexual abuse. *See* Abuse
Shelters for battered women, 14, 95
Social class. *See* Demographic factors

Stockholm syndrome, 75
Substance abuse. *See* Alcohol abuse;
    Drug abuse
Suicide: attempts by battered women,
    11–12, 25, 30; depression and, 68–
    70
Symonds, M., 71–72

Terrorism, conjugal, 73–75
Thomas, State v., 53–54
Threats: death, 24–28, 32, 35; injury,
    24; weapons used to make, 24, 30,
    32, 35–36, 40
Toch, H., 62
Torture, 9
Totman, J., 28–31, 37–38, 43

Traumatic bond between battered
    woman and batterer, 19–20, 75
"True man" rule, 81

Victimized self. *See* Self
Victimology, 70–73

Walker, L., 8–11, 18, 24–25, 27, 34–
    41, 46, 51, 57, 66–67, 70, 73, 78
Weapons used to kill, 24, 30–31, 39–
    40
Weapons used to threaten. *See* Threats
Weissman, M., 8
White, People v., 53

Zeisel, H., 62

About the Author

Charles Patrick Ewing, a clinical and forensic psychologist and attorney, is Associate Professor of Law and Clinical Associate Professor of Psychology at the State University of New York at Buffalo. After receiving a Ph.D. from Cornell University, he was a post-doctoral fellow at Yale University and received a J.D. from Harvard University. Dr. Ewing is the author of *Crisis Intervention as Psychotherapy* (Oxford University Press, 1978) and editor of *Psychology, Psychiatry and the Law: A Clinical and Forensic Handbook* (Professional Resource Exchange, 1985). He is also the author or co-author of numerous articles and chapters dealing with psychology and law, psychotherapy, professional ethics, and violent behavior. He has testified as an expert in many criminal and domestic trials.